P9-AFX-564

Visual Rhetoric

Series Editor, Marguerite Helmers

VISUAL RHETORIC
Series Editor, Marguerite Helmers

The Visual Rhetoric series publishes work by scholars in a wide variety of disciplines, including art theory, anthropology, rhetoric, cultural studies, psychology, and media studies.

Other Books in the Series

Writing the Visual: A Practical Guide for Teachers of Composition and Communication, edited by Carol David and Anne R. Richards (2007)

Ways of Seeing, Ways of Speaking

The Integration of Rhetoric and Vision in Constructing the Real

Edited by

Kristie S. Fleckenstein

Sue Hum

Linda T. Calendrillo

Parlor Press
West Lafayette, Indiana
www.parlorpress.com

Parlor Press LLC, West Lafayette, Indiana 47906

© 2007 by Parlor Press
All rights reserved.
Printed in the United States of America.

SAN: 254-8879

Library of Congress Cataloging-in-Publication Data

Ways of seeing, ways of speaking : the integration of rhetoric and vision in constructing the real / edited by Kristie S. Fleckenstein, Sue Hum, Linda T. Calendrillo.

   p. cm. -- (Visual rhetoric)

Includes bibliographical references and index.

ISBN 978-1-60235-032-8 (pbk. : alk. paper) -- ISBN 978-1-60235-033-5 (hardcover : alk. paper) -- ISBN 978-1-60235-034-2 (adobe ebook)

1. Visual communication. 2. Written communication. I. Fleckenstein, Kristie S. II. Hum, Sue. III. Calendrillo, Linda T.

P93.5.W397 2007

302.2--dc22

2007041905

Cover image © 2007 by Angel Herrero de Frutos. Used by permission.
Cover design by David Blakesley.
Printed on acid-free paper.

Parlor Press, LLC is an independent publisher of scholarly and trade titles in print and multimedia formats. This book is available in paper, cloth and Adobe eBook formats from Parlor Press on the World Wide Web at http://www.parlorpress.com or through online and brick-and-mortar bookstores. For submission information or to find out about Parlor Press publications, write to Parlor Press, 816 Robinson St., West Lafayette, Indiana, 47906, or e-mail editor@parlorpress.com.

P93.5
W397
2007

Contents

Illustrations

Acknowledgments

This project began in 2001 with a kernel of an idea and slowly grew to this collection of essays. Throughout that long evolution, we have been supported by generous institutions and colleagues.

Kristie S. Fleckenstein thanks Ball State University for an internal grant to defray the costs of permissions. She also thanks Florida State University's Department of English for similar support. Important to this project were student interns Liza Cunnington, who organized and began the process of soliciting permissions for the many images in the collection; Kyle Ford, who carried on her work by learning more about fair use laws than he wanted; and Michael Vermilyer, who juggled permissions, images, and chapters. In addition, she thanks Carmen Siering for her careful readings of and responses to the introduction. Finally, she thanks Jamie Miles for his expert preparation of the images that appear in this collection.

Sue Hum thanks her colleagues Bernadette Andrea, Elissa Foster, Nancy Myers, Mona Narain, and Carlos Salinas for their patience and wisdom in helping midwife this project to its birth. Their individual expertise contributed to the interdisciplinary approaches of this collection. Particularly crucial were the painstaking efforts of Laura Ellis and Lee Lundquist, who proofread the entire manuscript carefully and exhaustively.

Linda T. Calendrillo thanks Valdosta State University for supporting this project with a Faculty Research Grant to help with expenses. She also thanks Linda Holloway in the Dean of Arts and Sciences office for her generous help in keeping the work on track for this book. Finally, she thanks John Z. Guzlowski for his prodigious proofreading skills, which he provides so thanklessly.

Lastly, though certainly not least in importance, the editors thank David Blakesley for seeing the potential in this project, Marguerite Helmers for her careful guidance and detailed response, and Paul

Lynch for his meticulous copy editing work. And, we wish to thank our esteemed contributors for their continued, gracious commitment to this collection, all of whom responded thoughtfully and patiently to our suggestions for revision, enabling us to craft out of separate essays, a coherent yet interdisciplinary argument about ways of seeing.

Ways of Seeing, Ways of Speaking

1 Testifying: Seeing and Saying in World Making

Kristie S. Fleckenstein

> *The animals other than man live by appearances and memories, and have but little of connected experience; but the human race lives also by art and reasonings.*
>
> Aristotle, *Metaphysics*

> *How do we transform images, and the imagination that produces them, into powers worthy of trust and respect?*
>
> W. J. T. Mitchell

The 1744 edition of Giambattista Vico's *New Science* opens with a frontispiece, or title page (see Figure 1), which, in his first sentence, Vico describes as a "*Tableau of civil institutions.*" "Before reading my work," he continues, "you may use this tableau to form an idea of my New Science. And after reading it, you will find that this tableau aids your imagination in retaining my work in your memory" (1). Reminiscent of emblem book traditions popular during the Renaissance in which images (*picturae*) and word (epigram and/or motto) were joined as a means of externalizing memory, the frontispiece serves three roles for Vico: a prelude to reading, an organizing principle during reading, and a mnemonic device after reading.[1] Vico's elaborate, highly symbolic title page, as well as his philosophy of meaning, places at its center a theory of imagery and of imagination as the knowledge making facility that undergirds all other meaning making. For Vico, professor of Latin eloquence at the University of Naples, image making was essential to learning. However, image did not function alone. Rather,

Fig. 1. Vico's Frontispiece, Giambattista Vico, *New Science: Principles of the New Science Concerning the Common Nature of Nations.* 3rd ed. 1744. Trans. David Marsh. London: Penguin Books, 1999..

word and image were fused in world making, in the communal human activity of shaping a material reality.

Language plays an essential and complementary role in Vico's frontispiece. Beyond the language in the image itself, the text of the entire first chapter of more than 30 pages consists of a detailed exposition of the meaning of the various elements. While image is the foundation of knowledge for Vico, image does not function apart from word. Rather, like the Renaissance emblem book, image and word interweave to shape the world. Knowable reality is neither the sole province of language nor of image. Rather, it is the dance of both.

A third element in Vico's frontispiece is also important to world making: the eye of God, which Vico describes as an all-seeing divine providence that forges humans into a society, a community, saving them from isolation where, according to Vico, they are at the mercy of their animal natures. God's eye—or, in my interpretation, a shared vision—is crucial to the constitution of a cultural order and the shaping practices of that culture; it is complicit with image and word in world making. Thus, Vico's title page adds a choreographer to the *pas de deux* of word and image: a dominant way of seeing—a scopic regime—that serves as an organizing power for community. The role of that imperial eye highlights vision as the noblest of human senses. In *Metaphysics* Aristotle tells us that all men "by nature desire to know," delighting as they do in the senses. Above all, for both pleasure and usefulness, men prefer seeing. The reason for this preference, he explains, is that this "most of all the senses, makes us know and brings to light many differences between things" (980a26–27). But the power of the eye extends beyond knowledge and delight, important as both may be. For Vico this dominant eye ensures the cultural and communal nature of human congress. Via a shared way of seeing and being seen, humans act together within the material context of their immediate environments to craft through their labor a common reality. Community is constituted as much by the images we see and the visual conventions we share as it is by the words we speak and the discourse conventions we share.

Vico's frontispiece—a graphic image permeated with and surrounded by words—encapsulates the tripartite dynamic that serves as the focus of this collection. Three interwoven elements—image, rhetoric, and scopic regimes—transact in the creation of our realities throughout the range of communal labors and activities.[2] As we work together, we learn to see in ways that privilege the perception of a particular array of words and images; we learn to organize words and images similarly, which, in turn, leads us to work together in one fashion rather than another.[3] The essays in *Constructing the Real* explore the intersections among rhetoric, imagery, and scopic regimes in the shaping of our realities and subjectivities. Each author addresses the following question: how are the constitutions of our world and our identities composed of the intricate interweaving of word, image, and shared ways of seeing? Central to the nine essays comprising this book is the belief that how we articulate our realities and identities is inseparable from how we see and what we see. That is, the rhetoric by which we invent, validate, and disseminate our understanding of our multifaceted realities and identities is inextricably interwoven with images and shared ways of seeing. Understanding any aspect of our existence—from our beliefs about our universe, to our understanding of gender and ethnic identity, to our interfacing with technology—requires attention to the dynamic of word, image, and shared ways of seeing that constitute our experiences.

Our integration of image, rhetoric, and scopic regime in world making comes at an important time in Western culture. Many have pointed out that our world and lives have taken a linguistic turn so that world making has been increasingly analyzed for its constitution as a set of linguistic practices that "persuade" phenomena such as science, gender, ethnicity, and technology into existence. At the same time, we live in a migratory, fragmented, and diasporic visual culture. "Never has there been an age like ours," E. H. Gombrich said in 1956, "when the visual image is so cheap in every sense of the word" (8). Almost 50 years later, in the wake of the digitization of Western culture, that "cheap image" is even more widely distributed. A blitzkrieg of images bombards us in everyday life through television, road signs, bill boards, graphic novels, store windows, talk radio, and World Wide Web multimedia graphics. Visual experiences all rush at and by us during our waking and, if we count dreams, our sleeping moments. We construe who we are, where we are, and what we are imagistically as well as linguistically. However, the rising interest in the role of language in world making has been accompanied by a declining interest in, even a denigration of, the mediating role of vision in constructing the real.[4] The contributors to this volume re-establish that dialectic, striking a balance between rhetoric and vision by exploring the interplay of both without belittling the contribution of either. Drawing on diverse perspectives and different disciplinary orientations, these authors illustrate that we dilute our understanding of our physical universe, our sense of gender, our experience of ethnicity, and our relationship with technology when we fail to account for, one, the role of the visual, and, two, the relationship between the visual and the verbal.

The tangle of terms in the title of my introduction—testifying, seeing, saying, and world making—indicates the intersections that these individual essays highlight. First, these essays testify to the importance of the body in vision, implicitly and explicitly responding to Donna J. Haraway's call to rescue vision "from the leap out of the marked body and into the conquering gaze from nowhere" (*Simians* 188). The word "testifying," derived from the Latin root "testis," emphasizes the embodied quality of seeing and saying, for at one time men held their testes as they verified through language the validity of their seeing (Carver 47–48; 137). A shared vision about the material world communicated through words is attested to by the integrity of one's body. The palpable existence of the body provided the ground on which witnesses' testimonies—the words of their seeing—established the authority of that seeing. Furthermore, the insistence on the embodied nature of rhetoric and vision underscores the importance of the body doing the seeing and saying. Not all bodies are perceived as equal, a truth intrinsic to testifying, for how can a body born without testes testify? Thus, these essays insist on the "embodied nature of all vision," reclaiming vision as located and marked (Haraway, *Simians* 188).

Second, these essays testify to the importance of world making, of constructing the real: the complex processes of perception and articulation that persuade a community that a certain material reality, including the reality of the body, exists. Rhetoric, image, and scopic regime may be grounded in the real, but that construction of the real exists as a result of the integration of rhetoric, image, and vision. Rhetoric, image, and way of seeing interinanimate, to use I. A. Richards's term; they give life, give meaning, mutually to each other and to the real. They exist "only through the interplay of the interpretative possibilities of the whole utterance" (55). Thus, one's testimony to a particular configuration of the world is a reflection of both the world and one's perception-articulation of that world.

Third, these essays testify to the importance of community. Growing out of the interweaving of image, rhetoric, and scopic regime, our construction of the real gains validity only when it is shared—rendered compelling—by the judgment of the ambient community. This dynamic social construction of the real involves three interlocking processes: emergence, appropriation, and resistance. Emergence is the process by which a perception, articulation, or shared vision evolves. Neither image, rhetoric, nor way of seeing is instantly and unproblematically enfranchised by a culture. Rather, each emerges at a kairotic moment from a particular historical, situational matrix, carrying with it traces of its own making. Appropriation is the process by which a community takes as its own a perception, articulation, or shared vision, making it a part of its taken-for-granted reality, its construction of the real. Once an image, rhetoric, or scopic regime emerges, it is co-opted and absorbed by the culture so that it becomes a habitual part of a member's personal and cultural existence, so deeply ingrained that, like perception, the social constructedness of the real is difficult to recognize. Finally, resistance is the process by which a segment of the community posits alternative perceptions, articulations, and shared visions, calling into question previous constructions of the real. There is always an excess of chaotic reality that escapes the formative shaping of image, rhetoric, and way of seeing. In addition, there is never any perfect isomorphy among image, rhetoric, and scopic regime. Thus, members of a community can turn around on their visual-verbal habits, recognize what is highlighted and hidden by those habits, and resist the construction of the real privileged by dominant images, rhetorics, and ways of seeing. This dynamic of emergence, appropriation, and resistance is revealed within the nine essays of this collection and between them as they engage in an implicit dialogue. This dynamic serves as the organizing principle of the collection.

Ways of Seeing, Ways of Speaking: The Integration of Rhetoric and Vision in Constructing the Real, then, is ground breaking in three ways. First, it is an exploration of the way in which our construction of the real is a communal activity involving image, way of seeing, and rhetoric. Second, it provides insight into the dynamic of emergence, appropriation, and resistance. Third, these essays, jointly and individually, provide a template for further work in other constructions of the real. The physical constraints of a book limit the arenas of the real that these essays can explore. The constraints also restrict the number and kinds of strategies of emergence, appropriation, and resistance that individual authors examine. However, the essays provide a methodology that can be extended beyond the confines of this collection to explore other categories of the real, such as the interweaving of image, vision, and rhetoric in the configuration of disability, age, class, and marginalization.

The purpose of this introduction is to provide a context for the collection. I begin by defining our key terms: material rhetorics, scopic regimes, and image. I explore the ways in which these concepts interinanimate each other as much as they interinanimate the real. I then link this reciprocity to the specific essays, providing a preview of the individual chapters.

DEFINITIONS OF KEY TERMS

The soul cannot think without an image, Aristotle argues in *De Anima;* however, the *human* soul cannot think without both word and image. To understand our configuration of the world around and within us, we must understand our material rhetorics, our array of images and the conventions by which we perceive them, and the interinanimation of rhetorics, images, and conventions.

Material Rhetorics

Polysemic and ambiguous, the definition, as well as the value, of rhetoric has been up for grabs for the last 2500 years. Ranging from a language performance to a theory of language performances, from content to form, the meaning of rhetoric shifts from situation to situation, from era to era. Thus, rhetoric can be a description of verbal persuasion, which seems to be Aristotle's intent, for he defines rhetoric as the art of discovering the available means of persuasion, an "*antistrophos* to dialectic" (1354a). Rhetoric also can also be a primer, as in "a rhetoric," which is a set of guidelines and conventions for teaching (and learning about) the art of persuasion. Or rhetoric can refer to the specific enactments of persuasion, an array of language performances, which is, in part, Kenneth Burke's approach to rhetoric. Because, according to Burke, all language is a species of action by which we seek to move the world and move in the world, all language is rhetorical. In addition, because such rhetorical acts involve choices and all choices involve conflict, all rhetorical performances are dramatic, subject to analysis as drama.

From Aristotle's art of finding the available means of persuasion to Burke's dramatism, rhetoric refers to the use of language to evoke cooperation among a group of people. It is the means by which we participate individually and collectively in the life of a community, doing the work and exploring the pleasures of that community. In *Ways of Seeing, Ways of Speaking,* we focus on and theorize about a narrowly construed rhetoric: those language performances that convince participants—both rhetor and audience—that a particular configuration of reality exists and is truthfully represented by language. Thus, we approach rhetoric as a theory of persuasion concerned with understanding the symbolic performances that persuade phenomena—our beliefs about realities such as the physical and biological worlds, female identity, and ethnicity—into existence. The phrase "persuade phenomena into existence" highlights two tacit assumptions underlying that definition of rhetoric. First, it emphasizes that our realities are socially constructed, not given, and that they are constructed, in part, via language. This assumption requires us to focus on the discursive acts that lead a community to believe that one version of reality—one account of sexual desire, one account of space and time, one narrative of evolution, one story of racial identity—has precedence over or greater validity than a competing version. The second assumption emphasizes that our construction of those realities is a collaborative project, calling us to examine not just symbol systems but *shared* symbol systems and the dynamic process of emergence, appropriation, and resistance by which they come to be shared and contested.

The material aspect of rhetoric lurks within this definition of rhetoric. Material, like any good adjective, limits the scope of the noun or pronoun it describes. Thus, *material rhetorics* restricts the purview of rhetoric in this collection to language acts concerned with establishing our sense of an embodied or concrete reality. Unfortunately, material, like rhetoric, is polysemic and ambiguous, thus making our understanding of material rhetorics equally slippery. For example, on one level, every rhetorical act, regardless of its content or subject, is material by its very existence as an action, thereby rendering all rhetoric material. Words vibrating the larynx, black marks marching in a line on a white page, pixels of lights blinking on a cathode ray tube—all of these are physical, embodied aspects of our experienced reality. In addition, those words, marks, and pixels escape the confines of their medium to affect the world, although the degree and range of that impact varies. Thus, the minister intoning, "I now pronounce you husband and wife" creates at that precise moment a legally binding union, just as the civil court judge affixing her black mark to the white pages of a divorce decree dissolves those legal bonds. Finally, a particular array of flickering pixels on a cathode ray tube can fling a Titan missile into the air. Thus, rhetoric is always material.

On another level, however, the content, the subject matter, of those words, marks, and pixels can be either material or abstract. For instance, the *res,* or the "matter," of a rhetorical performance can be an embodied reality, such as language detailing a frog's DNA, describing a view through a telescope, or explaining sickle cell anemia. On the other hand, *res* can be abstract, as in a dissertation on the sublime or an explanation of the nature of epistemology. The former discourse takes as its subject matter specific aspects of the world, rendering those aspects capable of being shared. The other discourse takes as its subject matter discourses about discourses, abstracting from those discourses an account of how we experience the world or an account of how we know the world. Thus, while no rhetoric is immaterial, in that all rhetoric has a perceptible impact and is created out of physical elements of the world, not all rhetorical performances are focused on specific aspects of the real, such as our understanding of our biological and physical universe or our sense of ourselves as raced, gendered, and sexualized beings. For the purposes of this book, *material rhetorics* refers to those discourses specifically designed to shape, identify, analyze, and validate aspects of our lived reality. Material rhetorics persuade our realities into existence. They testify to community members that the world is configured in one way and not another; by so doing, they weld those members into a community.

Central to our definition of material rhetorics is a reliance on nonlinguistic elements in those rhetorics, specifically vision. Performances of material rhetoric are comprised of imagery and ways of seeing as well as of language. Shared symbol systems, not just shared language systems, are involved in constructing the real.

Scopic Regimes and Images

Essential to all rhetoric is vision, both in terms of a shared way of seeing and a shared network of visual images. Rhetoric is not, nor has it ever been, a solely verbal performance, either oral or print. It has always been immersed within a visual context and permeated with visual elements. Let me first explore that visual context, beginning with the concept of scopic regimes.

According to Martin Jay, a culture organizes itself by means of a dominant way of seeing, or a scopic regime, a term that he borrows from Christian Metz. A scopic regime consists of visual conventions that determine how and what we see. For example, one visual convention that all scopic regimes address concerns the relationship between the gazer and the object of the gaze. To illustrate, consider the way in which that relationship is configured in Cartesian perspectivalism, the scopic regime that Jay argues is pervasive in the West. In Cartesian perspectivalism the gazer is always separated from the object of the gaze. Trained from childhood in the West in this mode of seeing, members of the dominant culture detach themselves—psychologically, emotionally, and physically—from the object they wish to perceive and treat it as something that can be, should be, analyzed. Thus, the first convention of perspectivalism reveals an analytical, rational bias that interprets reality as something that can be graphed along the X-Y axes of a Cartesian plane. An outgrowth of this analytical, detached stance is the belief that observers are able to perceive everything pertinent about the object of study. That is, by detaching themselves from the object, the gazers simultaneously free themselves from the limitations of a single, constrained point of view. They are seemingly able to escape the confines of the individual body to claim a panoptic view of phenomena. Immersion in Cartesian perspectivalism leads to the "eye outside of time and history" that Nietzsche attacks. David Michael Levin calls this visual convention a "terrible double bind" in which "the subject is invariably positioned either in the role of a dominating observer or in the role of an observable object, submissive before the gaze of power" (4).

What, then, does Cartesian perspectivism constrain us to see? Or, perhaps an equally valid and somewhat easier question to answer, what does it prevent us from *not* seeing? Consider the human genome project, which seeks to map the human genome as the first step to investigating and addressing genetically linked diseases. Perspectivalism inclines us to envision DNA as an entity that can be mapped on a two-dimensional grid or even a three-dimensional model. It leads us to see those aspects of DNA that lend themselves to such arrangements. We perceive, collect, and accumulate the discrete bits of information about DNA that further our agenda without realizing all the bits of information that remain invisible because they do not fit within our frame. For example, one element that disappears from the human genome project is the degree to which DNA formation is subject to its reciprocal relationship with environments internal and external to the cell. Geneticist R. C. Lewontin protests that an organism does not compute itself from its DNA.

> A living organism at any moment in its life is the unique consequence of a developmental history that results from the interaction of and determination by internal and external forces. The external forces, what we usually think of as "environment," are themselves partly a consequence of the activities of the organism itself as it produces and consumes the conditions of its own existence. (63)

Such a reciprocal view of reality, however, is foreign to both Cartesian perspectivalism and the genome project. In addition, driven by Cartesian perspectivalism, we fail to see the mimetic logic of stories, metaphors, and myths that pervade our grasp of DNA. Thus, we are unable to see the degree to which a particular orientation to reality— a metaphor—organizes our approach to a scientific project (Keller, *Reflections* 131). In sum, a scopic regime dictates what can be seen because it dictates what aspects of the world are seen.

While a single scopic regime may dominate one historical era, that single regime does not dominate all historical eras. Thus, the second characteristic of a scopic regime is its historical variability. For instance, Jay presents scopic regimes as a useful way to critique the creation of meaning within a precise moment of history because scopic regimes are subject to historical shifts. Different periods and different cultures manifest different ways of seeing. To illustrate, diverse scholars assert that the Middle Ages were organized by a participatory way of seeing that merged viewer and object so that knowing about was inseparable from identifying with. As Owen Barfield describes:

> The background picture then was of man as a micro-cosm within the macrocosm. It is clear that he did not feel himself isolated by his skin from the world outside of him to quite the same extent that we do. He was integrated or mortised into it, each different part of him being united to a different part of it by

> some invisible thread. In his relation to his environ-
> ment, the man of the middle ages was rather less like
> an island, rather more like an embryo, than we are.
> (78)

Shaped by this highly engaged, highly imagistic way of knowing, people during the Middle Ages developed a "horizon of expectations" that
predisposed them to see aspects of reality that confirmed their belief in
the connectiveness of physical, spiritual, and emotional realities as well
as the connectiveness of the individual with the universal.[5] It predisposed them as well to *not* see aspects of reality that disconfirmed that
belief. For example, if one is mortised into a reality, then the position
of one's birth within a particular class structure is also mortised into
a reality. Impossible to perceive is the constructedness of social positions and the way in which political and religious policies ensure the
continuation of a rigid class hierarchy. The invisible threads that bind
also blind.

To further complicate this account, multiple scopic regimes exist
within any one historical period. A culture is rarely organized by means
of a single hegemonic regime. Instead, competing ways of seeing clash
and contend for organizational power within a culture. For instance,
on the cusp of the twenty-first century, the detached, analytical vision of Cartesian perspectivalism is contested by the highly participatory way of seeing Ernest G. Schachtel calls allocentric perception.
Allocentric perception is characterized by "profound interest in the
object, and complete openness and receptivity toward it, a full turning toward the object which makes possible a direct encounter with it"
(220). Such perception yields insights impossible through Carteisan
perspectivalism as Barbara McClintock, a Nobel laureate in plant cy-
tology, illustrates. McClintock describes her research approach as acquiring a "feeling for the organism," in which she opens herself up to
what the "material has to say" (qtd. in Keller, *Feeling* 198). McClintock
describes studying corn plants in the field and through her microscope so intently that she achieved an unexpected intimacy, which
was a necessary prelude to her insights concerning the transposition
of genes (198). Thus, Evelyn Fox Keller, McClintock's intellectual bi-
ographer, can conclude that the long delay in scientific recognition
of McClintock's remarkable discoveries resulted, in significant part,
from the radically different way of seeing McClintock enacted.

Four points concerning scopic regimes, then, are important to *Ways of Seeing, Ways of Speaking*. First, a culture is shaped as much by its scopic regimes as by its language conventions. A scopic regime exercises a formative power over what is knowable, sayable, and doable. Second, scopic regimes are never singular. A dominant regime jostles with competing, even if repressed, ways of seeing. Third, scopic regimes implicate rhetoric. Visual conventions affect discourse conventions. Thus, the prevailing means of persuasion within a period cannot be excised from the shared ways of seeing—from the visual culture—of that period. Fourth, scopic regimes implicate images. What counts as an image, what can be perceived and named an image, is affected, although not entirely determined, by the central regime that organizes a culture. Let me first define image, then return to the relationship between image and scopic regime.

Just as polysemic and ambiguous as material rhetoric, image is difficult to define in part because of the variability in image itself. When we define image, a key question to ask is "what kind of image?" To illustrate, in one context, image for Aristotle is a mental evocation of a reality, although not necessarily a "true" reality, in the absence of reality. As he explains in *De Anima*, "when the mind is actively aware of anything it is necessarily aware of it along with an image; for images are like sensuous contents except in that they contain no matter (432a6–9). At the same time, however, Aristotle is also concerned with the perceptual image, which is a product of the body, not the imagination. Then, to further complicate the picture, Aristotle also explores the verbal image, especially metaphor, according it a place of power in both *On Rhetoric* and *Poetics*. Finally, image shifts one last time when, in *Poetics*, Aristotle asserts the importance of, first, the impact of media on modes of representation, and, second, the role of "spectacle" in tragedy, created on the stage and created in readers. This variability is rendered even more confusing when we consider that an image can be all of these things at once. Depending on the moment and the manifestation, a graphic image is a perceptual image at the same time it is a mental image, one that can easily morph into a verbal image. That range and variability are reflected in this collection. The essays in *Ways of Seeing, Ways of Speaking* explore in turn scientific diagrams and verbal descriptions, feminist art and a website game, films, novels, and vivid literary metaphors, as well as the technologies of image production. Despite the shifting nature of image, certain common features characteristic of all images regardless of modality can be ascertained.

First, any image is the result of a highly active process of organizing the chaos of stimuli into a recognizable or nameable form whether that stimuli is present or absent. For instance, in perception, as Gombrich explains,

> What we get on the retina, whether we are chick-ens or human beings, is a welter of dancing light points stimulating sensitive rods and cones that fire their messages into the brain. What we see is a stable world. It takes an effort of the imagination and a fair-ly complex apparatus to realize the tremendous gulf that exists between the two. (60)

Seeing requires interpretation; it requires creating relationships, for an image is composed of relationships. Whether a percept, a mental configuration, a graphic incarnation, or a verbal flourish, an image shapes itself out of the relationships. As such, no image is ever a mere unproblematic copy of some reality, never a reproduction mediated by an innocent eye. Second, no image, once created, remains static. An image is an event. As Suzanne K. Langer points out, an image exists in time. As such, images are constantly reorganizing and reshaping themselves, for even as we create an image we experience that image, and in the very act we change the image. The fluidity of imagery is a constant even for those images seemingly welded into shape, such as architecture or art.

The relationship between image and scopic regime is circular rather than linear. While a scopic regime determines in part what we see and how we see, it is also subject to the unruliness of the image, of the chaotic stimuli out of which image constructs itself. The visual conventions that we learn dictate in general terms the images that we construct. However, the range of stimuli, as well as competing conventions, affects the construction of specific images. Thus, we have a continuous process of regimes reorganizing themselves to accommodate images until they can no longer do so. At that point, scopic regimes shift. This dynamic is especially evident during those liminal points in history when the scopic regime of one era undergoes seismic shifts into a new era. For example, one such moment of transition occurred during the seventeenth century in England. Poised between the

Renaissance and the Enlightenment, this period in England was torn by tension between the "iconic plenitude of the Renaissance imagination and the Reformist conception of a language purified of affective intent" (Cable, *Carnal* 2). On the one hand, we have the Renaissance love of the image, manifested in the popularity in the seventeenth century of emblem books and its rich pamphlet culture. Here was a time in which advances in print technology enabled a wide distribution of broadsides that merged image and rhetoric. We also have the Renaissance savoring of verbal imagery, the schemes and tropes that Renaissance scholars obsessively catalogued. On the other hand, we have the Reformation and the Enlightenment where images—graphic, verbal, and mental—were associated with the irrational, chaotic, uncontrollable, and illusory, calling forth distrust, disdain, and the drive to control their power. This, after all, was the tail end of Reformation, where the attack on idolatry, on devotional images, called for a literal pulling down and breaking up of those images. In addition to physical images, however, the image-making power of the mind was suspect because that power was tainted by carnality.

The licensing laws as well as the systematic destruction of devotional images illustrate the potentially disruptive relationship between scopic regime and image. Efforts to control the kind of images available in a culture required instituting a "correct" way of seeing and thinking. Thus, English religious-political leaders sought through legal means to legislate a scopic regime and a rhetoric. By reducing the occurrences of verbal and visual images, the ruling party believed it could control what was thought within the population at large, particularly among the more radical elements. In 1660, Samuel Parker, an official licenser and later bishop of Oxford argued: "Had we but an Act of Parliament to abridge Preachers the use of fulsome and luscious Metaphors, it might perhaps be an effectual Cure of all our present Distempers," for it is the "gawdy Metaphor" and "lascivious Allegories" that authorize the workings of private, and dissenting, conscience (qtd. in Cable, "Licensing" 244). A similar dynamic was at play in the calls for the plain rhetoric associated with Thomas Sprat and the fledgling Royal Society. Here language was shorn of images and of metaphors, each of which, it was argued, distracted the reader from the truth of the scientific insight.

We can no more escape vision than we can escape language. Blinding ourselves as Democritus supposedly did to gain greater intellectual insight does not prevent a way of seeing from becoming what Foucault in *The Birth of the Clinic* calls the pure gaze, the speaking eye (35). What we can do, however, is multiply our vision, increase our repertoire of images. By acknowledging and embracing images and scopic regimes, we can assume responsibility for the visual fields, social practices, and institutional spaces defined by those images and regimes. David Michael Levin holds out that hope: "Vision is nature's gift of a possible adventure in the social, or cultural order. It is not only an opportunity for individuation; it is also at the same time a project of responsibility for the social order as a world" (56). But a necessary step in the realization of that hope is understanding the reciprocal constitution—the interinanimation—of rhetorics, images, and ways of seeing.

Interinanimation

Material rhetorics, images, and scopic regimes interinanimate; they acquire meaning through their mutual dependence on the other as well as through their relationship to the whole utterance, whether that "utterance" is in the form of an image, a word, or a visual convention. This interinanimation is evident throughout the history of rhetoric, which is permeated with imagery. Gombrich claims that Quintilian "inserts a brief history of art [...] to illustrate the rise of Latin oratory and its change in character from rough vigor to smooth polish" (10). He claims that arguments throughout the history of rhetoric concerning oratorical style are, in fact, arguments about the nature of images and the nature of the morality those images promulgate. Image, word, and way of seeing function reciprocally to create our selves and our worlds. Nowhere is this interinanimation more clearly illustrated than in the constitution of community.

We have long accepted the proposition that community is created through linguistic action. Community is an amalgamation of language events shared within a specific geographical (or virtual) site, marked by a common pool of values and communicative competence. Any social structure, Peter Berger and Thomas Luckmann claim, is a sum total of a continuum of typifications or conversations, and community is the institutionalization of those shared language games (32; see also 50–63). "Language provides the fundamental superimposition of logic on the objectivated social world," they explain. "The edifice of legitimations is built upon language and uses language as its principal instrumentality" (61). Richard Rorty concurs. We live, think, and speak conversationally; therefore, we create and change community conversationally. Shifts in the European community from the idiom of the Enlightenment to the idiom of Romanticism, Rorty reminds us, was a process of gradually losing the habit of using certain words and acquiring the habit of using others (68).

However, community is not only the product (and producer) of language; it is also the product (and producer) of a particular orientation to vision. Perception and language are inextricably linked, a point that Burke captures so succinctly in his concept of terministic screens: "Even if any given terminology is a *reflection* of reality, by its very nature as a terminology it must be a *selection* of reality; and to this extent it must function as a *deflection* of reality" (*Language* 45). The terms we use affect our perceptions; our observations are, in part, "the spinning out of possibilities implicit in our particular choice of terms" (46). Language influences perception. But perception also influences language, as Burke's choice of the term "terministic screen" suggests. The concept of terministic screens, Burke explains, grew out of photographs that he saw, ones where different colored filters, or screens, affected the texture and the form of that which was pictured. Thus, his shifting perception of a visual image affected his choice of terminology, even as his choice of terminology recursively affected his perception. While a way of speaking may be a way of not speaking, that is, by saying one thing we choose not to say others, a way of seeing is also a way of not seeing (Burke, *Permanence and Change* 48).

A community is crafted out of its habits of speaking *and* its habits of seeing. Simon Goldhill offers a clear illustration of the interrelationship between scopic regimes, images, and rhetorical conventions in community building. Integrating the visual and the rhetorical, Goldhill argues that the regime of display permeated classical rhetoric. Successful persuasion in fifth and fourth century BCE Greece was effected by means of a visual spectacle acknowledged and judged by the collective gaze of the *polis*. Citing three major public institutions by which Athenian culture was characterized as "supremely Greek,"—the assembly, the law-court, and the theater—Goldhill claims that Greek society was a performance culture, in which participation as an audience member was an integral part of one's democratic citizenship. Participation during one moment as audience member could transform quickly and easily into participation during another moment as speaker. The boundaries between spectator and performer were permeable, not only because spectator could so easily become performer but also because spectating itself was a performance: an enactment of one's democratic duty as a citizen. Spectating was the "doing" of citizenship. Goldhill explains that *theoria,* the Greek root of theory, implies a participatory kind of visual regard, one that captures the "caring" aspect of regard in addition to its visual aspect. He reminds us that the word *theoria* is also the normal Greek "for official participatory attendance as a spectator in the political and religious rites of state" (19) in which spectatorship was a performance of duty.

Goldhill turns to the theater as an exemplar of the regime of display in which visuality cannot be severed from rhetoric in community participation. The institutional spaces of Athens were fashioned so that the gaze of Athenian citizenry became the field where individual and collective identities were validated. Military, religious, and political spaces provided an extensive overlap between spaces for viewing and spaces for discussing viewing. One such space was the theater, which offered a visual map of the city. The major theatrical occasion of the year, the Great Dionysia, positioned citizens in wedges of seats arranged according to their tribal divisions, displaying other social groups in differently marked ways. Rituals, Goldhill claims, before the beginning of the plays, promoted the ideas of citizen participation. In addition, sponsorship, what he calls "conspicuous beneficence," garnered political capital. "In short," he concludes, "the theater was a space in which all the citizens were actors as the city itself and its leading citizens were put on display" (19). The validity of one's place within a community and the constitution of the community were inextricably tied to the regime of the display that integrated rhetoric and vision.

Poised between the stability of community and the vitality of change, we live amidst the flux of vision and rhetoric. If we limit ourselves as scholars solely to an exploration of the language in reality building, then we understand only a small portion of the story of meaning. Reclaiming vision allows us to turn our gaze to the hegemony exercised by particular scopic regimes in conjunction with particular rhetorical conventions. The essays in this collection explore the intersections of material rhetorics, images, and scopic regimes, teasing out what Jacqueline Rose calls the "moment of unease" that points to competing visual and verbal regimes within a community (qtd. in Jay,

"Scopic Regimes" 3). Poised at these moments of unease, the essays in *Ways of Seeing, Ways of Speaking* uncover the "masked sutures existing in all patched-together modes of communication" (Stafford 78) and the dynamic by which we create, appropriate, and resist ways of seeing and ways of saying in constructing our sense of the real.

CONSTRUCTING THE REAL

These essays are organized into three sections based on the dynamic among emergence, appropriation, and resistance. Each essay highlights an aspect of that dynamic. In addition, all the essays spotlight three key points. First, they focus on the material substrate of the real in two ways. The essays stress a symbol's medium, whether the symbol is an image or a word. The technology of symbol production and setting, such as film, digital technologies, HTML, print, and websites, is accorded importance. The essays also underscore connections among vision, rhetoric, and diverse constructions of the real, from knowledge about our galactic and biological worlds to the configuration of our gendered, raced, and sexualized bodies. Second, the essays tease out the formative impact of production, that is, the inculcation of a dominant image, rhetoric, and scopic regime in a particular culture and, thus, the inculcation of a particular version of the real. Third, the essays illustrate the interinanimation of image, rhetoric, and scopic regimes in constructing the real.

We begin with essays that reveal different aspects of the emergence of a governing image and scopic regime. Optical technology as a vehicle for "different styles of imaging" is the concern of Don Ihde in "Hermeneutics and the New Imaging." With the development of optical technologies that capture aspects of the universe imperceptible to the human sensorium, Ihde argues that a *new imaging* is shaping itself, one that influences the discovery and production of scientific knowledge of the physical universe. Beginning with the Ice Age images on a cave wall in Niaux, France, and proceeding to the twenty-first century, Ihde identifies three imaging trajectories: isomorphic trajectory of early science, which delineates phenomena within familiar spatial and dynamic forms, thus making recognition easy and quick; hermeneutic trajectory, a quasi-textual basis for imaging derived from technologies that no longer construct an image that resembles the phenomenon; and critical trajectory, evolving out of digitally transmitted code that is re-constructed into a picture, but a picture which includes "translations" of phenomena not directly perceptible by the human senses. The critical, like the hermeneutic, trajectory joins language activities with perception, requiring a style of imaging that is analogous to map reading and art criticism. It is this style of imaging, this scopic regime, that is emerging in the physical sciences and diffusing throughout the culture at large.

Where Ihde explores a sea change in the scopic regimes central to our construction of our physical universe, Alan Gross in "Darwin's Diagram: Scientific Visions and Scientific Visuals" explores a sea change in the biological sciences that results from a change in the nature of the image itself. This change is so radical that it elicits the emergence of a new way of seeing in which diagrams are no longer "a means of looking *at* the world, but a means of looking *through* it to its causal structure." Gross focuses on a single diagram in Darwin's *Origin of Species* as an example of the growing trend in scientific illustrations to depict theories, not things. These illustrations are visual-textual compounds, object-sided, on the one hand, and theory-sided, on the other. Gross argues that this fusion of image and word is central to what he calls a Heideggerian science, for, through this union, image and word compensate for each other's limitations in constructing the real. To illustrate this, Gross engages in a historical, conceptual, and biographical analysis of the single diagram in *Origin of Species*, demonstrating how this diagram embodies and creates a scientific theory and, in the process, evokes a "new kind of seeing."

In exploring the phenomenon of emergence from the perspective of optical technology and graphic diagrams, these essays hint at the process of appropriation, the means by which a new way of seeing or a new image-word integration is diffused throughout and reproduced by members of the culture at large to stabilize and privilege certain constructions of the real. Focusing especially on children as the site of cultural reproduction, the essays in our second section deal more explicitly with the process of appropriation. A specific array of visual and rhetorical conventions cannot converge and gain dominance until appropriated by and reproduced in a culture's children. These three essays investigate different modes of appropriation and the effects of that appropriation on constructing the real.

Exploring children's evolving sense of embodiment in "body pixel child/space time machine," Anne Frances Wysocki describes the process by which repeated encounters with an online game can shape children's perception of their bodies. Through a thoughtful and careful analysis of repetition, space, and time in the online game *Lilo and Stitch,* Wysocki demonstrates that the designed visual structures ask the audience to repeat particular (but different) bodily rhythms in order to "activate" the texts. Children inhabit these visually repetitive spaces of the texts as they read and interact. Wysocki argues that the visual and textual aspects of an interactive computer game do "thick work" on children, dictating how children experience space and time and hence controlling how they experience themselves as embodied. From these visual-textual repetitions, small children evolve a sense of self as a "seeing self" that sees self as whole, "a body given to sight and experienced through sight." Bound into a way of seeing encouraged by the screen, children evolve a focused and "circled-back-upon-itself" sense of body and attention that both isolates and conforms.

The (re)construction of a particular kind of body in time and space through visual-textual technologies is also central to Sue Hum's essay; however, the visual technology in question is *Mulan,* a film designed and marketed for children but popular with adults as well. Also, the scopic regime in question serves as the vehicle of appropriation, and a particular configuration of the real is the image-textual fusion appropriated. In "The Racialized Gaze: Authenticity and Universality," Hum analyzes Disney's *Mulan* to demonstrate the existence of what Christian Metz calls the "scopic regimes of the cinema," a dominant way of seeing that contributes to the replication and reproduction of a (racist) cultural order. Hum argues that issues of race and ethnicity in hegemonic white America, as reflected in its popular films, are reinscribed and appropriated by means of a racialized gaze that constructs and promulgates a reductive configuration of race. This racialized gaze constructs racial and ethnic identity as inconsequential, first, by reducing differences to a compendium of aesthetic and surface markers, such as iconography, a process that denies the existence of deep differences that result from historical oppressions. Second, the racialized gaze erases even those superficial markers by superimposing the assumption of universality, where all human beings are essentially the same in needs, desires, and aspirations. Appropriated and appropriating, the racialized gaze inculcates within culture's members a way of seeing that (re)confirms a racist order.

The dynamic of appropriation, then, operates in children's play space through the integration of words and images, yielding a particular way of seeing that "selects" a specific reflection of reality. However, appropriation also occurs in schools where constructing the real is an overarching agenda. Gunther Kress, in "Making Meaning in 'School Science': The Role of Image and Writing in the (Multimodal) Production of 'Scientificness,'" explores the ways in which school children in England become enculturated into the visual and verbal conventions of scientific reality building. "The task of the science curriculum," he explains, "is, still, to induct young people into the practices that constitute 'doing science.'" By analyzing students' creation of a multimodal text that reports on students' observations of a plant's cellular structure, Kress reveals the mechanisms of that induction. He focuses closely on the affordances of the different modes (speech, writing, image)—that is, the unique view of reality "afforded" by a particular mode—and traces how these modes (re)appear in the students' representations. He argues that students rearrange visual and verbal discourses, particularly "transducing" one mode into another, a process of transforming into image what initially appeared in speech or writing. This transduction highlights that students are active participants in their enculturation into science, making design decisions about what aspect of the real is constructed by which mode: image or text. Kress concludes by recommending an "outcomes-based curriculum," a curriculum that encourages learning as design so that children are agents able to conceive a goal and achieve it by fashioning visual-verbal texts out of the available resources.

Images, rhetorics, and regimes emerge and are appropriated within a culture, in the process evoking and stabilizing constructions of the real. But, as these essays also illustrate, neither images, rhetorics, nor regimes emerge out of a vacuum; they jostle and wrestle with other competing images, rhetorics, and regimes. The interinanimation of images, rhetorics, and regimes holds within it the seeds of resistance because, as Kress points out, image and language function according to different logics and thus can foster contradiction. Wysocki notes as well the lack of direct isomorphy between the visual-textual structures of a game and the embodiment of a child. There are, after all, many games and many experiences that children juggle to construct their sense of the real. Thus, each point of emergence and appropriation is also a potential point of resistance, suggesting the ways in which our construction of the real is also the site of resistance and contestation. The last set of essays examines in detail the dynamic of resistance to dominant ways of seeing and saying the world, a resistance that results in disruptions of the real.

We open this section on resistance with two essays that deal with perhaps the most material of all experiences: birth. Focusing on the creation of the category women, Catherine Hobbs in "What Do Pictures Want (Of Women)? Women and the Visual in the Age of Biocybernetics" turns to images of reproduction, arguing that we can find in the work of feminist visual artists efforts to shape a new imaginary that reorganizes our rich semiotic world. Taking as her starting point a talk by W. J. T. Mitchell, University of Chicago art historian and theorist, in which he asks, "What do pictures want?" Hobbs asks, "What do pictures want of women?" Building on Mitchell's inquiries into the cultural emergence of "biocybernetics," Hobbs reads in women's visual art concerning birth and the female body the bioinformatic traces that have changed and will continue to change human reproduction. She asserts that depictions of reproduction are created in a historically emergent cultural context that has interpretive and interactionist effects on artists, viewers, materials, and other factors. Reciprocally, the work of feminist visual artists steeped in this culture work on that culture to sculpt a new imaginary. Ultimately, she answers her motivating question with hope. Perhaps, she concludes, pictures want women to create and save the world by "troping on the codes and icons that make up its [this cultural moment's] historical debris." Through laughter "in the field of human women's vision," the dream of biocybernetic perfectability can be "embraced as well as exploded."

Hobbs highlights insurgency tactics founded on the definition and celebration of difference. However, resistance can also be predicated on union, on community. The last two essays in this section on resistance suggest methods to disrupt appropriation through new ways of seeing that grow out of immersion, not separation. Focusing, in turn, on the construal of sexual desire and race, each essay advocates alternative ways of seeing that enact resistance by forming relationships among the perceivers and between perceivers and the perceived.

In "Far Encounters: Looking Desire," Mieke Bal examines the gaze and its role in fixing, colonizing, and appropriating the subject of the gaze, especially when motivated by sexual desire. She focuses on a single verbal image in Proust, finding in that verbal image the outlines of the "sexogenic look," a way of seeing that enables one to see without co-opting that which is being seen. For Bal, Proust foregrounds the

visual element in the kind of encounters that generate sexuality, especially sexual interactions that are banned as a result of cultural taboos.
In a novel that explores desire and its unavoidable consequence, jealousy, imaged desires represent a kind of heroics or magic of semiosis:
visualizations that reveal and conceal unspeakable desires. Emblematic of the complexities of visual culture, the sexogenic look negotiates
between the individual subject and the social environment that we call
"culture." The non-colonizing sexogenic look joins perceiver and perceived through "hetereopathic identification," making it possible for
the marginal—the closeted—to shine and subvert appropriation.

David Palumbo-Liu in "Blood, Visuality, and the New Multiculturalism" not only critiques the impact on race of the hypervisiblity
of mass mediated culture, but also proposes an alternate way of seeing based on the invisibility of the deep "bond of social obligation."
Drawing on Clint Eastwood's film *Blood Work*, Palumbo-Liu focuses
on racial identity as it is manifested both visibly and invisibly. At once
a murder mystery and a tale of personal and racial redemption, the
film is a surprisingly liberal plea for hybridity, Palumbo-Liu argues,
one that revolves around not only connection but also modes of connection. The exchange of hearts and minds and the dynamic of vis-
ible/invisible challenge the stability of racial categories, offering a new
way of seeing that undermines appropriation and colonization. For
instance, Palumbo-Liu demonstrates that throughout the film "the visual, the evidentiary, is transmogrified and metaphorized into a synthetic image that discloses the interior, the psychic connecting tissue
between characters." As a result of the paradoxical play of the rhetoric of the visible and invisible, the film presents a "capacious notion
of human sympathy and social life" that resists divisive categories of
being. Through a kind of visual decoding that reveals the surface to
be deceptive and that presents a vision of society "demoting" contrived
narratives and images, the film argues for resistance based on finding
and nurturing the (invisible) private spaces of microcommunal sympa-
thies and generosity.

We close our collection with an interview with rhetorician, composer, and film-maker Trinh T. Minh-Ha, finding in her discussion
of her documentary film, *The Fourth Dimension*, a fusion of the major
arguments in this collection. Inextricable from the previous discussions of emergence, appropriation, and resistance in constructing the
real are issues of technology. Ihde looks at optical imaging technolo-

gies. Wysocki explores a complex website. Hobbs's starting point is the technology of human reproduction as well as the wild technological proliferation of images. Hum and Palumbo-Liu tease out a new vision by analyzing a film. The question of technology, both as a medium for images and words, and as a medium created by images and words, is addressed explicitly in an interview with Trinh T. Minh-ha, conducted by Valentina Vitali. In the process, this interview also crystallizes the focal points of this collection: the interinanimation of images, rhetorics, and scopic regimes in constructing the real and the dynamic processes of emergence, appropriation, and resistance in that interinanimation.

Without ever using Richards's term of interinanimation, Trinh in "The Cyborg's Hand: Care or Control?" highlights this phenomenon through her exploration of the rhythm of music, text, and image in *The Fourth Dimension*. Trinh argues that the integration of verbal fragments and visual returns propels the film. In addition, Trinh explains that she produces films that are first and foremost "boundary events," consisting of "boundary images" that merge language and vision, such as the "hearing eye": the image looks at itself, hears what it says, and tells of the moment of consumption even as it is being consumed. Through the creation of boundary images, Trinh seeks in her films to manifest reflexive play, a space created to expose film-making processes. Such a goal is not pursued for the mere sake of reflexivity—a notion whose significance is often taken in a very shallow way—but as a means to deconstruct the visual-textual context in which we operate. "It is through the finite," she argues, "through the rituals of imaging (or framing, scanning, panning, traveling, and editing, for example) that infinity is made tangible." Thus, the way we frame people tells not only about how and what we see, but also about the off-screen, the space excluded or not visible in the frame. This realization of the constructedness of our realities, "may bring about a shift in one's reception of the visual and aural material," she says, shifts in one's habits of perception.

The nine essays in this collection reveal how the language of prose—the rhetoric of reality building—is inextricable from the design of the visual image. They point to the ways in which our construction of the real, reliant as it is on the interinanimation of images, rhetorics, and regimes, is in constant flux, enacting ongoing processes of emergence, appropriation, and resistance. Gombrich argues that

"[j]ust as the study of poetry remains incomplete without an awareness of the language of prose, so, I believe, the study of art will be
increasingly supplemented by inquiry into the linguistics of the visual
image" (8–9). Guided by these essays, we can celebrate and critique
the formative power of the linguistics of the visual image and the design of the word.[6]

NOTES

[1] Characterized by ellipsis, enigma, and paradox, emblem books consist of changeable relationships between picture and epigram (2–3). Alastair
Fowler, in a defense of emblem books as a distinct literary genre rather than
as a subject of media studies, notes that emblems were "once dismissed as
popular, trivial, and visually second-rate" (1). "Emblems seem to have had
close interconnection with mnemonic images," Fowler argues, a connection
between emblem and *ars memoria* that Linda T. Calendrillo explores. She
argues that Renaissance emblem books grew out of the memory-art tradition
and assumed the function of externalizing memory, of stabilizing in print the
association of words and ideas with specific images.

[2] The degree to which the phenomenon of blindness radically changes
the nature of participation in a world of sighted people underlines the importance of the thesis we argue here. While memoirs by such individuals as
Erik Weihenmayer, who—among other things—climbed Mt. Everest, attest
to the power of sightless individuals to accomplish feats amazing even for a
sighted person, they also reveal the degree to which blindness requires of the
individual a different way of thinking. John M. Hull articulates this clearly.
In losing his sight as an adult, he explains, he had to learn to dismantle all of
the visual conventions that structured his realities. Central to the shift from
sightedness to blindness is the release of the visual conventions by which
one automatically functioned in the world and the subsequent shaping of
different conventions. Furthermore, the move from blindness to sightedness
is equally fraught. Oliver Sacks recounts a case study of Virgil, whose life-
long blindness was surgically corrected during his middle years. However, he
could not see; that is, he had to learn new ways to interpret the stimuli bom-
barding his optic nerve. In mythology, the most powerful prophets and poets
were blind. They were able to achieve insights denied the sighted because
they were not bound by the conventions governing that seeing. My point
is not to denigrate physical blindness by privileging sight. My point is that
physical sight is already by its nature limited and limiting. By learning to see
in ways privileged by our culture, we learn to not see.

[3] Nowhere is this privileging more evident than in those eras where the
dominant way of seeing begins to morph into new form, such as the first half
of the seventeenth century, during which, Alastair Fowler argues, "[S]emiotic

relations of words to images were altering profoundly, so that different concepts, old and new, existed simultaneously" (8).

[4] According to David Michael Levin, Hannah Arendt dates this decline from Henri Bergson, specifically the switch in attention in philosophy from *nous* to *logos* (2). On the other hand, W. J. T. Mitchell argues that the entire history of Western culture can be plotted according to the rise and fall of the image, which suggests that this particular dynamic is repeated throughout our 2500 years of recorded history in the West.

[5] I borrow "horizon of expectation" from E. H. Gombrich, who uses this term to discuss the role of perceptions in art history and aesthetics.

[6] I wish to thank Sue Hum and Linda T. Calendrillo for their help with this essay.

Works Cited

Aristotle. *De Anima*. Trans. J. A. Smith. *The Complete Works of Aristotle: The Revised Oxford Translation*. Ed. Jonathan Barnes. Vol. 1. Princeton: Princeton UP, 1984.

—. *Metaphysics*. Trans. W. D. Ross. *The Complete Works of Aristotle: The Revised Oxford Translation*. Ed. Jonathan Barnes. Vol. 2. Bollingen Series 71.2. Princeton: Princeton UP, 1984.

—. *On Rhetoric*. Trans. George A. Kennedy. New York: Oxford UP, 1991.

—. *Poetics*. Trans. I. Bywater. *The Complete Works of Aristotle: The Revised Oxford Translation*. Ed. Jonathan Barnes. Vol. 2. Bollingen Series 71.2. Princeton: Princeton UP, 1984.

Berger, Peter L., and Thomas Luckmann. *The Social Construction of Reality: A Treatise in the Sociology of Knowledge*. Garden City, NY: Doubleday, 1966.

Barfield, Owen. *Saving the Appearances: A Study in Idolatry*. 2nd ed. Hanover, NH: Wesleyan UP, 1988.

Burke, Kenneth. *Language as Symbolic Action: Essays on Life, Literature, and Method*. Berkeley: U of California P, 1966.

—. *Permanence and Change: An Anatomy of Purpose*. Indianapolis: Bobbs-Merrill, 1965.

Cable, Lana. *Carnal Rhetoric: Milton's Iconoclasm and the Poetics of Desire*. Durham, NC: Duke UP, 1995.

Calendrillo, Linda Theresa. "The Art of Memory and Rhetoric." Diss. Purdue University, 1988.

Carver, Craig. M. *A History of English in Its Own Words*. New York: HarperCollins, 1991.

Foucault, Michel. *Discipline and Punish: The Birth of the Prison*. Trans. Alan Sheridan. New York: Vintage Books, 1979.

—. *The Birth of the Clinic: An Archaeology of Medical Perception*. Trans. A. M. Sheridan Smith. New York: Vintage Books, 1994.

Fowler, Alastair. "The Emblem as a Literary Genre." *Deviceful Settings: The English Renaissance Emblem and its Contexts.* Ed. Michael Bath and Daniel Russell. New York: AMS P, 1999. 1–32.

Gombrich, E. H. *Art and Illusion: A Study in the Psychology of Pictorial Representation.* Princeton: Princeton UP, 1969.

Goldhill, Simon. "Refracting Classical Vision: Changing Cultures of Viewing." *Vision in Context: Historical and Contemporary Perspectives on Sight.* Ed. Teresa Brennan and Martin Jay. New York: Routledge, 1996. 15–28.

Haraway, Donna J. *Simians, Cyborgs, and Women: The Reinvention of Nature.* New York: Routledge, 1991.

Hull, John M. *Touching the Rock: An Experience of Blindness.* New York: Pantheon Books, 1990.

Jay, Martin. *Downcast Eyes: The Denigration of Vision in Twentieth-Century French Thought.* Berkeley, CA: U of California P, 1993.

—. "Scopic Regimes of Modernity." *Vision and Visuality.* Ed. Hal Foster. Seattle: Bay P, 1988. 3–23.

Keller, Evelyn Fox. *A Feeling for the Organism: The Life and Work of Barbara McClintock.* San Francisco: W. H. Freeman, 1983.

—. *Reflections on Gender and Science.* New Haven, CT: Yale UP, 1985.

Lewontin, R. C. *Biology as Ideology: The Doctrine of DNA.* New York: HarperPerennial, 1992.

Langer, Suzanne K. *Philosophical Sketches.* Baltimore: Johns Hopkins P, 1962.

Levin, David Michael. *The Opening of Vision: Nihilism and the Postmodern Situation.* New York: Routledge, 1988.

Metz, Christian. *The Imaginary Signifier: Psychoanalysis and the Cinema.* Trans. Annwyl Williams. Bloomington, IN: Indiana UP, 1982.

Mitchell, W. J. T. *Iconology: Image, Text, Ideology.* Chicago: U of Chicago P, 1986.

Richards, I. A. *The Philosophy of Rhetoric.* London: Oxford UP, 1936.

Rorty, Richard. "The Contingency of Language." *Contingency, Irony, and Solidarity.* Cambridge: Cambridge UP, 1989. 3–22.

Sacks, Oliver. *An Anthropologist on Mars: Seven Paradoxical Tales.* New York: Alfred A. Knopf, 1995. 108–152.

Schachtel, Ernest G. *Metamorphosis: On the Development of Affect, Perception, Attention, and Memory.* New York: Basic Books, 1959.

Stafford, Barbara Maria. *Good Looking: Essays on the Virtue of Images.* Cambridge: MIT P, 1996.

Weihenmayer, Erik. *Touch the Top of the World: A Blind Man's Journey to Climb Farther than the Eye Can See: My Story.* New York: Penguin, 2001.

Vico, Giambattista. *New Science: Principles of the New Science Concerning the Common Nature of Nations.* 3rd ed. 1744. Trans. David Marsh. London: Penguin Books, 1999.

Part I: Emergence

2 Hermeneutics and the New Imaging

Don Ihde

Imaging, if we mean making depictions, has been with us for a very long time. And, if making inscriptions may also be considered to be a kind of imaging, this practice has also been an ancient one. Perhaps the most dramatic personal experience I had of this was in 1968 during a visit to the cave at Niaux, France, as one of the first visitors to that site after the "Events of May." After more than a kilometer of following our guide into the cave's darkness, we came upon some abstract marks in ochre reds, somewhat like spears. Only later do the famous Ice Age paintings of bison, aurochs, horses, and mountain goats begin to appear, obviously ancient since many are encased in the translucent overlayment of minerals deposited during the fourteen millennia since their fabrication.

What struck me was not only the intense "realism" of the animal depictions, especially dramatic when lighted with a candle, the flicker of which seemed to make the bison breathe, but also the instant recognizability of each species. My twentieth century book and zoo experience was more than enough for me to experience the "aha" phenomenon of this recognition. This stood in contrast to the previously mentioned abstract line figures which also occurred in the cave. Whatever these inscriptions may have signified remained opaque to me, I could not "read" them.

I now take this nearly forty-year-old experience to have been my first "image and logic" recognition of two different styles of imaging.[1] In an overly simple sense, "seeing" a picture and "reading" an inscription each calls for somewhat different hermeneutic acts.

In what follows, I shall focus particularly upon some aspects of the history of imaging, primarily in the sciences, and follow two trajectories of imaging suggested above into what I now take to be a revolution that begins to take shape in the mid-twentieth into the twenty-first centuries, a new imaging. Beginning with picture-like depictions, which I shall call isomorphic images, early modern science begins with observations made possible by optical technologies which are also imaging technologies.

Imaging technologies have always played a major role in the discovery and production of scientific knowledge. Early modern imaging technologies often were optical, and the new discoveries through Galileo's telescope and Leewenhoek's microscope come to mind. The former, by transforming apparent distance, brought into view the four main lasting discoveries reported by Galileo: the satellites of Jupiter, the mountains of the Moon, sunspots, and the phases of Venus. The latter, by magnifying the micro entities within liquids or the hairs of fleas, and even sperm, brought human vision into the realm of previously unsuspected bacteria, cells, and single-celled animals.

These early optical technologies followed a line of development which I call isomorphic imaging; that is, they depict the entities within recognizable spatial and dynamic forms which made perceptual recognitions relatively easy and quick to spot. One of these technologies,

Fig. 1. Camera obscura by Athanasius Kircher, *The Great Art of Light and Shadow,* 1646, as a portable room from which to sketch scenes illuminated upon the blank screens inside (tabula rasa).

the camera obscura, was of particular importance and became useful in a wide variety of applications. These ranged from a device to produce verisimilitude in the production of art, as in Alberti's 1430 use, later similarly used by Da Vinci in 1450.

But it was also used for scientific purposes, a variant of which was the helioscope invented by Galileo, which allowed him to observe sunspots. Still later, both Descartes and Locke used the camera obscura as a metaphor machine, or epistemology engine, to describe the knowledge process itself.[2]

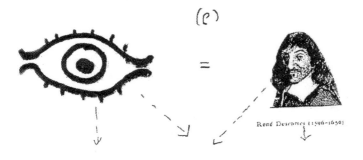

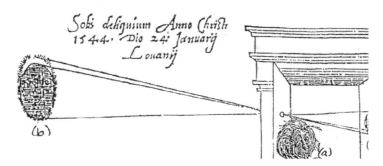

Fig. 2. A Knowledge Machine. Collage and drawing by Don Ihde, 14 February, 2000.

In this variation of the camera obscura, the newly invented "subject" (a) is distinguished from the "external object" (b), who sees only the "representation" (c), on the blank screen [*tabula rasa*] (d), which, to be true, must correspond to the real object (b) guaranteed only by the ideal observer (e), who simultaneously sees both the inside and the outside of the camera (God or the philosopher inventing the epistemology engine). This metaphor operates upon knowledge in somewhat the same way as the earlier notion of a "clockwork universe," suggested by Bishop Oresmus in the thirteenth century, did for celestial movement (White 98).

Before leaving the trajectory opened up by optical devices that deliver isomorphic images, I need to note preliminarily that isomorphism, no matter how "realistic," always remains partial. For while the camera obscura, for example, automatically displays the spatial forms of things imaged, it reduces or transforms the things imaged into two, rather than three, dimensions. It also inverts things, and transforms depth into a non-depth geometical display. Note that each of these features of the technological "construction" are values of early modern epistemology.

Not all imaging technologies employ isomorphic strategies. Peter Galison and Don Ihde have argued separately that a second strategy is one which prefers a "logic," "counting," or "quasi-textual" basis for imaging. The image produces something like a *code*, which must be "hermeneutically" interpreted or "read." An early example of such an imaging technology emerged from Isaac Newton's transformed version of a camera obscura combined with a prism, which produced rainbow spectra. Newton gained an insight into refraction from the spectrum by recognizing that each color within "white light" had a different frequency. He was thus able to produce better astronomical images by means of a reflecting telescope, which avoided what is known as the "chromatic aberration." But he did not invent the device which became a genuine non-isomorphic imager, the spectroscope. A century later, continued experimentation with prisms included in camera obscura devices did lead to spectroscopy and what today constitutes a major class of instrumentation used in disciplines as diverse as astronomy and pathology.

A simple spectroscope, rather than reducing the object imaged into a two dimensional display, transforms the light emissions from the object into something like a "bar code."

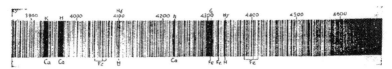

Fig. 3. Spectroscope, from J. B. Hearnshaw *The Analysis of Starlight*. (Cambridge: Cambridge University Press, 1986) 36, 38. Reprinted with the permission of Cambridge University Press.

Spectroscopes, in the simplest sense, replace the earlier round hole or lens with a slit, plus a prism to cast a more clearly refined spectrum complete with darkened absorption lines never seen by Newton. Without going into the finer points of the history of spectroscopy, refinements in the nineteenth century led to the recognition that these spectroscopic "bar codes" were signatures of chemical composition, for example, of the sun and different types of stars (see above).

In this image trajectory, what is "read" or interpreted is the image which no longer "resembles" the thing imaged. The image is, rather, a quasi-text phenomenon which has to be "read" using the proper hermeneutic techniques. And, just as in learning to read a natural language (or a set of mathematical equations), there must be a set of preparations and the learning of the now-spectroscopic "language" if the chemical recognition is to occur.

Peter Galison's version of this process is the one he calls the "logic" tradition. The "images" in this tradition, for example, are displays of the number of events recorded by logic machines ranging from Geiger counters to Cernekov counters, with results frequently displayed as graphs. These statistical displays contrast with the *image* tradition in physics, which favors a "golden event," or an isomorphic image of, say, an electron trail or a positron track.

Moving rapidly now, it can be seen that the two imaging trajectories, isomorphic and non-isomorphic, differently transform the objects imaged through technological constructions. (The image is *not* the thing, nor the map the territory. But the type of transformation differs from technology to technology, and this has not often been focused upon.) The instruments magnify and reduce different aspects of the object being investigated. Yet, also in both trajectories, the development of instrumentation has been one following ever deeper and more extreme interventions with macro- and micro-phenomena. I have called this a technological trajectory. In one sense, it is simple: if some magnification reveals more than we previously thought to be there, isn't greater magnification likely to yield more? And, phenomenologically speaking, whether the observational intervention is aimed at the macro or the micro, the bringing-into-view is equivalent. Whether the object is a galaxy brought "near" by a reflecting telescope, or an amoeba brought near by being made large, both appear as focal objects within the instrumental field of vision of the relevant instrument. Indeed, in these cases the tube of the telescope or microscope creates a similar frame for both image styles, and both produce a basically flat or depthless depiction.

Both these highly foreshortened histories, however, refer to the sciences produced through optical devices, microscopes, telescopes, and their variant uses within camera obscurae instruments. And, one could even add, *photography* to this family of camerae from the mid-nineteenth century. Historically speaking, all these visualizations did bring into the field of human knowledge a multitude of new and never-before-seen entities: from Galileo's mountains on the moon, the Jupiterian satellites, sun spots, on into galaxies begun to be recognized in the early twentieth century, and down to Leeuwenhoek's sperm, cells, the seven labia of bees recognized by the Society of Lynxes (Freedberg 272–96), and into the range of new microscopic structures of early microbiology. Still, in another sense, both isomorphic and non-isomorphic imaging could be called variations upon the human sensorium. If one is picture-like, it is seen with eyeball vision; if the other is text-like, it is read with those same eyes embedded in a reading practice. To be sure, one could also recognize through the magnified, amplified optical imaging processes both the pictorial-like perceptual gestalten of isomorphic processes and the text-like interpretive processes of the non-isomophic styles of imaging. In both optical example lines which I have used, however, there is retained something of a "realist" thesis. Objects "out there"—stars, galaxies, light sources—emit their radiations to and through the imaging devices which transform these emissions into "images" that can be seen/read, all within the analogue range of visual perception.

Yet, there is more than that which can be *seen*. In antiquity, Chinese scholars noted that there is sound beyond sound, experienced by feeling the bell's vibrations continue on beyond and below what could be heard with one's ears (Chen 10). Similarly, and in the tradition of the spectroscope, Herschel felt warmth at a point beyond and below what the red colored spectrum shone (today we call this phenomenon *infra*red).[3] Such experiences point to phenomena which lie beyond our sensory ranges, but which nonetheless are "real" or emitted. Today, such extreme phenomena are routinely *imaged*. I shall call this new style of imaging, constructed imaging.

Apart from scattered references such as those above, detection of phenomena lying beyond our normal sensorium, even when suspected, were quite rare.[4] In astronomy, clearly one of the sciences with a long modern history, observation until the twentieth century was *optical* both in the sense of optical technologies and within the range of optical or visible light. In what is now the early twenty-first century, astronomical imaging regularly detects and images emissions that include nano-emissions at the level of gamma rays up to the kilometer-long wave lengths of radio emissions. As Nigel Henbest and Michael Marten point out, optical light is now realized to be a very narrow band within the gamma-to-radio spectrum such that, "The range of light is surprisingly limited. It includes only radiation with wavelengths 30 per cent shorter to 30 per cent longer than the wavelength to which our eyes are most sensitive. The new astronomy covers radiation from extremes which have wavelengths less than one thousand-millionth as long [. . .] to over a hundred million times longer [than visible light]" (6). Radio reception, and especially the development of radar in World War II, was a dramatic technological break-through that began to make the heavens speak with non-light voices. Radio sources from distant astronomical objects began to be detected and in many cases these did not match up with optical objects. Later the "background hiss" of what is now known as the background radiation of the entire universe was also detected, and while it took some time to "decode," as a source, the eventual identification yielded Robert Woodrow Wilson a Nobel Prize in 1978. I shall not cite the equivalent histories that led to the detection of the now known spectrum, gamma to radio waves, but by the twenty-first century the technological embodiment of astronomy is filled with arrays of detectors that again can image in both isomorphic and non-isomorphic displays. But there is a difference: the visualizable and "readable" displays now also have to be understood as something different; I shall call this *translation*.

Behind what I am terming translation are actually two technologically constructed practices and processes. First, there is data/image reversibility. Any well-informed reader of science news should know about this. When a space probe approaches a planet, armed with an array of detectors and sensors—for purposes here let us include photographic as well as some set of non-optical range devices—it gets within range, engages its sensors and detectors, and then must send the results back to Earth. The photo taken needs to be digitally transformed into a transmittable code, sent, and then re-constructed back into a picture at the base. From photographic image to data back to image: this is reversibility. We can now have an earth-side experience of this process with digitally produced photographs through email. Some four years ago my then text-only computer got the following message:

Fig. 4. Data/Image Reversibility. Electronic digital communication, Eric Ihde to Don Ihde, 6 March 2000.

Not knowing what this code was, I had to ask my wife to have it reconstructed on her higher-end computer, and the image of my new grandson was produced. Image-data-image reversals lay behind the depiction.

Here a clue to the hermeneutics of contemporary imaging may also be discerned. I simply could not "read" the data; indeed, I doubt anyone could. Yet the data has the appearance of being a "text." On the other hand, with very ordinary experience, I could easily recognize the isomorphic image of my grandson, and even folk who would not know the identities of the individual could easily recognize the depiction of the baby. This is one clue about imaging which shows an apparent advantage to isomorphy: its instant and gestalt recognizability. But it also gives a clue to the non-isomorphic "text-like" data: to be able to "read," one needs special training and skills, analogous to learning a language or an arithmetic.

This example, however, remains within the range of simply modern isomorphic imaging. It is merely a more complex set of photographic, optical processes and thus remains within the ordinary range of our sensorium. So now we must push the process to its next set of translation processes, the transformation of data from sources lying beyond our bodily capacities, translated into images which can be seen/read.

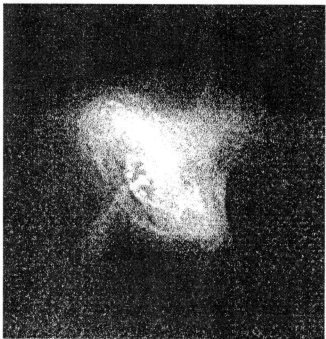

Fig. 5. X-Ray Emission (NASA Image. 24 Nov 2002 <http://science.nasa.gov/chandra/>). NASA and Chandra Science Center.

The same data-image reversibility is present with any remote sensing and with any sensing which produces constructed images from phenomena not directly sensed with our human bodies.

Galileo's optical observations of the sun, some of which yielded the discovery of sun spots, remain within magnified visual perceptions.[5] If, now, however, we substitute for his early drawing of sun spots some imagery from contemporary detectors—here an X-ray emission (Figure 5)—we must note something very different from the Galilean context. This image, while clearly isomorphic in that it shows regions of intensity and thus shape and configuration, cannot be bodily sensed. Instead, the image must be translated into perceivable depictions and conventionally displayed in "false color." [Here in black and white.] Such images remain strangely "realist" in the sense that they are displaying emission patterns from the distant sun, but they are also "irreal" in the sense that we are now perceiving the unperceivable (through the technological translation made possible by our detectors). Here the anthropological invariant is clearly implied. For us to "see" the X-ray (or any other frequency patterns, such as radio-wave patterns), the phenomena must be translated into perceivable form. In short, our bodily constraints, position, and sensory range is implicitly taken into account in the imaging technologies. Our bodies, in other words, are implied within the imaging process. The same observations apply to other slices from the entire microwave spectrum. Figure 6 shows the same Crab Nebula depicted in other frequency slices:

Fig. 6. Crab Nebula (NASA Image. 24 Nov 2002 <http://science.nasa.gov/newhome/headlines/ast28sep99_2.htm>.) Credit: NASA and Chandra Science Center.

Each of the examples I have just shown can be called slices, that is, slices of the vast spectrum of microwave activity coming from the sun. Slices work as "instrumental phenomenological variations," and each variant shows some distinctive feature of the phenomenon; for example, the X-ray image of the Crab shows the radiation jets which stream out from its central pulsar or highly radioactive neutron source.

The advantage of slices is that particular features which would not be visible in a composite image, that is an image which combines all the wave lengths but which could be constructed through the computer and a tomographical process, and these show the "full" range of emissions but lose the clarity of the selective reduction to the previous x-ray spectrum. One can see here also how the image may be manipulated, tuned, enhanced—a machinic set of interventions. This imaging is far from "passive"; it is, rather, highly "active." To recapitulate some of the process: first, as with all imaging, the image is technologically produced. Without an instrument—and its associated transformations—no production of scientific knowledge of these phenomena is possible at all. Second, each imaging process produces whatever phenomenon is displayed through the magnification and reduction which the instrument allows. And, third, the image, to be perceived-interpreted, must be translated into a "perceivable-readable" result. The technologically produced translation is the production of a humanly perceivable-readable result, thus indirectly pointing to what I called above the anthropological invariant.

In the examples I have just used, the translation process yields a "perceivable" image; thus it appears to be similar to the isomorphic or image tradition. However, there is a caveat, since the informed observer must also know that the use of "false color," the displays of X-ray dimensions are not simply observable, but observable only under the conditions of the translation. Whatever seeing-reading is going on must therefore be *critical.* The implication posed by the critical is one which argues that the hermeneutics which go with this process of seeing/reading is one which must include specific forms of background knowledge. Here a wider range of authors have partially described this process, including Galison and Ihde, but also Isabelle Stengers and Bruno Latour.

What the new technologically constructible imagery introduces is actually more than manipulability, variation, contrast, and the like; it adds a set of innovative "add-ons" which emerge from the machinic process itself. Here are two examples: the data/image examples I have cited above have been limited to detection or sensor devices, reversed into data, and reconstructed back into images. But this reversibility can also be made to produce images from algorithms or algorithms from images; this is what computer processes can now do with an astonishing number of applications. My first example comes from the emergence in mathematics and modeling practices in the field of chaos and fractal phenomena. Data, algorithmically produced, can be imaged.

Fig. 7. Imaged Algorithmic Data. a@a_F_rActAl__a@a_. 2006. <http://news-fractal.free.fr/news4/page1.htm. Philippe de Courcy>. Used by permission.

But, once imaged, the newly and clearly constructed depictions turn out to be amazingly suggestive of some natural phenomena (coastlines, erosion patterns, mountain ranges). Computer "embodied" thematical codes now turn out to be ways to model far more complex phenomena than previously have been available. And, by turning these into gestalt-perceptions, the astute observer can—at a glance—perceive the reiterative patterns shown. New knowledge is produced in this process.

This additive emergence from the reversibility of data/image works in any number of contemporary technologies. My second example comes from the composition practices of my youngest son, Mark. He has a digital keyboard connected to a music program in a computer. Its "design intent" was to make it possible for the composer to produce a score just by playing the composition on the keyboard. (Mark plays the piece, the computer prints out the score, and then he can come back and edit or correct as per his taste.) But this process is also reversible: he can produce a score and play it back through the keyboard, and it is here that the additive manipulation emerges. The composer can compose a score which includes more than ten notes at a time, that is, more than a human player could play with ten fingers, and he can program the play-out to be at a speed faster than any human player could play. In short, a new musical possibility can be produced through this reversibility and, given a young boy's fascination with electronic "toys," precisely such compositions began to be heard from his "studio."

In the two examples just given, it might seem that the instrumental construction possibilities clearly break the bonds and constraints usually associated with science praxis, that is, the constraint which aims at "knowledge of the real" of whatever phenomena range one is exploring. Clearly, the fractal patterns are not of any "real" thing and the music produced is no longer that of a human performer (at least not in its traditional understanding). Instead, both are, in different senses, *simulations.* But simulations can be taken in multiple directions.

Within science praxis, simulations are usually used in fairly conservative ways to produce visible displays which purport to show something about a phenomenon being studied. What the new, computer enhanced, or even produced, imagery does is to make available depictions of complexity previously unavailable to earlier instruments. In medicine, for example, data produced through very different physical processes by MRI, PET, and CAT X-ray scans, can be combined and tomographically depicted through computer imagery to show a 3-D, complex image of some pathology: a brain tumor, cancerous growth, and so forth. This production of a virtual object is now an ordinary feature of much medical practice. Moreover, there is a reversibility which is made possible by alternating between the imaged or virtual tumor and the "real" one when it comes to an operation.

But a virtual or simulative process also produces an even higher level image in such problems associated with what I call "whole earth measurements." The question seems simple: is there global warming?

And, if so, one of the presumably measurable phenomena would be the level of the earth's oceans. But while the question is clear and simple, its answer is complex and until very recently impossible to undertake. Figure 8, however, is an example of a contemporary answer.

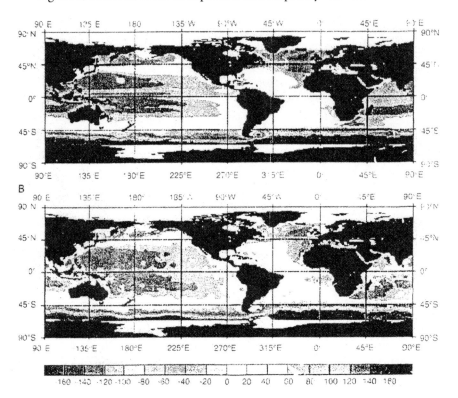

Fig. 8. Computer Modeled Simulation. © 1995 by Robin T. Tokmakian and Detlef Stammer. Reprinted with their permission from *Science*, V. 269. 8 Sept. 1995, 1384.

This image is a computer-modeled simulation of the levels of all oceans combined, claiming the 16.8 cm rise between 1993 and 1994. And this simulation is an excellent example of today's highly constructed imaging of complex objects. The measurements which went into this ultimately produced image include vast amounts of data produced by satellites (TOPEX/POSEIDON altimery data), tomographically analyzed by computer processes, and then displayed in these whole earth-depictions. I have often said that this "picture" (which is not really a picture) is more expensive than any multi-million dollar art work sold through contemporary auction houses: it is a multi-million dollar image if the costs of its production were to be counted. Yet, as with all perceivable visualizations, it can be taken in at a glance and now, under the stipulation of a critical hermeneutic reading, shows the overall ocean level rise. I contend that this scientific image is neither a picture nor a text. And for that I will have to explain what goes into the distinctive visual hermeneutics that science practices have developed.[6]

First, however, a brief summary of the developments which lie behind this new style of visualization: ever since early modernity, science practice has been inextricably tied to forms of instrumentalization, to technologies of vision. The earliest examples above (lenses and camera obscurae) gave distinctive shape to the kinds of vision preferred and/or provided the transformations of phenomenological distance ("apparent distance") that allowed the macro- and microscopic to be made visually present. More extensively, even in early modernity, scientific investigations of all phenomena beyond face-to-face, eyeball observation are possible only through forms of technological embodiment or instrumentation that bring these phenomena into view.

Variations upon visualism, however, included both picture and text analogues, isomorphic and non-isomorphic imaging in my terminology, but both are seen/read and imply the humanly embodied experiencer; this is the anthropological invariant in experienced observations.

Once beyond ordinary experience, imaging—and I argue that this is a continuum of ever-increasing distinctions, from simple magnification to magnification beyond any eyeball/instrument alternation, to and beyond the horizons of the sensorium itself—points to the growing need to develop translation techniques which transform the phenomena into humanly perceivable images. This, in turn, calls for special skills of a hermeneutic or critically interpretive order to "read" or understand the phenomena involved.

Third, having followed the progression into ever higher degrees of complexity and compounding technologies, I would argue that there is an implicit trajectory that emerges which can be stated as: the higher the degree of technological construction, the more precise the scientific result, the more integral the display in a gestalt pattern can be. This is a special case in which what is "most constructed" is simultaneously "most real."

Fourth, philosophically and epistemologically, all this implies that
the kind of epistemology involved in scientific imaging is very much a
type of constructive activity, embodied technologically, and is "inter-
ventional" not simply "representational." It is also actively hermeneutic
in the sense that the seeing/reading of a scientific image must be critical since the "image" in this sense is neither a "picture" nor a "text"
in any usual sense. Thus, whereas the traditional approach to imaging
has often remained stuck or sedimented in an early modern, represen-
tionalist framework, I am arguing that imaging is better understood as
an interventionist and constructive activity which takes place through
a material hermeneutic embodied in instrumental variations.

Finally, then, parallel what has clearly been a technological history
in imaging to what is equally needed, a hermeneutic history. I conclude with some observations about the expanded hermeneutics which
are called for.

Return to the opening example, Ice Age art in the Cave of Niaux.
I would claim in this example that some, but not very much, common
experience is needed to both appreciate and recognize the animals depicted. But more would be needed to recognize the "world" to which
they belonged. Contemporary France no longer even has these animals
roaming in its landscape, nor do we know very well what the fabrica-
tors of the depictions were doing. A larger and deeper background in
cultural anthropology, knowledge of geological changes, and knowledge of comparative religions enrich the hermeneutic aura of these
depictions. Generalizing: it is probably better to know more than less,
more broadly and deeply than more narrowly and shallowly. This adds
to the implied context for the observations. But nothing new here.

What about technical production? In some caves the pigments have
been found (ground ocher clays, charcoal, etc.) of the limited palette
of the archaic painter. Brushes, a blow technique (for the hand prints
at many sites), are known. Yet none of this knowledge by itself adds
much to our limited understanding of the depiction and its "world."
And the situation is even worse for the abstract or non-isomorphic
marks accompanying the animal depictions. Were these numeric? Cal-
endaric? Iconic? Again, with some knowledge of how some marks seem
associated with moon cycles combined with archeological and anthropological knowledge, only small bits of knowledge seem probable.

Now, jump to the end of my image progression, and the simulation of a whole earth measurement of oceanic levels. What would we

naively recognize? Again, from common late-modern experience, we recognize a whole earth projection (the entire globe displayed on a two-dimensional spread, with recognizable continental shapes). And we recognize the multicolors of the ocean areas and can surmise some sort of intensity scale being shown; but without more clues, what is being shown? In short, more background knowledge is needed to "see" at the informed and critical glance what can be "seen." And while that need not be full knowledge of which satellites and measuring devices were used, it must be at least general knowledge that what is being measured is ocean height rather than temperature. Then, if I know that, I can "see" at a glance which parts of the ocean are "higher" than its other parts on the global scale and that may (or may not) tell me something more.

Here the visual hermeneutic calls for "reading" skills that are much more analogous to map reading, and perhaps in a surprise, also more analogous to art criticism than might be thought. We are now entering very complex and difficult territory, the details of which lie far beyond the limits of a single essay, but clues can be provided. In map reading, the reader must know the conventions embodied in the map. For example, contemporary maps contain the convention that north is to the top; south to the bottom; west to the left; east to the right (this convention is fairly modern: Medieval T-maps had south on top). Unless this is part of the sedimented reading practice of the reader, the map could be misaligned and not provide any, or provide a contradictory, clue to what it shows. It is worthwhile to pursue this a bit farther: ordinarily in "reading" a map, we do not actually align the map with the terrain, that is, lay the map down with south to south, and so forth, but take this into account in our reading practices. In contrast, we do ordinarily align a picture with head on top, feet on bottom to "see" the picture aright. In my camera obscura examples, our imagined Alberti, I would guess, knew enough to re-invert his drawn-by-the-lines depiction when he showed it to his audience. But the practices of painting from an inverted image apparently also taught artists to "see" differently as well, if Philip Steadman is right about what Vermeer learned![7] Our whole earth map includes the south-is-up convention, and it is "read" by making the double interpretive move indicated. But it also incorporates another convention. In its original false colors, the intensity patterns follow a "rainbow spectrum" convention in which the most intense, in this case, the highest points, are at the infrared or hottest horizon, while the coolest or lowest lie at the ultraviolet horizon. Here what I am calling conventions are taken for granted in the "reading" of the images, but all are part of an acquired hermeneutic practice. These are map reading analogues.

The art criticism analogues are similar in that items within the painting are recognizable for their symbolic and informative roles to the critical analyst. Here I am relying upon two hopefully more familiar examples of paintings which contain well discussed iconographic items: Van Eyck' s *Arnolfini Wedding* (1434) and Velazquez's *Las Meninas*. The Van Eyck painting is often called a marriage contract, with each gesture, the mirror, positioning, each element analyzed; whereas *Las Meninas* is, according to Foucault, a painting about painting in which the observer(s) are subtly included within the painting (the royalty in the mirror). Both are more than "mere" pictures calling for more than naïve sight. The critical art hermeneutic identifies the elements going into the make-up of the complex gestalt. Scientific images have that same character, although with different meaning contexts (usually emphasizing measurements, dimensions, intensities, and so forth) and, in the case of the new imaging, the types of non-sensory elements must also be taken into account. Critical hermeneutics, in short, pervade all three practices (maps, art objects, scientific images) in their distinctive ways. One clear implication is that there may be far less difference between what once was taken as the divide between the sciences and the humanities than once thought.

NOTES

[1] Although not then writing explicitly about imaging technologies, I differentiated between embodiment perceptual-bodily technology relations and hermeneutic or linguistic-reading relations in my early *Technics and Praxis*. More recently, these human-technology relations were seen to apply in both directions, isomorphic and non-isomorphic, which I now see in image technologies. My 1998 *Expanding Hermeneutics* made these two directions clear. Peter Galison, in his masterful *Image and Logic,* calls these two styles of instrument reading "image" and "logic" traditions.

[2] See my millennium essay "Epistemology Engines."

[3] Infrared was discovered as a "heat wave" beyond the extent of visible light in the nineteenth century, but was not yet imaged at that time. See Hearnshaw.

[4] I refer here to physical or natural phenomena, not to the long history of imaginative phenomena which might have been called "supernatural" in

a previous era, since ghosts, demons and angels have long been "literary" inhabitants of our cultural worlds.

[5] But even these got him into trouble in his early modernity. His publication about sun spots was the first publication to bring him to the attention to the Inquisition, and he was issued a warning about "blemishes" on the sun.

[6] See my *Expanding Hermeneutics.*

[7] There has been a lot of controversy and publicity surrounding the rediscovered use of the camera obscura in Renaissance art. David Hockney's *Secret Knowledge* has gotten the most attention, but Philip Steadman's *Vermeer's Camera* seems to me the better work. However, this "rediscovery" is hardly that: my favorite 1929 *Encyclopedia Britannica* has an extensive article on the early artistic use of camera obscuras that deals with what has clearly been a well-known history of mechanical devices in Renaissance times.

Works Cited

Chen, Cheng-Yih. "Acoustics in Chinese Culture." *Encyclopedia of the History of Science, Technology and Medicine in Non-Western Cultures.* Dordrecht: Kluwer, 1997.

Freedberg, David. "Iconography Between the History of Art and the History of Science, and the Case of the Urban Bee." *Picturing Science, Producing Art.* Ed. Carolyn A. Jones and Peter Louis Galison. New York: Routledge, 1998. 272–96.

Galison, Peter Louis. *Image and Logic: A Material Culture of Microphysics.* Chicago: U of Chicago P, 1997.

Hearnshaw, J.B. *The Analysis of Starlight.* Cambridge: Cambridge UP, 1986.

Henbest, Nigel and Michael Marten. *The New Astronomy.* Cambridge: Cambridge UP, 1996.

Hockney, David. *Secret Knowledge: Rediscovering the Lost Techniques of the Old Masters.* New York: Viking, 2001.

Ihde, Don. *Expanding Hermeneutics: Visualism in Science.* Evanston: Northwestern UP, 1998.

—. "Epistemology Engines." *Nature* 6 July 2000: 21.

—. *Technics and Praxis.* Boston: Reidel, 1979.

Latour, Bruno. *Science in Action.* Cambridge: Harvard UP, 1988.

Steadman, Philip. *Vermeer's Camera: Uncovering the Truth Behind the Masterpieces.* New York: Oxford UP, 2001.

Stengers, Isabelle. *The Invention of Modern Science.* Trans. Daniel W. Smith. Minneapolis: U of Minnesota P, 2000.

White, Lynn T. *Medieval Technology and Social Change.* Oxford: Clarendon, 1962.

3 Darwin's Diagram: Scientific Visions and Scientific Visuals

Alan Gross

In the third book of *Gulliver's Travels,* Jonathan Swift abandons his tight narrative and indulges forthrightly in broad satire. In his account of the Grand Academy of Lagado—read the Royal Society—he is particularly merciless. Among his targets are the attempts to reform the language. He takes as his particular target Thomas Sprat's pronouncement that scientific communication must "return back to the primitive purity and shortness, when men delivered so many things in an equal number of words" (II xx). His wicked lampoon takes this pronouncement literally, and has as its climax two "sages" exchanging views without the benefit of natural language, both burdened with heavy bags of "things" that they laboriously pass to and fro in order to communicate (190–91).

Swift has been proven right: science has found natural language indispensable. But Swift has also been proven wrong. Artificial languages, such as those of mathematics and logic, though ultimately they depend on natural language for their meaning, *are* more perspicuous, the notation that Leibniz invented for his calculus being a good example. Equally important, science has found that "things" (in the form of scientific visuals) are as indispensable to its communication as is natural language. As we gathered data for our book, *Communicating Science,* my collaborators and I discovered,[1] though we did not anticipate, the increasing centrality of visuals to scientific communication and thought, a centrality more and more evident as the nineteenth century unfolded. Over the centuries, the visuals of science also altered in their character; more and more, they depicted, not things, but theories as well; they became diagrams and, later, data graphics, visual-textual compounds, object-sided on the one hand, theory-sided on the other.

I would like now to focus on the single diagram in Darwin's *Origin of Species* as an example of this trend. Although well-known, it is little commented upon. This error of omission is perhaps due, in part, to the relentless concentration of philosophers of science on sentences and their underlying propositions. In this chapter I would like to place Darwin's diagram in three contexts: the historical, the conceptual, and the biographical. First, I integrate the diagram into the historical development of visuals. Then I focus on the diagram itself as a visual-textual compound, a mediator between the world and its explanation. Finally, I place the diagram in the context of Darwin's own intellectual development.

The Historical Context

In his essay, "The Age of the World Picture," Martin Heidegger remarks that "the fundamental event of the modern age is the conquest of the world as picture" (134). This, Heidegger says, "does not mean a picture of the world but the world *conceived and grasped* as a picture" ("als Bild *begriffen*" 129, emphasis added). Heidegger is aware that we speak consistently and cogently of the Greek world view, and the world view of the Middle Ages. But his point is that this way of speaking would be foreign to the Greeks and to the Middle Ages. He differentiates the science of Greece and of the Middle Ages from that of the modern age by distinguishing between the occasional theoretical depiction of the world, as, say, in Theodoric's fourteenth century discourse and diagram on the rainbow (Boyer 118), and the relentless and wholesale objectification of the world as illustrated in the theory-infused scientific visuals that meet us now at every turn.

This is how Heidegger puts it in his rebarbative prose, the product less of a desire to obfuscate than of the need to muster the meager resources of language in the service of creative thought: "It is one thing to preserve the horizon of unconcealment that is limited at any given time through the apprehending of what becomes present (man as *metron* or the measure of all things). It is another to proceed into the unlimited sphere of possible objectification, through the reckoning up of the representable that is accessible to every man and binding for all" (147, translation slightly modified).[2] If Heidegger is right, theoretical diagrams are not only central to science, but also to the spirit of the modern age.

It might seem that astronomy speaks loudly against Heidegger's claim. But this conclusion may be overhasty. The many figures in Ptolemy's *Almagest* are not pictures of anything, nor are they evidence that Ptolemy conceived and grasped the world as a picture. These constructions are a means of calculating the positions of the moon, the stars, and the planets rather than representing their actual motions. In a passage from his prefatory letter to Copernicus's *De Revolutionibus,* Osiander speaks of Ptolemy when he says:

> Perhaps there is someone who is so ignorant of geometry and optics that he regards the epicycle [calculated path] of Venus as probable, or thinks that it the reason why Venus sometimes precedes and sometimes follows the sun by forty degrees and even more. Is there any one who is not aware that from this assumption it necessarily follows that the diameter of the planet at perigee [its nearest distance from the Earth] should appear more than four times, and the body of the planet more than sixteen times, as great as the apogee [furthest distance]? (II,xvi and 336)

Nor is it clear that Copernicus affirmed the reality of the orbits he constructed. (This point must not be confused with the realism Copernicus plainly evinces when he speaks of the centrality of the sun.) My example is his solution to the problem of the inequality of the solar apsides, the sun's positions relative to the Earth. Of his exceedingly complex diagram, which offers two solutions to the same problem, he says: "since so many arrangements lead to the same result, I would not readily say which one is real, except that the perpetual agreement of the computations and phenomena compels the belief that it is one of them" (164). Even Copernicus's faith that one of these arrangements is true seems misplaced: it is hard to see how these motions would be possible in any coherent physics. But the same cannot be said for Galileo's explanation of the retrograde motion of Jupiter as observed from the Earth in his *Two Chief World Systems.*[3]

In the diagram in Figure 2, the outer arc is a component off the circle of the zodiac in the stellar sphere: imagine it as a screen on which the image of the planet Jupiter is projected. The inner circle is the

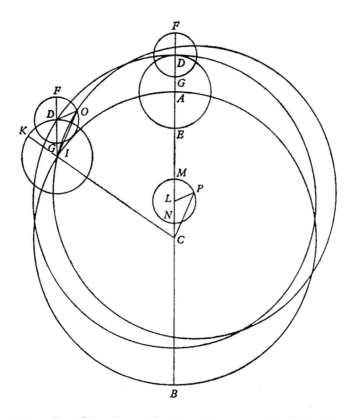

Fig. 1. Inequality of the solar apsides. From Copernicus, *On the Revolutions,* 163.

Earth's orbit, the outer, Jupiter's. The illusion of retrograde motion is caused by the differential orbital circuits of the Earth and Jupiter: the Earth one year, Jupiter, 12. When we observe Jupiter from B on Earth, we see it in the circle of the zodiac at position P. When we move to positions D, E, and F, Jupiter seems to slow down. At positions G and H, Jupiter appears to move backward. For Galileo this is a true picture of the cause of the phenomenon; moreover, setting down such pictures, conceiving and grasping the world as a picture, is not Galileo's occasional but his habitual practice.

Galileo may serve equally well as an example of the Heideggerian transformation of physics. Reproduced is a diagram from *Two New Sciences,* a simple and elegant demonstration of the law of uniform accelerated motion.

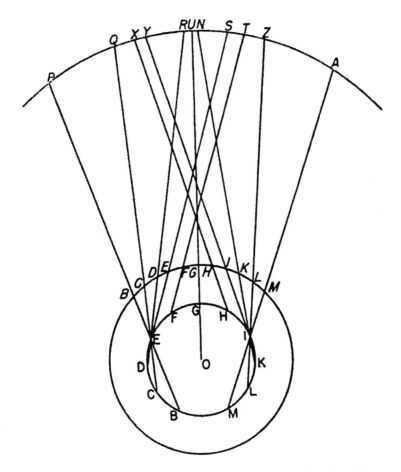

Fig. 2. Retrograde motion of Jupiter. From Galileo, *Two Chief World Systems*, 343.

Of a body beginning at rest and moving from C to D with uniform accelerated motion, the law states that the time of traversal is equal to the time in which the same space would be traversed by the same body in a uniform unaccelerated motion if its speed were one-half the final speed of the latter body. The proof is geometrical. Line AB represents time traveled in uniform unaccelerated motion, Line EB, the maximum and final speed of a body traveling in uniform accelerated motion. Given these two lines, we can construct right triangle AEB. Given line AB, we can construct rectangle AGFB, equal in area to triangle AEB. Since the triangles IEF and GIA are identical, line

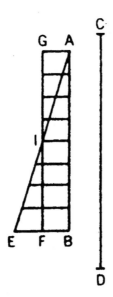

Fig. 3. Law of uniform accelerated motion. From Galileo, *Two New Sciences*, 165.

segments EF=GA=FB. Therefore, line segment FB is one half line segment EB. But by definition line segment EB is the final speed of the accelerating body, while line segment FB is the final speed of the unaccelerated body. QED.[4]

Irrelevant is the extent to which Galileo's work is indebted to the Mertonian school of medieval Oxford. Only salient is the thoroughness with which Galileo pursued this vision, the extent to which he saw geometry not only as a means of solving problems in the real world, but also as an accurate representation of the real structures of that world. That this is his view is clear from a well-known passage from *The Assayer* of 1623:

> Philosophy is written in that vast book which stands forever open to our eyes, I mean the universe; but it cannot be read until we have learnt the language and become familiar with the characters in which it is written. It is written in mathematical language, and the letters are triangles, circles and other geometrical

figures, without which means it is humanly impossible
to comprehend a single word. (qtd. in Crombie 142)

Consequently Galileo's QED differs from that of Ptolemy; his proof is
not a theorem that merely accounts for the phenomena and is without

TABLEAU DES SUBSTANCES SIMPLES.

	NOMS NOUVEAUX.	NOMS ANCIENS CORRESPONDANTS.
Substances simples qui appartiennent aux trois règnes, et qu'on peut regarder comme les éléments des corps.	Lumière............	Lumière.
	Calorique..........	Chaleur.
		Principe de la chaleur.
		Fluide igné.
		Feu.
		Matière du feu et de la chaleur.
	Oxygène...........	Air déphlogistiqué.
		Air empiréal.
		Air vital.
		Base de l'air vital.
	Azote.............	Gaz phlogistiqué.
		Mofette.
		Base de la mofette.
	Hydrogène.........	Gaz inflammable.
		Base du gaz inflammable.
Substances simples, non métalliques, oxydables et acidifiables.	Soufre............	Soufre.
	Phosphore.........	Phosphore.
	Carbone..........	Charbon pur.
	Radical muriatique....	Inconnu.
	Radical fluorique....	Inconnu.
	Radical boracique.....	Inconnu.
Substances simples, métalliques, oxydables et acidifiables.	Antimoine.........	Antimoine.
	Argent	Argent.
	Arsenic...........	Arsenic.
	Bismuth...........	Bismuth.
	Cobalt............	Cobalt.
	Cuivre............	Cuivre.
	Étain.............	Étain.
	Fer	Fer.
	Manganèse.........	Manganèse.
	Mercure..........	Mercure.
	Molybdène.........	Molybdène.
	Nickel............	Nickel.
	Or...............	Or.
	Platine...........	Platine.
	Plomb	Plomb.
	Tungstène	Tungstène.
	Zinc.............	Zinc.
Substances simples, salifiables, terreuses.	Chaux	Terre calcaire, chaux.
	Magnésie..........	Magnésie, base de sel d'Epsom.
	Baryte............	Barote, terre pesante.
	Alumine...........	Argile, terre de l'alun, base de l'alun.
	Silice.............	Terre siliceuse, terre vitrifiable.

Fig. 4. Table of simple substances. From Lavoisier, *Traité*, 135.

realist pretensions; it is rather a theorem that explains the behavior of bodies, their actual and potential motions, a step in the uncovering of the causal structure of the world.

With Lavoisier's revolution at the end of the eighteenth century, chemistry also became a modern science in Heidegger's sense. In his "Table of Simple Substances," Lavoisier also conceives and grasps the world as a picture (Figure 4).

Though it bears a superficial resemblance to its predecessors, this is no ordinary table (Roberts); rather, it is a precursor to Mendeleev's periodic table of 1869. Like Mendeleev's, Lavoisier's Table is meant to be a true reflection of the elements of which the material world is composed:

> The perfection of the nomenclature of chemistry, en-
> visioned in this account, consists in conveying the
> concepts and the facts truly, omitting nothing, and
> above all adding nothing; nomenclature must be a
> faithful mirror, because—and we cannot repeat this
> too often—it is never nature or the facts that she
> presents to us, but our own reasoning processes, that
> deceive us. ("Nomenclature" 359, my translation)

But there is another, equally important aspect of Lavoisier's Table: its structure is a faithful mirror not only of the elements themselves, but also of the structure existing among them. Even such unknowns as the "Muriatic radical" ("Radical muriatique. . . . Inconnu") have their place in Lavoisier's scheme of things, which is also the scheme of things, purportedly, the causal structure of the world as meant by chemistry.

This is not to say that his particular model of nature's working is the final word: "Chemistry progresses toward its goal, and towards its perfection," Lavoisier says, "by dividing, subdividing, and subdividing once again, and we do not know where it will all end. We cannot be sure that what we regard as simple today will be simple in the final analysis" (*Traité* 137, my translation). But whatever may be discovered, Lavoisier implies, the science of chemistry will always consist at bottom of simple substances named for what they actually are and structured within the science exactly as they are structured among themselves in nature. This is the Heideggerian point.

It may be that a fine-grained study of the context from which the practices of Galileo and Lavoisier emerged will weaken any claim to their uniqueness in the transformation of natural philosophy into Heideggerian science. This would modify, though it would not undermine, my claim. In the one case where we have a longitudinal study of scientific visuals, Martin Rudwick's essay on geological illustrations, the transformation is plainly social rather than individual. In this ground-breaking work, Rudwick shows conclusively that, in the period from 1760 to 1840, geological illustration became more and more theory-sided: illustrations became "highly abstract statements in a visual language" (168). Both types of geological sections, for example, the transverse and the columnar, were theory-based, the first in that it actually contained theory-based extrapolations, the second in that in addition it omitted quasi-realistic conventions indicating a mine shaft or a quarry face (164, 167). Most important, after about 1820, these sections represented a causal theory of the strata: "after about 1820 these truly geological forms of illustration were modified still further to enable them to become the vehicles of cognitive goals that reached beyond the analysis of three-dimensional structures in causal terms" (180). This trend conforms to the Heideggerian criterion for a modern science.

Charles Darwin's depictions of the slow elevation of mountain chains, which also conforms to this Heiddeggerian standard, may exemplify the state of geological illustration in mid-century (Figures 5, 6, and 7).

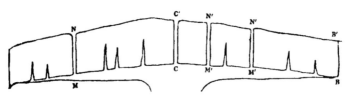

Uplifted square masses.

Fig. 5. Uplifted square masses. From Darwin, *Collected Papers, 77.*

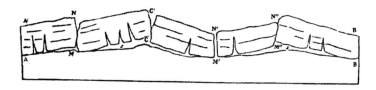

Fig. 6. Dislocated square masses. From Darwin, *Collected Papers,* 77.

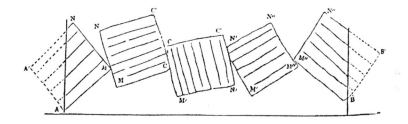

Fig. 7. Overthrown crustal masses. From Darwin, *Collected Papers,* 78.

According to Darwin's thesis, this elevation is caused "by a long succession of slow movements" (*Collected Papers* 76). The three diagrams in his paper are to be read as stop-action photographs of a dynamic process, the third being a variant of the second in which the thickness of the sections matches their width. These are not pictures of actual mountains in the process of growth through upheaval, or of actual volcanic formation. Rather, these figures make a general claim: the growth of mountains and volcanoes is a consequence of underlying and general dynamic processes. The diagrams are a representation of Hutton's theory in which "the repetition of small causes [produces] great effects," a theory "which Mr. Lyell has already brought distinctly to bear on this particular subject" (80).

According to Darwin, the cause of the elevation of mountains is now known: "Mountain chains are the effects of continental elevations; continental elevations and the eruptive force of volcanoes are due to one great motive power, now in progressive action; therefore the formation of mountain-chains is likewise in progress, and at a rate which may be judged by either phenomenon, but most nearly by the growth of volcanoes." Moreover, "we are to include the entire globe in the foregoing hypothesis." This means "that the configuration of the fluid surface of the Earth's nucleus is subject to some change." While "its cause is completely unknown," as in the case of the 'empty' spaces in Lavoisier's table or in Mendeleev's periodical table, it is a place waiting to be filled by further science (80–82).

By the end of the first quarter of the seventeenth century, astronomy and physics were modern sciences fully Heideggerian in character, the world conceived and grasped as a picture of "spatiotemporal magnitudes in motion" (119).[5] By the middle of the nineteenth century, chemistry and geology had also arrived at this point. To align biology with the rest, to make biology a Heideggerian science, seems to have been Darwin's achievement.[6] His diagram in *Origin* is the concentrated essence of this achievement, a tribute to the power of his visual imagination as a conceptual instrument. I now pursue this point.

Darwin's Diagram as Textual-Visual Compound

In a Heideggerian science, I claim, visual-textual compounds are central: only the fusion of words and pictures can overcome the limitations of each in disclosing and explaining relevant aspects of the world. Let us begin our exploration of this claim with a contrasting use of scientific visuals, not in the service of theory, but of identification. Here is the description of the Common Speedwell from an Audubon Society Field Guide:

> Common Speedwell
> (*Veronica officinalis*)
> Snapdragon Family (Scrophulariaceae)
> Description: *Prostrate, mat-forming plants* have spike-like clusters of pale lavender or blue flowers arising from the leaf axil.
> Flowers: about 1/5" (5mm) wide; petals 4; stamens 2.
> Leaves: about ¾-2" (2–5cm) long, opposite, elliptic, toothed, downy.
> Height: creeper with flower stalks to 3–10" (7.5–25 cm) high.
> Flowering: May-July.
> Habitat: Dry fields, open woods.
> Range: Nova Scotia south to North Carolina; west to Tennessee and Wisconsin; north to Ontario. (Niering and Olmstead 799; photograph 523; scientific name and prominent features italicized)

The description is very detailed. But the writers of the *Guide* recognize that verbal description alone will be inadequate for unerring identification: a photograph is also provided. The real instrument of identification, then, is a visual-textual compound that must be constructed by amateur botanists as they fuse photograph and verbal description in their mind's eye.[7]

While visual-textual compounds designed for identification maximize relevant detail verbally and visually, those meant to serve theory exhibit a different pattern: they exclude any detail that turns the reader too far toward the world we perceive and too far away from its explanation. In his *Notebooks,* what is Darwin's drawing a drawing of?

We know it is of a bird's wing and not of a river delta but only be-

Zoolog. Garden. Sept 16." Hybrid between Silver & Common Pheasant. Male bird, said to be infertile.— spurs rather smaller than in ‹ma› silver male— Head like silver except in not having tuft,— back like do.— but the black lines on each feather instead of coming to point ‹are›

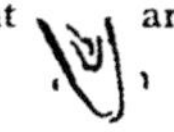

more rounded.

Fig. 8. Pheasant's wing. Reprinted from Charles Darwin. *Charles Darwin's Notebooks, 1836–1844: Geology, Transmutation of Species, Metaphysical Enquiries.* Ed. Paul H. Barrett, Peter J. Gautrey, Sandra Herbert, David Kohn, and Sydney Smith, p. 383. © 1987 by Paul H. Barrett, Peter J. Gautrey, Sandra Herbert, David Kohn, Sydney Smith. Used by permission of the publisher, Cornell University Press.

cause he tells us: he has minimized the detail and eliminated the immediate visual context that would make such identification possible in the interest of confronting an objection to the theory of natural selection, that posed by the existence of infertile hybrids. Why should hybrids be selected for, if they are infertile? In the *Origin,* Darwin provides a response to this question:

> On the theory of natural selection the case is especially important, inasmuch as the sterility of hybrids could not possibly be of any advantage to them, and therefore could not have been acquired by the continued preservation of successive profitable degrees of sterility. I hope, however, to be able to show that ste-

rility is not a specially acquired or endowed quality,
but is incidental on other acquired differences. (245)

In the case of the single diagram in *Origin,* the mode of depiction also
serves theory: lines and curves depict aspects of the world only insofar
as those aspects serve evolutionary theory. In its first appearance in
Chapter IV, the diagram's vertical dimension is time; its horizontal
dimension, organic diversity. The further up we go, the nearer we get
to the present; the further apart species are, the more they have differentiated themselves from their parent species through evolutionary
processes. Reading the diagram (Figure 9) vertically, we trace descent.
We see that a^1 and m^1, and a^{10} and m^{10} have the same remote ancestor
A. Reading horizontally, we see that far greater evolutionary divergence exists between the latter pair than between the former.

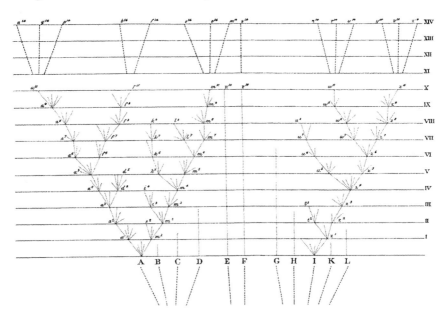

Fig. 9. Diagram of Divergence of Taxa. From Darwin, *Origin of Species,*
end-papers.

Extinction is also represented in the diagram, literally, by the end
of a line. Species s^2, the descendent of A, becomes extinct in Era II;
species u^8, a descendant of z^4, which is, in turn, a descendant of I, becomes extinct in Era VIII[8]. The diagram also embodies the cause of
extinction, the struggle for existence. It is no accident that A, F, and

I, whose ancestors are still living, were originally nearly the most divergent from each other, for the nearer species are along the horizontal dimension the more likely they are to compete for the same territories and resources in the battle for survival, the more likely they are to become extinct. In many cases, B, C, and H, for instance, there is no evolutionary change over time, but only in the case of F do we still have a living species, a living fossil. In other cases, the branches of evolutionary trees eventually crowd out these lines of descent.

Finally, Darwin makes a theoretical point about the significance of the numbered letters: "In our diagram the line of succession is broken at regular intervals by small numbered letters marking the successive forms that have become sufficiently distinct to be recorded as varieties. But these breaks are imaginary, and might have been inserted anywhere, after intervals long enough to have allowed the accumulation of a considerable amount of divergent variation" (119). Despite their individuation as points, species a^1, a^2, a^3, etc., are not real; even the lines of divergence are conjectural; they are *dotted* lines. Only the processes that create divergence are real. Evolution embodies an ontology of process, rather than product.

Moreover, as the time scale of the process is open, the amount of evolutionary change each incremental coordinate represents may legitimately vary. Darwin says: "If we suppose the amount of change between each horizontal line in our diagram to be excessively small, these three forms may still be only well-marked varieties [. . .] but we have only to suppose the steps in the process of modification to be more numerous or great in amount, to convert these three forms [a^{10}, f^{10}, and m^{10}] into well-defined species" (120). But the time scale can also change enormously. Darwin asks us to imagine the vertical increment represents "a million or hundred million generations" (124). This variation in time scale and, consequently, in the span of evolutionary change blurs distinctions between species and variety, genus and species. In effect, Darwin turns the diagram into an argument for these intellectual leaps.[9]

Thus far, we have seen Darwin's diagram as a representation of evolution, but it is equally a representation of the geological record, "a succession of the successive strata of the Earth's crust including extinct remains" (124), a record of evolution. In the first case, the vertical dimension is metaphoric: space represents time. In the second case, the vertical dimension is denotative: space represents only space: the geological column. But the geological column is, as it were, time made visible; therefore the vertical dimension also represents time. Really, it is time: looking at the fossil embeddings in the geological column, we are, in a very real sense, looking at the past. It is a past, moreover, that the first reading of the diagram allows us to understand. Looking at the geological record, Darwin says, "we find [. . .] such evidence of the slow and scarcely sensible mutation of specific forms, as we have a just right to expect to find" (336). The location of these forms and their fossil remains, it should be noted, is not their physical but their evolutionary location, not where they are found, but where, once found, they belong in the evolutionary sequence.

It is crucial that the diagram has gone half-way to meet theory, divesting itself in the process of those features that facilitate pattern recognition in the case of middle-sized objects such as real trees and real geological columns. It is precisely this divestment that permits the diagram to mediate between the world and its explanation.

We can see the argumentative value of the graphic presentation when we compare Darwin's diagram with its verbal "equivalent"; Darwin ends this chapter with an extended simile based on the analogy between evolutionary development and the growth of a tree. Up to a point, the comparison holds:

> The green and budding twigs may represent existing species; and those produced during each former year may represent the long succession of extinct species. At each period of growth all the growing twigs have tried to branch out on all sides, and to overtop and kill the surrounding twigs and branches, in the same manner as species and groups of species have tried to overmaster other species in the great battle of life. (129)

But the argument from analogy soon outwears its theoretical welcome. In the verbal expansion, disanalogy undermines Darwin's theoretical purpose: in the case of the real tree that must be the vehicle of Darwin's extended simile, the lower branches, trunk, and roots must be alive or there can be no top branches. The minimalism of his diagram permits Darwin to evade this fatal implication: the diagram represents only those characteristics of a tree that serve his theoretical purpose.[10] Darwin's strategy in his crucial fourth chapter is not to rely solely on verbal argument or graphic presentation or metaphorical representation, but to avail himself of *every* available modality of persuasion. As a consequence of this rhetorical assault, the visual-textual compound that is the single diagram in Darwin's *Origin* becomes more than a depiction of evolutionary theory; it also becomes an argument in favor of that theory. The geological column is evidence for the theory of descent; the theory of descent explains the geological column.

But the analysis thus far does not exhaust the diagram's argumentative possibilities. The diagram also presents us with a paradox, a visual figure of speech: death is life. Death and life are dramatically juxtaposed, the living beings of the tree with the fossils of the geological column, revealing that continuing life depends upon continued death. In addition, the diagram functions as a conceptual oxymoron. It juxtaposes actual continuity, the tree of life, with apparent discontinuity, the fossils in the geological column; it demonstrates that the discontinuity evidenced in the column is really evidence of continuity, revealing that seeing must not be believing.[11] We know from the work of Jeanne Fahnestock that the figure "is a verbal summary that epitomizes a line of reasoning. It is a condensed or even diagram-like rendering of the relationship among a set of terms, a relationship that constitutes the argument and could be expressed at greater length" (24).

A final effect results from another paradox: in the diagram, descent is ascent. Although Darwin does not exploit the possibilities of this trope, others will, and Social Darwinism, the eugenics movement, and "scientific" racism will be some of the results:

> The system of universal evolution worked out in the late nineteenth century treated biological and social progress as integral aspects of the same phenomenon. The technological backwardness of non-European societies indicated that they were culturally inferior, and this in turn was taken as a sign of the biological inferiority of the other races. (Bowler 285)

We may say with some justice that, so interpreted, Darwin's diagram is his theory, his argument. On this view, once we understand the diagram, we understand Darwin. On this construal, our view of the *Origin* as a book with one diagram is mistaken; it is really a diagram so complex that it takes a whole book to unfold its meaning. Such a view, however, misrepresents the division of labor that the fourth chapter so elegantly exemplifies. Necessarily, Darwin's diagram falls short of depicting the complexity of the processes involved. It altogether omits sexual selection, the effects of inbreeding that would retard change, and the environment that is change's motor:

> The diagram illustrates how natural selection, the principle of divergence, and the evidence for the extinction of many species in time [can be conceived and grasped as a single picture]. It goes far in exemplifying the complexity Darwin needs, but cannot do it all. Darwin needs the rest of the book, not [only] to explain the diagram, but to explain to his readers the complexity of the process that is missing from the diagram. (Reidy, personal correspondence)

Darwin's Diagram as a Product of Conceptual Evolution

The materials for the analysis of the origin of Darwin's diagram as a product of conceptual evolution are particularly rich: we have three tree diagrams in the *Notebooks* and a suite of four related tree diagrams in *Natural Selection,* the "big book" Darwin was writing when interrupted by Alfred Russel Wallace's independent discovery of natural selection. Between May and July 1837, Darwin made the following entry in *Notebook B.*

The tree of life should perhaps be called the coral of life, base of branches dead; so that passages cannot be seen.— this again offers

contradiction to constant succession of germs in progress.— «no only makes it excessively complicated.»

Fig. 10. Tree of Life. Reprinted from Charles Darwin. *Charles Darwin's Notebooks, 1836–1844: Geology, Transmutation of Species, Metaphysical Enquiries.* Ed. Paul H. Barrett, Peter J. Gautrey, Sandra Herbert, David Kohn, and Sydney Smith, p. 177. © 1987 by Paul H. Barrett, Peter J. Gautrey, Sandra Herbert, David Kohn, Sydney Smith. Used by permission of the publisher, Cornell University Press.

Right after this diagram (Figure 10), he goes on:

Is it thus fish can be traced right down to simple organization.–

birds— not.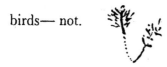

Fig. 11. Fish and bird lineage. Reprinted from Charles Darwin. *Charles Darwin's Notebooks, 1836–1844: Geology, Transmutation of Species, Metaphysical Enquiries.* Ed. Paul H. Barrett, Peter J. Gautrey, Sandra Herbert, David Kohn, and Sydney Smith, p. 177. © 1987. Used by permission of the publisher, Cornell University Press.

In this diagram, the solid lines represent the evolutionary development for which we have evidence; the dotted lines, development for which we do not, while evidence for the evolutionary development of the fish is available; it is not available for birds. As a consequence, common origin in the latter case must remain a hypothesis.

Ten pages later Darwin writes "I think," and produces, not an assertion, but a third version of his branching diagram (Figure 12) (180).

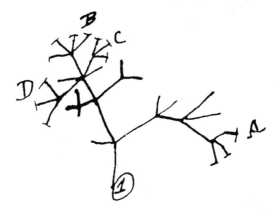

Fig. 12. Diversity Diagram. Reprinted from Charles Darwin. *Charles Darwin's Notebooks, 1836–1844: Geology, Transmutation of Species, Metaphysical Enquiries.* Ed. Paul H. Barrett, Peter J. Gautrey, Sandra Herbert, David Kohn, and Sydney Smith, p. 180. © 1987. Used by permission of the publisher, Cornell University Press.

He adds:

> Case must be that one generation then should be as
> many living as now. To do this & to have many spe-
> cies in same genus (as is). REQUIRES extinction.
> Thus between A. & B. immens [sic] gap of relation.
> C and B. the finest gradation, B & D rather greater
> distinction [...].

From this Darwin draws a conclusion:

> Thus genera would be formed.—bearing relation to
> ancient types.—with several extinct forms, for if an
> ancient species (1) is capable of making, 13 recent
> forms.—Twelve of its contemporarys [sic] must have
> left no offspring at all, so as to keep number of species
> constant [. . .] .

From this Darwin draws an implication:

> This requires principle that the permanent varieties
> produced by confined breeding & changing circum-
> stances are continued & produce according to the
> adaptation of such circumstances & therefore that
> death of species is a consequence (contrary from what
> would appear from America) of non adaptation from
> circumstances. (180)[12]

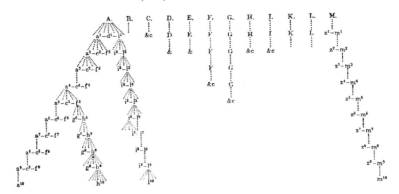

Fig. 13. Descent through natural selection. Reprinted from Charles Darwin.
*Charles Darwin's Natural Selection: Being the Second Part of his Big Species
Book Written From 1856 to 1858.* Ed R. C. Stauffer. London: Cambridge
UP, 1975, 237. Used by permission of Cambridge University Press.

There are no further diagrams of this sort in the *Notebooks*. None is needed, as this last already includes the key concepts of descent, diversity, and extinction: descent represented by branching, diversity by horizontal distance, extinction by branches without a foot.[13]

It is these aspects of evolutionary theory that are exhibited in the four related diagrams (Figures 13, 14, 15, and 16) in Darwin's big book on evolutionary theory. Each represents a single aspect of the theory. Figure 13 is devoted to descent through natural selection; Figure 14, parallel to the first, illustrates descent in the absence of natural

Diagram II

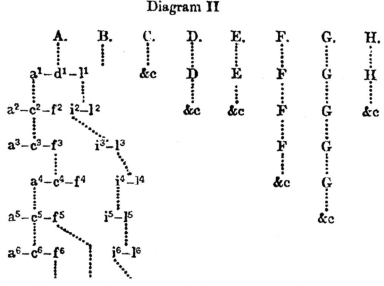

Fig. 14. Descent in absence of natural selection. Reprinted from Charles Darwin. *Charles Darwin's Natural Selection: Being the Second Part of his Big Species Book written from 1856 to 1858.* Ed R. C. Stauffer. London: Cambridge UP, 1975, 237. Used by permission of Cambridge University Press.

selection, showing that diversity is also virtually absent. Figure 15 concerns itself with evolutionary distance as a consequence of divergence; Figure 16, with extinction.

In *Origin*, Darwin refashions these diagrams. He omits the second and combines the other three into one. Then he turns the resulting combination 180 degrees on its axis so that he can superimpose it on a series of parallel horizontal lines that represent evolutionary and geological eras.[14] There is another change. In the big book, Darwin speaks

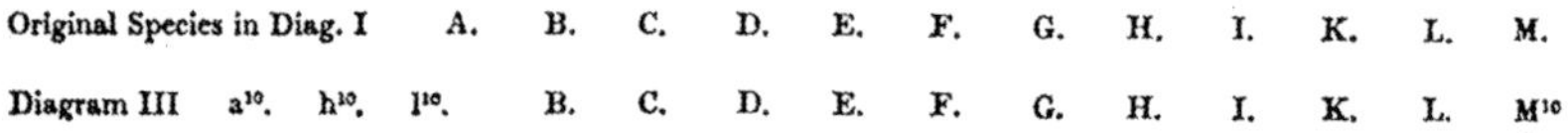

Original Species in Diag. I   A.   B.   C.   D.   E.   F.   G.   H.   I.   K.   L.   M.

Diagram III a^{10}. h^{10}. l^{10}.   B.   C.   D.   E.   F.   G.   H.   I.   K.   L. M^{10}

Fig. 15. Evolutionary distance as a consequence of divergence. Reprinted from Charles Darwin. *Charles Darwin's Natural Selection: Being the Second Part of his Big Species Book written from 1856 to 1858.* Ed R. C. Stauffer. London: Cambridge UP, 1975, 237. Used by permission of Cambridge University Press.

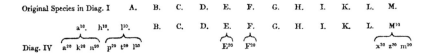

Fig. 16. Extinction. Reprinted from Charles Darwin. *Charles Darwin's Natural Selection: Being the Second Part of his Big Species Book Written From 1856 to 1858.* Ed R. C. Stauffer. London: Cambridge UP, 1975, 237. Used by permission of Cambridge University Press.

of the diagram's imperfection (238) and its description of events as taking place in an "imaginary country" (239). As modified in the *Origin,* the diagram has ceased to be imperfect, and the imaginary country of the big book has vanished. This is because both of these cautionary hedges had undermined Darwin's central point: evolutionary theory is not imaginary and applies to every real country.

Can a case be made that the diagrams that begin in the *Notebooks,* resurface in *Natural Selection,* and culminate in the *Origin* are not a mere sequence but represent conceptual evolution in the strict sense, that is, differential survival in the face of selection pressures of an evolving theory, a changing conceptual environment that shapes a changing diagrammatic species? To James Griesemer and William Wimsatt, scientific diagrams can indeed be viewed as units of selection in conceptual evolution. As such, they are adaptations, cost-effective means for increasing the probability of survival of the concepts they embody. They increase this probability by reducing "demands on memory, computation, or other limited resources" (99). Griesemer and Wimsattt's example is the sequence of diagrams that represents August Weismann's germ theory of heredity. Weismann's founding diagram of 1893 concerns the lineage of the germ-plasm within the context of the individual development: it depicts a single organism and a single generation.

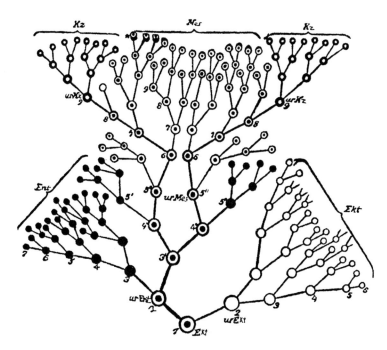

Fig. 17. Germ-track of *Rhabditis nigrovenosa*. From August Weismann, *The Germ-Plasm* (1893), 196.

While Weismann focuses on hereditary continuity as mediated by development, his heirs have very different aims. In his 1896 diagram in *The Cell in Development and Heredity*, E. B. Wilson's point is argumentative, his target, the rival theory of inheritance of acquired characteristics: "The child inherits from the parent germ-cell, not from the parent-body, and the germ-cell owes its characteristics, not to the body which bears it, but to a pre-existing germ-cell [. . .] . As far as inheritance is concerned, the body is merely the carrier of the germ-cells, which are held in trust for coming generations" (13).

In this diagram (Figure 18), say Griesemer and Wimsatt, "Wilson virtually accuses those who believe in the inheritance of acquired characteristics of confusing correlation with causation" (114). An inspection of the diagram reveals that, while the line of inheritance is continuous, the line of succession is not: the source of continuity is always and invariably the germ-plasm. Wilson's diagram is an adaptation of Weismann's, one geared to the specific function of refuting believers in the inheritance of acquired characteristics.

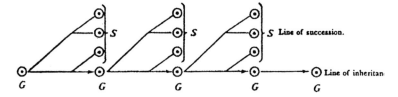

Fig. 18. E. B. Wilson's view of Weismann's theory of inheritance. From Wilson, *The Cell in Development and Heredity*, (1900), 13.

The Wilson diagram has had many progeny. One on which Griesemer and Wimsatt comment extensively is John Maynard Smith's representation of heredity in his 1965 *Theory of Evolution* (Figure 19). It is the lower section of this diagram that reveals the real purpose of Maynard Smith's visual adaptation; in this, the conceptual parallel is

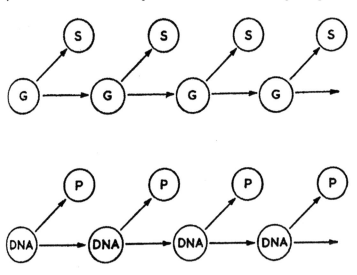

Fig. 19. J. Maynard Smith's view of the central dogma of molecular genetics, from John Maynard Smith. *The Theory of Evolution* (2nd ed., London: Penguin, 1965) 67. © 1958, 1966, 1975. Reproduced by permission of Penguin Books Ltd.

made explicit between the continuity of the germ-plasm as a source of phenotypes and the continuity of DNA as a source of proteins. Smith's is an adaptation of Weismann's diagram with the specific purpose of creating a historical and conceptual link between theories he regards as analogous. Simultaneously, he reaches back to the pioneering work of 1893 and moves forward to the cutting edge of current theory.

Griesemer and Wimsatt conclude that the diagrams they have examined "show a number of interesting patterns, including descent without modification, descent with modification, differential proliferation, adaptive radiation, extinction, relict survival in a changed and specialized niche, and successive simplification for efficient specialization to a simplified niche" (128). Wilson's and Maynard Smith's diagrams are examples of the last of these categories. They exemplify that "what is passed on [in visual succession] is a relatively compact generative structure which, in the right conceptual and social environment, generates the theory-phenotype of the next generation" (89).

In a fashion analogous to Weismann's original diagram and its progeny, Darwin's evolves from a simple depiction of branching to a full depiction of the essentials of evolutionary theory. In doing so, Darwin unites the lines of two very different parents: the genealogical trees that decorate royal and noble houses and contemporary scientific depictions of the geological column. C. M. Heyes and H. C. Plotkin describe the process in the general case:

> What happens when two pictures are put together? Do they tend to overlap, or is one superimposed on the other, or do the features of both contribute to the product? Is each feature modified, or are various features of each picture maintained intact? [. . .] The blending inheritance of cultural replicators may sometimes result in the generation of novel variants outside of the existing range. (159)

In Darwin, both features—the tree and the column—contribute to the product: we have a case of blending inheritance, the generation of a novel variant that acts as a depiction of evolutionary theory and as an argument in its favor.

The single diagram in *Origin of Species* does not refute Rudwick's contention that Darwin was a poor draftsman and that his imagination was not essentially visual (185). That such a visualization is an exception to Darwin's usual practice, that in the midst of his lucubrations about evolutionary theory in *Notebook B,* he is virtually compelled to shift from the verbal to the visual, says more about the nature of his theory than about his habitual style of thought. To Kitchter, his is a theory that is essentially qualitative, with low axiomatability (qtd. in Hodge 179). While it cannot be perspicuously embodied in propositional form, graphic form is ideal for its presentation. As a consequence, graphic form intervenes at two points in Darwin's intellectual biography: theory creation and theory exposition. At first, graphic form permits him to think through his theory at a crucial point in its development. Later, when he addresses the very different task of conveying his theory persuasively to his public, Darwin revisits and reworks his early diagrams. Initially, we have a draft, the set of diagrams in the "big book"; finally, we have the diagram in the *Origin,* a visual-textual compound that represents the essentials of his theory. While the diagram is a product of Darwin's genius, it is, simultaneously, a product of its time and place, of a general movement in scientific communication toward the visual representation of theory.

Conclusion

The central insight of M. A. K. Halliday and J. R. Martin's *Writing Science* is that scientific communication is a semiotic system, a complex network of meaningful signs that represents "a reworking of common-sense classifications into un-commonsense ones" (24). While "common-sense classifications" are based on what can be directly observed with the senses, scientific classifications "organize reality differently" (205–6), that is, according to the underlying causal structure of the world. A commonsense taxonomy might organize diseases into childhood and general; a scientific taxonomy would organize them into viral and bacterial. Halliday and Martin's theory is correct as far as it goes, but it is incomplete. Scientific communication is a convergence of two semiotic systems, the verbal and the visual. *The Origin of Species* is one example.

The status of the visual in the dual semiotic at the heart of scientific communication was not a given. In *The Eye of the Lynx,* art historian David Freedberg explores the unsuccessful efforts of Federico Cesi, Galileo's fellow, in depicting the flora and fauna scientifically. Freedberg shows that Cesi's depiction of these in all their variety was self-defeating. Diagrams were needed, not pictures; not a means of looking *at* the world, but a means of looking through it to its causal structure. The diagram was a vehicle for this new kind of seeing; it "appealed for its effectiveness to order, logic, and reduction. Each of its marks was significant. Take away a line from a diagram, and it is nonsense. Take away a mark from a picture and all that is lost, in the worst of cases, is some part of its affect" (396). Physicist Richard Feynman generalizes the discovery that Cesi's missed: Feynman says that "there is [. . .] a rhythm and a pattern between the phenomena of nature which is not apparent to the eye, but only to the eye of analysis" (qtd. in Kemp, 101).

This metaphor is more than a metaphor. Feynman's insight means that this new way of seeing is also a new way of knowing: what science sees is, invariably, the causal structure of the world. This is true, even in the case of visuals that stop at surface features: when a new species of animal or plant is depicted, what is of interest to science is nevertheless invisible: the ordering of the living world as an evolving system. What is depicted is cognitive, not sensuous: the strong and implicit claim is that only through science can we know the world as it really is and only by means of a dual semiotic system can we communicate our knowledge to others.[15]

Notes

[1] I say discovered, but it would be truer to say rediscovered, since ours is merely a generalization of Martin Rudwick's insight into illustrations in nineteenth century geology.

[2] The German is as rebarbative as the English.

[3] The observation that at some points in its orbit as observed from the Earth the planet seems to move backwards.

[4] The mean speed theorem implies that the ratios of the distances traveled are proportional to the square of the times taken for those distances. The proof is algebraic. The speed of an accelerating body equals its acceleration times its time. According to the mean speed theorem, to get the average speed of an accelerating body starting from rest, we divide the final speed by two: acceleration x time/2. But distance equals speed times time. Substituting, the distance traversed by an accelerating body starting from rest equals acceleration x time/2 x time or, more perspicuously, $d=at^2/2$.

[5] Whether this "mathematization" became actually mathematical, actually a matter of numbers, was not crucial to Heidegger (118–19); once the world is so conceived and grasped as a picture, mathematization becomes merely the actualization of an ever-present possibility.

[6] The degree of Darwin's originality depends on further investigation of the social context in which this diagram arose, an investigation parallel to Rudwick's.

[7] It is a deficiency of the *Field Guide* that, prompted solely by financial considerations, 276 pages separate the two instruments of identification that, to be effective, must combine in the amateur botanist's mind.

[8] The break between Eras X and XI is unexplained. Perhaps it was meant to indicate the indefinite future, as the similar converging dotted lines at the bottom of the figure are meant to represent the indefinite past. If so Darwin changed his mind, labeling the topmost era Era XIV.

[9] Paraphrased from a letter of Michael Reidy, October 2, 2002.

[10] Perhaps Darwin would have been better off with an alternative comparison, mentioned in the *Notebooks:* "the tree of life should perhaps be called the coral of life, base of branches dead" (177). But for his nineteenth century audience coral would have lacked the cultural resonance possessed by the tree.

[11] Fahnestock makes the additional point that only if it were in three dimensions, as in a computer graphic, could the diagram do full justice to branching (121).

[12] Only Darwin's final thoughts are presented. For all interim changes, see Barrett's edition of *Notebooks*.

[13] My treatment depends on the earlier, incisive treatment of Gruber 141–44.

[14] I have already pointed out an unintended consequence of this rotation.

[15] I would like to thank Randy Allen Harris, who reminded me that I had once read Heidegger, though without profit; Paul Thagard for his incisive critique of my more extravagant claims; and Michael Reidy for his careful commentary, some of which I have pilfered.

WORKS CITED

Bowler, Peter J. *Evolution: The History of an Idea.* Berkeley: U of California P, 1984.

Boyer, Carl B. *The Rainbow: From Myth to Mathematics.* Princeton: Princeton UP, 1987.

Copernicus. *On the Revolutions* Trans. Edward Rosen. London: Macmillan, 1978.

Crombie, A. C. *Medieval and Early Modern Science.* Rev. 2nd ed. Vol. II. New York: Doubleday, 1959.

Darwin, Charles. *Charles Darwin's Natural Selection, Being the Second Part of his Big Species Book Written from 1856–1858.* Ed. R. C. Stauffer. Cambridge: Cambridge UP, 1975.

—. *Charles Darwin's Notebooks: 1836–1844.* Ed. Paul H. Barrett. Ithaca: Cornell UP, 1987.

—. *The Collected Papers of Charles Darwin.* Ed. Paul H. Barrett et al. Chicago: U of Chicago P, 1977.

—. *On The Origin of Species.* 1ˢᵗ. ed. Cambridge: Harvard UP, 1964.

Fahnestock, Jeanne. *Rhetorical Figures in Science.* New York: Oxford UP, 1999.

Freedberg, David. *The Eye of the Lynx.* Chicago: U of Chicago P, 2002.

Galileo. *Dialogue Concerning the Two Chief World Systems.* Trans. Stillman Drake. Berkeley: U of California P, 1967.

—. *Two New Sciences.* Trans. Stillman Drake. Madison: U of Wisconsin P, 1974.

Griesemer, J. R. and W. C. Wimsatt. "Picturing Weismannism: A Case Study of Conceptual Evolution." Ruse 75–138.

Gross, Alan G., Joseph E. Harmon, and Michael Reidy. *Communicating Science: The Scientific Article from the 17ᵗʰ Century to the Present.* New York: Oxford UP, 2002.

Gruber, Howard. *Darwin on Man: A Psychological Study of Scientific Creativity.* 2ⁿᵈ ed. Chicago: U of Chicago P, 1981.

Halliday, M. A. K. and J. R. Martin. *Writing Science: Literacy and Discursive Power.* Pittsburgh: U of Pittsburgh P, 1993.

Heidegger, Martin. "The Age of the World Picture." *The Question Concerning Technology and Other Essays.* Trans. William Lovitt. New York: Harper, 1977. 115–54.

Heyes, C. M. and H. C. Plotkin. "Replicators and Interactors in Cultural Evolution." Ruse 139–62.

Hodge, M. J. S. "Darwin's Theory and Darwin's Argument." Ruse 163–82.

Kemp, Martin. *Visualizations: The* Nature *Book of Art and Science.* Berkeley: U of California P, 2000.

Lavoisier, Antoine. *Elements of Chemistry.* Trans. Robert Kerr. New York: Dover, 1965.

—. "Nomenclature de la Chimie." *Oeuvres,* V. Paris: Imprimerie Nationale, 1892. 354–64.

—. *Traité Élémentaire de Chimie. Oeuvres,* I. Paris: Imprimerie Nationale, 1892. 1–407.

Niering, William A., and Nancy C. Olmstead. *The Audubon Field Guide to North American Wild Flowers: Eastern Region.* New York: Knopf, 1979.

Ptolemy. *Ptolemy's Almagest.* Trans. G. J. Toomer. New York: Springer Verlag, 1984.

Reidy, Michael. Personal correspondence. October 2, 2002.

Roberts, Lissa. "Setting the Table: The Disciplinary Development of Eighteenth-Century Chemistry Read Through the Changing Structure of its Tables." *The Literary Structure of Scientific Argument: Historical Studies.* Ed. Peter Dear. Philadelphia: U of Pennsylvania P, 1991. 99–132.

Rudwick, Martin J. S. "The Emergence of a Visual Language for Geological Science, 1760–1840." *History of Science* 14 (1976): 149–95.

Ruse, Michael, ed. *What the Philosophy of Biology Is.* Dordrecht: Kluwer, 1989.

Sprat, Thomas. *History of the Royal-Society of London, For the Improving of Natural Knowledge.* London: J. Martyn and J. Allestry, 1667.

Smith, John Maynard. *The Theory of Evolution,* 2nd ed. Midddlesex: Penguin, 1965.

Swift, Jonathan. *Gulliver's Travels,* New York: New American Library, 1999.

Weismann, August. *The Germ-Plasm: A Theory of Heredity.* Trans. W. Parker and H. Ronnfeldt. New York: Scribner's, 1893.

Wilson, E. B. *The Cell in Development and Heredity.* 3rd ed. New York: Macmillan, 1896.

Part II: Appropriation

4 body pixel child / space time machine

Anne Frances Wysocki

Repetition and the bodies of small children are the figures of my concern in this writing. How is it that the bodies of small children can be carved, through various repetitions, into focus for themselves as well as for others, a double-edged focus of visuality and visibility? And through a game, just an online game, from Disney.

If the Internet can be construed as a wavering sea of glances, of attentions accelerated to the point of fracture, of identity split and split again so that a mesh of diffuse multiplying communities—scattered through space and not bound by proximal time—is the resulting structure, then I want to think of the little game I've found as a structure of actions, asked of a viewer, that makes that viewer a solidified visible identity before others. This game—available at a website that in September 2003 had 1,061,000 visitors between the ages of 2 and 11 (USA Today)—is a little technological machine for producing bodies that find sense of self in being seen whole. This game is a moment of reaction against diffusion. Though it is not planned by its designers to be anything other than a fun way to build attachment to Disney, in its own little ways it acts on its young viewers to set them into bodies without fracture, bodies that are meant primarily to see and be seen as wholes with finite edges. This game is a small model of how the visual and interactive aspects of an online game can work on us, and, especially, how often-overlooked visual and interactive aspects of computer games can do thick work in shaping how we see space and time and ourselves.

☌

Everybody in the world was once a child. We grow up. Our personalities change, but in every one of us something remains of our childhood. [. . .] [which] knows nothing of sophistication and distinction. It's where all of us are simple and naive without prejudice and bias. We're friendly and trusting and it just seems that if your picture hits that spot with one person, it's going to hit that spot in almost everybody [. . .] that fine, clean, unspoiled spot down deep in every one of us that maybe the world has made us forget and that maybe our picture can help recall.

Walt Disney, qtd. in Watts 109-10

The online game I'll be discussing is based on the Disney animated film for children *Lilo and Stitch*—and so I will first describe the movie before describing the game.

This movie starts in a faraway galaxy, in one of those galactic conventions whose visual dimensions—of endlessly vertical rows of delegates in small balconies—is familiar from the *Star Wars* series. Hanging among the endless rows of sentient creatures from many different planets is a platform on which the leader—a wasp-figured, cool, visibly female character—is questioning another character, who is of "mad scientist" appearance. Going against galactic law, this mad scientist has created a small creature designed to be nasty, designed to tear up and destroy cities and pretty much everything else it encounters. The leader orders this small dangerous creature to be contained, and we see it led to a container that is a mix of zoo and prison—but the creature escapes and ends up accidentally on Earth, on one of the smaller Hawaiian islands. Almost run over by a truck, the creature is taken by the humans who rescue it to an animal shelter because it looks like a puppy to them (once it hides its second set of arms and the spikes on its back). Later that day, the puppy-creature is adopted by Lilo—a young Hawaiian girl—and now the movie really starts, moving in two parallel threads.

In one thread, Lilo and Nani, her older sister, hope to stay together. Lilo and Nani are orphans, their parents having died in an accident some short time before the start of the movie. Nani—who appears to be between 17–21 and is trying to work to support the two of them but is having trouble holding onto a job because she is strong-willed. Lilo, who is even more strong-willed, is also upset, acting up and out, fighting with other children, throwing herself around the house, probably (although this is never discussed in the movie but implied) in response to the abrupt loss of her parents. There is a large social worker (named Cobra Bubbles) looking in on Lilo and Nani; he threatens to take Lilo away if Nani cannot find a steady job, but after the little alien arrives with its own hard-to-control obstreperousness, nothing holds together, and Nani cannot hold down any job. The movie's first thread is therefore about the possible break-up of this small family, about how families can come apart first through accidents and then through outside social response to a child out of control.

The other thread in the movie is about the small alien, who is named "Stitch" by Lilo (without any reason given for the name). After the little alien escapes, the leader of the galactic conference orders two other creatures (including the "mad scientist") to bring Stitch back; they go to Earth and try to capture Stitch. Because of their mishaps, even more aliens come to Earth to try to get Stitch, to take the little alien away from Lilo and Nani, whom Stitch has come to regard as family. This other thread in the movie, then, is about how Stitch, another child in size and shape and also out of control, can be brought into a family by desiring their love and so changing its behavior.

At the end of the movie, just as it looks as though everyone will be separated, as though Stitch will be taken back to the far-away galaxy and Lilo will be taken from Nani, Lilo produces her $2 receipt from the animal shelter to show that she owns Stitch, which persuades the alien leader that Stitch is legally Lilo's, and the social worker turns out to be an ex-CIA agent/Roswell investigator, who recognizes the potential of Nani, Lilo, and Stitch to live together well, given what Lilo and Stitch are both learning about living in and as a family. The expected happy ending shows them all—Nani, Lilo, and Stitch, as well as the two aliens who were ordered to capture Stitch—living together boisterously as a family, with warm visits from the social worker.[1]

There is in a sense no body of literature which rests so openly on an acknowledged difference, a rupture almost, between writer and addressee. Children's fiction sets up the child as an outsider to its own process, and then aims, unashamedly, to take the child in.

Jacqueline S. Rose, *The Children's Culture Reader*

At the Disney website there is a free computer game based on the movie. (The website offers only a few free games, but for $50 per year a child can have access to all the games and entertainments of the site.) The game is called "Stitch: Master of Disguise." Although it can be played by someone who doesn't know about the movie, it makes fullest sense in terms of the movie: the game takes place as though the movie has not yet ended, for the game's player is asked to keep Stitch from being taken out of the family by the two aliens who have been sent to take Stitch back to space.

The game takes place in what we assume to be Lilo's house. The first screen following the opening is of Lilo and Stitch in what appears to be a child's room that is "painted" onscreen in a style familiar to us from other children's cartoons and animations. It is Lilo who gives the motivation for the game, when—in the opening animation to the game where she is seen to be preparing to leave for school and so to leave Stitch alone—she tells Stitch, "If someone comes to the door, disguise yourself! Don't let those bounty hunters find you here!" Following these instructions, a player sees a wall of "photographs" of possible disguises, such as a cartoon Elvis or Marilyn Monroe, a goofy scubadiver, or even Lilo.[2] A child playing this game thus doesn't get to build a disguise for Stitch or even choose one of the ready-mades; instead, when she clicks a "Play" button to start the game, one of the available disguises gets large to indicate that this is the disguise the child is to give Stitch.

When a child clicks "Play" again, the game begins: the screen gives players a larger view of the child's room—with clearly delimited objects and a space that is given realistic representation in that the artists who made the scene followed the guidelines of single-point perspective (the edges of objects recede into space following the edges of lines receding to a vanishing point, for example)—with Stitch waiting to be disguised. (Before play starts, as well as during play, a player sees the alien "bounty hunters" drive by outside the window.) A player clicks the various cabinets, drawers, and chests around the room, which "open" to show trays of costume pieces; when a child then clicks one of the costume pieces, it appears on Stitch. A player can click as many costume pieces as she likes (if, for example, she's already clicked a hat or some sort of other head-piece, and then clicks another, the new head-piece will replace the previous one) until she either builds a costume to match the one she was given or until her time runs out (there is a timer at the bottom of the screen). When time is up, the two alien "bounty hunters" appear in the window of the room: if the costume is right, then they just pass by because they do not recognize Stitch, but if Stitch is not properly disguised, they take Stitch away from the home and back into space. If Stitch is taken away, the game ends, but if the player has properly disguised Stitch, the game continues: between 9 a.m. and 3 p.m., when Lilo returns from school, a player needs to give Stitch a new disguise every hour (according to the game's sense of what constitutes an "hour," which is the time needed for the slider to move across). At 3 p.m., Lilo comes home, and the game can stop.

⚛

As I play this little game, it asks me to step into a thick set of behaviors and understandings. A foreground emerges in which identity is visibly built. But there are also visual backgrounds in which space and time are shaped and identity is therefore built.

⚛

At center of the screen where Stitch is disguised is Stitch itself. Stitch is centered by position and color, being more saturated and darker than anything else and having a dark line around the body unlike any of the other objects. Stitch is emphasized also by being the only visual shape at all human. As E. H. Gombrich writes, "Whenever anything remotely facelike enters our field of vision, we are alerted and respond" (103). Stitch is also the center of a player's focus because of the directions and action of the game: when Lilo tells Stitch to get into disguise, Lilo is asking a player to help Stitch fit into the family by being made unrecognizable to the aliens. The game is thus a lesson to the child playing—sort of participatory fairy tale—about what children need to do if they wish to become a real part of a human family.

The first lessons are about identity and its structures, such as gender. Notice that Stitch, in its "natural" alien state, is visibly ungendered, having no visible genitalia or body shape coding. Stitch's head and body, however, do correspond to that of a small child and are much the same head and body shape of Lilo, the small girl. Stitch has none of the visible signs of gender we usually see with Disney animated characters such that Daisy Duck (for example) is just Donald Duck with curls, lipstick, and earrings. Throughout the movie, Stitch is verbally coded, called "him" (or, as in the name of this game, "Master of Disguise") but Stitch has no *visible* gender. You might point to Stitch's aggression in the movie or to the character's notched ears or the implied violence of Stitch's teeth and nails as indications of masculinity. The young girl Lilo, however, is just as aggressive as Stitch (and in the movie Stitch and Lilo are equivalent in the lessons they must learn about how to behave so as to be part of a family), and notched ears or sharp teeth and nails are no indicators of gender in (for example) turtles or lizards. In the predominant mode of this game, the visual, Stitch is not (yet) gendered, and neither is a child playing this game asked to play from within a set of characteristics we attribute in our time and place to girls or boys.

Instead, Stitch is presented in this game as almost a blank slate, a body visually separated from what is around it so that it can be seen as a body. By that separation, Stitch is then prepared and made available for the gendering—and the application of race and age—that is carried with each of the "disguises" a player is given to put onto Stitch. As I mentioned earlier, those who play this game do not get to choose an identity to put onto Stitch; the lesson of this game is instead that one's identities come to one from a range of ready-made sets that wrap gender together with race and age and certain kinds of social positioning. As Kaja Silverman argues is a condition of all identity-formation, "What must be demonstrated again and again is that all subjects, male or female, rely for their identity upon the repertoire of culturally available images and upon a gaze that [. . .] is not theirs to deploy" ("Fassbinder" 295). And further, it is not only that this process of understanding identity must be demonstrated again and again, but that the process of taking on identity itself must be repeated, as Judith Butler argues when she writes that "gender is produced as a ritualized repetition of conventions" (144). Within this game, the conventions of gender as well as of race and age and other characteristics are taken on over and over in the play. A child must then play the game within these constrictions; she cannot choose for Stitch to be just anything but can only give Stitch identities that others already recognize, that are already available as "images" recognized by others, provided by others. These identities are not self-created; they are ready-made, and they are made to be repeated over and over.

A child playing this game also does not get to mix and match identities and still stay at home: a child can only keep Stitch at home, part of the family, by finding and putting onto Stitch all the parts of the one indicated ready-made identity. A child can put onto Stitch parts of different identities, but then Stitch is still considered alien by the other aliens and is removed from the home. The little alien creature cannot stay on Earth—or become part of a human family—until it is covered with visible, socially recognized attributes. A child playing this game is learning that to tame its alien, savage tendencies it might have and move toward human adulthood, to be a safe part of the comforts of family, it must repeatedly take on these ready-made roles of gender, race, class, age, and so on.

In addition to this lesson about taking on these complex identities, however, a child is learning that these identities have a primarily visual function. In the logic of this game, identities are what we can see about each other. The child playing this game is being asked to regard Stitch as a visible being, to learn to see and think of a body and its characteristics as composing an object that is for others to see and judge; to use Silverman's words from the quotation above, a child playing this game experiences the alien bounty hunters in this game as "the gaze." Both Silverman—in *The Threshold of the Visible World*—and Martin Jay—in *Downcast Eyes: The Denigration of Vision in Twentieth-Century French Thought*—develop arguments about the gaze as Jacques Lacan discussed it. Although Jay gives a fuller background for Lacan's analysis as coming out of and responding to work by Merleau-Ponty and Callois, both Jay and Silverman show how Lacan's analysis develops centrally out of Sartre's discussion of *le regard,* where someone peeking through a keyhole—so lost into looking he has no sense of self—hears a sound (footsteps?) and becomes jarred into awareness of himself as an object for the apprehension of someone else; Lacanian analysis then stresses how "vision [. . .] may be understood as a conflictual field in which the looker is always a body to be observed" (Jay 368). As Silverman puts it, "we depend on the other [. . .] for our very confirmation of self. To 'be' is in effect to 'be seen'" ("Threshold" 133). In any act of looking, in the acts simply of being, whether in public or playing a children's online game, we are ourselves object for someone else; in this telling, we only exist by existing for others. In the game I've been discussing, that existence is, as I've argued above, visual: a player must take on what is in the terms of the game a coherently visible identity if Stitch is to be acknowledged as a rightful family member. And the acknowledgment is external, coming from outside the house, coming via the window through which the other aliens judge Stitch.

The game thus asks a child to play within a complex weave of claims about identity: a child is asked to see (both "understand" and "look upon") herself as a body that is separate from others so that the body can take on ready-made identities fit for staying within a human family. In learning that the judgments of fitness come from outside the family, the child learns not only to see herself as a visible body but also as a body to be judged; she learns that this process never ends, but must be repeated if she is to be seen as fitting.

And if this game is in no small part about teaching a child the necessity of repeatedly taking on ready-made identities and considering herself as visually separated from others, it is because other visual and interactive aspects of the game—aspects of the game that shape the spaces and times of the game—have prepared the child to be the sort of body that can take on such identities.

This Game's Space

The words I cited earlier from Silverman and Jay are about how a subject learns to see itself from the outside through one of a range of possible ready-made identities. In this game, then, a child learns about being visible in the world. But, in order to be visible, the child has at the same time to be placed within structures of visuality that make possible her visibility. The child playing this game, while she plays identifying with Stitch, must also then necessarily see her self in space, because it is by experiencing space that, as Elizabeth Grosz argues, one becomes a subject:

> The subject can take up a position only by being able to situate its body in a position in space, a position from which it relates to other objects. This anchoring of subjectivity in its body is the condition of a coherent identity and, moreover, the condition under which the subject has a perspective on the world, be-

comes a source of perception, a point from which vision emanates. (38)

By seeing herself as separate from other objects, which in the case of
this game is enacted by a player seeing herself spatially represented
on screen, a player sees not only that she has a delimited body always
available for others to see, identify, and judge, but she also sees that
she has a position relative to others, which enables her to be someone
who sees (and identifies, and judges). There are, I argue, (at least) two
kinds of space represented in this game that make such understanding
of visuality and so visibility possible: a space that gives abstract spatial
perspective and so relation (as Grosz describes), but also a space that
gives concrete—familial—perspective and relation.

The first space of this game is tied in part to the Newtonian conception of physics. To use the words of Michael Curry, it "can be characterized through the use of a mathematical system—in this case a
grid—that is independent of the features of the earth. Rather, that
grid is imposed upon the surface by a viewer. Further, the viewer is
imagined to be capable of imaginatively stepping outside the earth,
and viewing it as if from above" (507). If a player in this game is able
to see Stitch and so herself as if from outside, it is because she looks at
an online visual picture whose makers have used what we can see on
the computer's monitor as though it were the kind of abstract space
Curry describes. We use the grid Curry describes not only to picture
the Earth as if from above but also to picture—to give shape to—what
is around us. That grid is what also allows us to see our selves from the
positions of others because it is when sight is so tied to a grid that we
enable ourselves to construct what (we believe) can be seen from any
point on that grid. That grid is what, in other words, makes possible
what drawing instructors and historians of art call "artificial or scientific perspective" (Dubery and Willats 56), which has not only shaped
painting but how we understand what we see.

This kind of perspective is an invention of the fifteenth century
Italian Renaissance, a way for artists (and others) to "achieve a systematic representation of naturalistic space in pictures" (Dubery and Willats 56) through the use of a grid of lines on paper or canvas that allowed a painter to place and shape objects relative to each other within
the space of the grid. In the final painting, the grid is painted over, as
though it never existed. The art historian Erwin Panofsky describes
the development of perspective by quoting a contemporary writer;

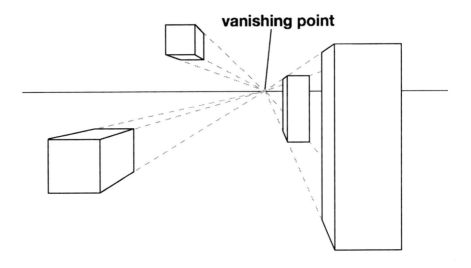

Fig. 1. Single-point linear perspective, as diagrammed in a picture plane.

Panofsky says that, with perspective, "There was now a generally valid and mathematically justifiable rule to determine 'how far two things ought to stand from one another, or how closely they ought to cohere, in order that the intelligibility of the subject matter is neither confused by crowding nor impaired by sparseness'" (Pomonius Gauruis, qtd. in Panofsky 65). With this kind of perspective, then, the grid serves not only to help painters figure out how to place objects (and others) coherently within a space, but it also teaches what the proper spatial relations are between objects (and others). To use a system of perspective in visual presentations is thus to give shape to what we see and hence to our seeing. To use perspective is, in fact and in act, to create ways of seeing, to create a particular way of making sense of how we use our eyes, the way of understanding how we as seeing beings fit into the visible world and are spatially and conceptually related to what we see. Panofsky, for example, says that because perspective is a "translation of psychophysiological space into mathematical space," it brings about "an objectification of the subjective" (66); perspective, he argues, "creates distance between human beings and things" (67). Similarly, Robert Romanyshyn articulates the development of perspective with the development of the split between subject and object; in addition, he sees perspective as bringing a de-emphasis on the physicality of the body because within the structures of perspective sight is both emphasized over the other senses and abstracted.

Because the processes of perspective have become so accepted and thus so naturalized in our sense of how photographs or representational paintings are supposed to look, we often do not know that visual artists originally carried with them apparati—mirrors, wood frames gridded with string, and other measuring devices and tools—for creating perspective, and that perspectival looking depends on the eye of a viewer being held steady and even with the horizon line shown in Figure 1. The software used to create three-dimensional computer scenes is based on these same geometries used in the Renaissance, translating painting space into pixel space, with the result that, as Lev Manovich argues, "A Renaissance painting and a computer image employ the same technique (of consistent depth cues) to create an illusion of space—existent or imaginary" (184). And so, for Manovich, drawing on the work of Norman Bryson and Jay, with these various tools, "It is as if the subject who attempts to catch the world, immobilizing and fixing it within the representational apparatus [. . .] is trapped by the apparatus himself. The subject is imprisoned. [. . .] In this tradition, the body must be fixed in space if the viewer is to see the image at all" (104). If a child playing the game I've been describing is able to see her self as a separate body, visible both to her and to others, available for judging and taking on identity, it is in no small part because the visual presentation of the room in which play takes place has been drawn perspectivally. The room, by being drawn with vanishing lines and perspectival placement and representation of objects, carries with it the other characteristics of perspective such that subjects and objects are held still and separated, placed in view of each other—made visible to each other. It is through this particular representation of space, then, that Stitch, the objects in the room, and the child playing the game as Stitch, are made available to their own eyes and to the eyes of others; it is through this particular representation of space that eyes are emphasized as the sense for being with—having an identity for and with—others.

The second kind of space made visible in this game is less experientially abstract than that of perspective, but it makes concretely visible and gives human weight to the spatial relations perspective prescribes: this is the space of houses, of home as we conceive it in the late twentieth and early twenty-first centuries: a private place for, usually, a single family, a place where money-making work is not supposed to intrude. A visual background of this game—that the game takes place in what is clearly but unremarkably a child's room with its toys, art-making supplies, and books—asks a child to flatten onto the computer screen her lived knowledge of being in a house with others; it draws in the relationships that a child experiences within her home.

Think of "home" as it appears in the floorplans published in newspaper supplements and in the many currently available magazines of floorplans: there is generally a public entry into a hallway, and then there is a front room—a room physically in front of the others—where we meet with those outside the family. There is a kitchen, which exists between the public and the private, and then there are the bedrooms, ideally, in our time and place, one for each person in the house. There is the master bedroom, larger than the others; there are the smaller bedrooms for the smaller (both physically and in terms of decision-making power in the house) inhabitants. Mark Wigley, writing about Alberti's fifteenth-century text on architecture, argues that, just as there was an initial separation of public from private as houses became homes and not places of mixed work and family life, there was in addition a further division and elaboration of privacy within the house:

> While one of the first signs of the growing desire for privacy for the individual, such that a "privacy within the house developed beyond the privacy of the house," was the separation of the bedrooms that Alberti prescribes, which established a masculine space, this space is not completely private, since women can enter it, albeit only when allowed. The first truly private space was the man's study, a small locked room off his bedroom which no one else ever enters, an intellectual space beyond that of sexuality. (347)

It is of such spaces that Pierre Bourdieu writes:

> Inhabited space—and above all the house—is the principal locus for the objectification of the generative schemes [of a culture]; and, through the intermediary of the divisions and hierarchies it sets up between things, persons, and practices, this tangible classifying system continuously inculcates and rein-

forces the taxonomic principles underlying all the arbitrary provisions of this culture. (89)

These home spaces make visible and experiential the mixed power,
gender, and other relations amongst those who live in the house, as
the child's room in the game I am discussing makes clear to a child
playing the game her position within the game. She is a child, someone
who can expect less privacy within the home than the larger others
with whom she lives, someone who needs to stay closer to home than
the others, someone who is, because of her relative smallness, vulnerable to the judgments and actions of others, someone whose room and
body are not yet marked by gender but are prepared for gendering.

But it is also home that, in this game, provides a ground for a player
to try on the presented identities because, as Iris Marion Young argues,
"Home is a concept and desire that expresses a bounded and secure
identity. Home is where a person can be 'herself'; one is 'at home' when
she feels that she is with others who understand her in her particularity. The longing for home is just this longing for a settled, safe, affirmative, and bounded identity" (157). A child can both bring to and take
from this game a sense that home is where you get to be your "real"
self (in this case, something not—or not yet—human) prior to taking
on the identities that allow you to be judged acceptable by those outside the home.[3] If it feels to us that home is where we have a "settled,
safe, affirmative, and bounded identity" and are affirmed within that
identity, it is not because home is where we get release or relaxation
from some messier outside; it is rather that (as Young argues and as the
computer game I discuss takes as a given) home is the primary space
where such identities are made possible because it is the place where
the subjects of such identities are first produced and grounded. To go
home is thus to be re-grounded, to have the machinery of the house
spaces work on us yet again, re-affirming what feels to be at our cores
because home is what from the first has surrounded and grounded and
prepared us.

And this is why, I think, the house in the *Lilo and Stitch* game is
just so quietly there, sitting in the background, not calling visual attention to itself, not requiring any odd or interesting interactivity. For
the game to do its perspectival home work, the house must just simply be there, drawn perspectivally into the background, unemphasized
for a player so that her attentions can be focused on what the game

teaches is the next stage of becoming human: taking on ready-made identities.

This Game's Time

If the workings of space in this game rely on home, and on how home is visually presented perspectivally, the workings of time come, like the aliens out to capture Stitch, into the house from the outside in several different ways, showing the permeability of the house—and home—and those who live within it.

The kind of time a child playing this game first encounters is time as a particular kind of visual event, made accessible to eyes by means of the timer that is drawn below the child's room but on which the room rests: this is the time of deadlines, of—visually—a short distance that a marker covers while some task is completed. This is like the homely time of baking cookies when we set a timer for the oven, for example, but it is much more often a temporality one finds outside the privacy of home, in the timed public tasks of school and other work. Similarly, the second kind of time present in this game, that of repetition, is also shaped as time coming into the home from the public outside. The player is given a task—to keep Stitch disguised over the course of the day while Lilo is at school—a task that must, within the logic of the game, be repeated every hour on the hour until Lilo comes home. This is the time of the assembly line, of work as well as of school, of time broken into discrete bits so that discrete actions (like the assumption of specific identities) can take place. In the interactivities of the game, the subject of the game—Stitch, with whom a player has been told to identify—is being prepared to see its self and its days shaped by these units. And notice how this subject is not asked within the game to be much alert to—to think about—the effects of such timing on itself: the mechanisms of this time are simply placed visually down low, represented mildly in the moving indicator, in the numeric time displayed at the bottom right of the screen; repetition for tasks and deadlines are instead simply a given in this game, the ground for what makes possible the central action of identity formation that relies on and that is impossible without repetition.

There is yet another kind of temporality to the game, that of succession, one of the three qualities of time for which Kant argued as he divided up what he considered to be the essential and inherent categories with which we comprehend the world. In doing work so central to modernist notions of self-in-the-world, Kant argued that there is the time of duration, of objects that appear to us to persist; there is the time of simultaneity, of objects (and others) existing alongside each other; and there is the time of succession, of objects taking the place of each other. In this game, identity is successive: not only must identity follow the ready-made, culturally available visual configurations I described earlier, but different identities cannot be held simultaneously, cannot be mixed or made complex. Instead, a lesson of this game is that identities come as complete configurations that can only replace each other whole. They may neither endure nor be simultaneously mixed, but they are complete and whole and successive, and as such they fit into the structures of time I've earlier described that require focused, deadline-shaped, repetitive work: someone who sees herself as holding successive identities can step into public and private identities, identities for work and for home, as the time requires. This is also preparation (perhaps) for taking on successive jobs rather than developing in a player the expectation that a single job with a single company awaits her.

Notice, finally, that there is nothing we might call "bodytime" in this game: although the game is to take place between 9 a.m. and 3 p.m., there is for a player no break for lunch, no break for the bathroom, no break for a nap. There is also no time for growth or change: the game is simply, visibly, in the present. There is, however, something like "private time" implied in the game, as my discussion of successive time would suggest: from the game's stretch of 9 a.m. to 3 p.m., Stitch—and the child playing the game—must work to be presentable to the outside. The implication is that, outside those times, there is no need to put on acceptable identities for others. Instead, the child then simply gets to be, to be what it is in some kind of home essence, prior to being visibly, publicly acceptable . . . but a still further implication, to carry out the logic of the game, is that public scrutiny will return, repetitively, during the public hours of the day, with its ability to reach into the house and remove the child, and that she must therefore always be ready to return to the repetitions of identity.

Outside and Encompassing the Game

I have in my writing over these pages kept our focus on what shines on the computer screen, on what happens within the visual field of the game itself, much as my attentions, like the attentions of children I watch playing this game or others on computers, are held on the computer screen when I play the game, but that is to miss still more shaping background, that of the screen and the monitor box around it and me in my chair not really aware of the mouse I move as I play. These too—a player in her chair, her hand on the mouse, her face rapt at the screen—figure into how the game does its work.

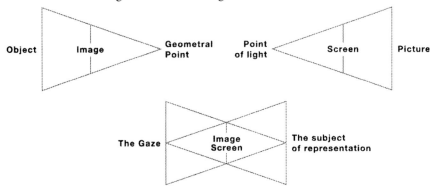

Fig. 2: The Lacanian field of vision. "Diagram on p. 91," from *The Four Fundamental Concepts of Psycho-Analysis* by Jacques Lacan, translated by Alan Sheridan. © by Editions du Seuil. English Translation © 1977 by Alan Sheridan. Used by permission of W. W. Norton & Company, Inc.

It is hard here not to align the computer screen with Lacan's notion of the screen, not because the two words align but because—just as particular notions of the gaze are made visibly operable in this game— the way a player sits raptly before the computer screen playing this game in which the gaze is so enacted seems so well to exemplify how on the surface of the computer screen seeing and being seen, visuality and visibility, entwine. Both Jay and Silverman describe how Lacan inverted the scheme of perspective—diagrammed at top left in Figure 2, with the viewer at what is called "the geometral point"—to consider (in the triangle at top right) "that figure as spectacle rather than as viewer" (Silverman, "Fassbinder" 289; the emphases in this quotation and the following are hers). In the triangle that schematizes perspective, Silverman argues that Lacan is demonstrating that there is a geometral point instead of an eye because "at the juncture where planar lines converge within a perspectival painting, drawing, or photograph, it is precisely the viewer him or herself who might be said to 'vanish' or 'fade away'" (288). When seeing is so understood—as a diagram— then the position of the viewer is a function, not a call for the particularities of any "real" person; in addition, the triangle describes how the processes of perspective separate a viewer/geometral point and any object being seen, for the image made through the tools of perspective must always stand between the two. The triangle at top right inverts this situation: the viewer is now considered in her or his visibility to others, made visible through the impersonal field of vision opened by light, indicating how the gaze functions impersonally, as the "presence of others as such" (*Threshold* 133) and within the general spaces of light; this diagram, according to Silverman, is "concerned with the process whereby the subject assumes the form of a representation or— to state the case somewhat differently—*becomes a picture*" for others ("Fassbinder" 289). For Lacan, we are always caught within both these processes, hence the third diagram that brings together the other two. There is always, that is, an image-screen between us and the gaze, a screen that Silverman interprets as meaning "the image or group of images through which identity is constituted": "What we are asked to understand by the last diagram is that it is at the level of what is variously called the 'image' and the 'screen' [that Lacan] in fact means the image or group of images through which identity is constituted" ("Fassbinder" 291). We are, that is, never available fully to others as any underlying essence or as a being unlike any other; instead, we can only be seen by others—through the impersonal gaze—through ready-made and comprehended cultural categories such as those of gender, race, age, sexuality, and so on, categories that function through this crossing of a subject who sees and is seen. We can control neither being seen nor the set of possibilities through which we are seen.

For Lacan, the image-screen is not a physical construct but rather a part of the processes of seeing and being seen. Nonetheless, it is hard not to understand the little computer game I've been describing as exemplifying the structures I've just described, similar to how Silverman discusses these structures through the other visual technologies of film and photography. In playing the game, a child sits on one side of the computer screen, looking at that opaque surface that throws light out onto her face; the game—itself a representation of its makers and their

particular temporal and spatial locations and hence cultural understandings—gazes upon her through the screen, seeing her through a
particular category of alien-child who needs subjectifying through the
range of identities available to the makers.

And if the computer screen can be seen as an exemplification of
Lacan's identity-producing image-screen, then there are also other ex-
emplifications at work in the little computer game I've been analyzing.
In my earlier, necessarily cursory, description of artificial perspective,
I did not describe how a frame—such as that of a window—is one of
the tools (conceptual or physical) used to create perspective: in order
to impose a perspectival grid on what she sees, an artist must first cut
out a rectangular scene from all that is around; the resulting art is also
rectangular. The frames that we put around paintings—to make them
into paintings ready for display—are generally not much discussed,
and often when they are, they are considered secondary to the art onto
which they put what we consider a finishing touch. Kant did this, for
example, when he discussed frames, calling them (along with the other
materials that support the presentation of art but are not themselves
the art) *parergon,* "outside the work." In our time, on the other hand,
Derrida—calling attention, as he so often does, to matters outside the
usual discussion—wrote that "the *parergon* is a form that has, as its
final determination, not that it stands out, but that it disappears, bur-
ies itself, effaces itself, melts away at the moment it deploys its greatest
energy. The frame is in no way a background" (61). Rudolf Arnheim
points out that paintings were not framed until the fifteenth century;
framed paintings, that is, appeared at the same time and alongside the
frame of perspective. Prior to this time, paintings were put directly
onto walls or altars for they were, as Arnheim describes, "integral components of architectural settings" (51), but as a merchant class with
surplus capital developed, artists started producing portable work for
this market, which required the support and protection of frames.
Arnheim argues that a frame

> defines the reality status of works of art as distin-
> guished from the setting of daily life. The frame
> makes its appearance when the work is no longer
> considered an integral part of the social setting, but
> a statement about that setting [. . .]. The frame indi-
> cates that the viewer is to look at what he sees in the

> picture not as a part of the world in which he lives
> and acts, but as a statement about that world. (52)

Through this framing, inseparable from the processes of perspective, spectators are distanced from what they see, and can look with what feels like objective distance. "The statement about that world" that Arnheim describes is not a part of the world in the sense that it comes directly out of that world; it is instead a statement that, in its ordering, explains that world and gives to the viewer the ordering patterns through which to see the world. The representational process at work in this framing is a process of seeing (through eyes as well as conceptualizations) the world through one particular set of categories, those bound with perspective, those that distance and order and calculate and rationalize and discipline. This is not visual representation in the usual sense, the representation of people, animals, places, or things; this is rather the making visible—on canvas, printed page, or computer screen—the pattern of order and arrangement and relation that framing sets onto its objects and that onlookers therefore see in a framed scene.

And with the game I am describing, the framing is multiplied beyond that of most paintings: there is the frame of the monitor; there is then the frame of the operating system on the screen itself, with its horizontal or vertical menus at the sides of the screen; there is the frame of the window of the browser software used to access the Disney website. There is within the browser a rectangular frame of advertising and other visual tempts to encourage a player (or, more likely, her parents) to pay the $50 that will give her access to all the entertainments available at the site, and, within that last frame, finally, is the visual field of the game itself, of Stitch visually isolated in an empty room, waiting for a player to give human identity to the little alien body, waiting to be judged by the others outside the window frame in the wall, a window frame that implies where Stitch—and a child playing the game—can go when they have learned to take on identities appropriately, into non-framed space outside the home. But the non-framed space is itself framed, of course, because it is only visible to a player who has first narrowed her attentions down through all those other frames, which, although they apparently do no work, are necessary for the particular focus of this game. The framing that works its way from the outward edges of a computer monitor down through all that is on screen is a structure—like the particular shapes of space and time in this game—providing underlying support for the production of a body ready to take on its necessary identities for going out into the particularly shaped work world outside the home. These levels of framing help visually isolate that body by placing it within, helping to structure, the particular spaces and times without which we could not see that body or see it as needing to take on successive identity.

But what, now, finally, of the body sitting in the chair looking into all this framing? The immobility of a monitor and the closeness with which we sit to computers encourage us to be immobile, although the question of the body is a question the game itself doesn't readily suggest, given how it instead asks a player to focus her attentions onto the center of the screen, Stitch, and the repetitions of identity. The practices of seeing that this game encourages do not ask us to understand seeing as connected to bodies with other senses. Not only are Stitch and the various successive identities given by the game available to us exclusively through vision—rather than or in addition to being smellable, touchable, tasteable, or hearable—but a player is asked, as I have earlier described, to think of sight as the only sense that judges whether any being (including herself) is fit to be human. At the same time, a player is asked to keep her eyes focused on the screen in order to play, her head steadily upright, her hand moving and clicking the mouse in small increments below her field of vision, the rest of her body unaddressed by anything in the game. If vision can take on the qualities of judging and identifying it does in this game, if a child learns that to be is to be visible, it is because her postures set her into structures of seeing that are repeated within the game. What is framed here—made into a statement about her world—are repetitions of a gaze onscreen and out from the screen, a focus onto the screen and away from a nonvisible body, a body given to sight and experienced through sight.

All the above is not meant to suggest that I believe the lessons of this game are overt, that the designers of this game have necessarily read Silverman, Butler, or Jay (for example), or that this game determines how any child who plays this game will go on to see. I want to be clear that this game, as I wrote in my introduction, functions like a machine, and one does not expect a machine, as it works on its products, to teach those products to attend to their origins. Nor does a game that so enmeshes theoretic understandings of sight, identities, and bodies have to be built with any awareness of those theories; the game simply repeats structures that are already in play in how we live, and that repetition—as Bourdieu and Giddens remind us—sets those structures into play yet again.

But even though this game sets those structures into play, that does not mean that a child will finish playing this game seeing and acting as a visible object in the ways the game organizes. Were this the only game children ever played—were these the only ways of seeing and being a (visible) body—my words on this paper would be typed with an urgency I'd hope you could touch. Children do play other games and do interact within many other structures—but I hope that what I've argued here about one game helps us be alert to the varying times and spaces that shape other games and so our selves. Our charge should be to hear Martin Jay's call at the end of *Downcast Eyes* to "encourage the multiplication of a thousand eyes, which, like Nietzsche's thousand suns, suggests the openness of human possibilities" (591): as much as we are capable of understanding how we create spaces and times in the representations we build, we should be attending to how particular embodiments of space and time, like the unobtrusive computer screen through which we see such games, necessarily figure into shaping the sensing body that plays. The body into which this game about a little alien would shape a child—a body not quite modern because of its successive identities but also not quite postmodern because of its underlying sense of sharply delineated unitary body and not even really posthuman because of its domestications of the technologically rendered alien—shows in its mixed status how such online machines need not be rigidly doctrinaire to be particularly constructive.

Acknowledgments

At Wayne State University and at the Feminisms and Rhetorics Conference at The Ohio State University, both in October 2003, I presented earlier versions of this paper; to the audiences who asked such thoughtful and change-suggesting questions, I give thanks. I also give thanks to Heidi Bostic and Dennis Lynch, who both read with such eyes for detail.

NOTES

[1] *Lilo and Stitch* (the movie) as well as the game that I discuss based on
the movie are exemplary of the arguments Vivian Sobchack makes in *Screening Space* about what she names "conservative" science fiction: the movie and
game (as I hope my following arguments show) are about display in shallow
space and hence about image rather than questioning how we live with each
other; they are about seeing aliens as similar to us so that we can erase any
fear and difficulty of working with real difference. Because the space of this
paper allows me to show how this game shapes a particular kind of body,
without being able to follow out various threads of consequence to that body,
I can only acknowledge this useful but only potential line of inquiry for my
work here.

[2] There is, of course, another whole chapter that could be written here
about the Disney Corporation and their self-conscious attempts—through
games such as I discuss here but also through Happy Meals, T-shirts, Hal-
loween costumes, and so on and so on—to build consumer loyalty to their
brand and products through encouraging children's identification with the
characters of their movies. The identities allowed in this game are all from
the movie on which the game is based (except for that of Marilyn Monroe,
which I can only assume was added for some sort of gender equity) and so
certainly function to limit children's imaginaries to the Disney-certified. My
interest here, however, is not in the particular identities offered to children
but rather that different successive identities are offered. I hope you will not
begrudge me this focus, and instead—if you want to question these particular identities—will wonder with me why it is that Lilo's doll (a lumpy hand-
made doll), the doll that in the movie is used to show Lilo's differences from
other girls around her (who all hold Barbies), is shown as a potential identity
in the game but is never one of the identities a child is asked to give Stitch:
the doll's parts—unlike those of Elvis or Marilyn or the surfer—simply do
not appear in the cabinets from which a child chooses pieces of identities.

[3] The particular relation between Stitch and the identities a player puts
onto Stitch can be interpreted as making visible Don Ihde's notions of a
"body one" and a "body two": "body one" is "motile, perceptual, and emotive
being-in-the-world" (xi) and the "necessary condition of all situated knowledges—but it is not the sufficient condition" (69); "body two" is the "body
upon which is written or signified the various possible meanings of politics,
culture, the socius. And it is the body that can have markers. It is the body
that can be female, of a certain age, from a certain culture, of a certain class,
and thus can have a *cultural perspective* as the embodied and enculturated
particular being we are" (70).

Stitch is, visually, body one in this game, a body prior to being marked;
the identities a player overlays on this body show us body two being created.
I am not comfortable with this division, however, because it can be taken as

saying we have a body prior to culture, a body we all share, which is certainly an implication of this game as well. I have given some consideration to Ihde's formulation in terms of how it can be interpreted as a body in a culture visually tied to books—to visual appearance of pages as support for inscription, for example—could conceive (see "A Bookling Monument"); in terms of the game I discuss in this paper, this body formulation could then be conceived as an attempt to hold onto some modernist notion of solidity in the face of the successive identities asked by the globalization and dispersal of the workplace and jobs.

Works Cited

Arnheim, Rudolf. *The Power of the Center: A Study of Composition in the Visual Arts.* Rev. ed. Berkeley: U of California P, 1982.

Bourdieu, Pierre. *Outline of a Theory of Practice.* Trans. R. Nice. Cambridge: Cambridge UP, 1977.

Butler, Judith. *The Psychic Life of Power.* Stanford: Stanford UP, 1997.

Curry, Michael R. "Discursive Displacement and the Seminal Ambiguity of Space and Place." *The Handbook of New Media.* Ed. Leah A. Lievrouw and Sonia Livingstone. London: Sage, 2002.

Derrida, Jacques. *The Truth in Painting.* Trans. Geoff Bennington and Ian McLeod. Chicago: U of Chicago P, 1987.

Dubery, Fred, and John Willats. *Perspective and Other Drawing Systems.* New York: Van Nostrand Reinhold, 1983.

Gombrich, E. H. *Art and Illusion: A Study in the Psychology of Pictorial Representation.* Princeton: Princeton UP, 1960.

Grosz, Elizabeth. *Architecture from the Outside: Essays on Virtual and Real Space.* Cambridge: MIT P, 2001.

Ihde, Don. *Bodies in Technology.* Minneapolis: U of Minnesota P, 2002.

Jay, Martin. *Downcast Eyes: The Denigration of Vision in Twentieth-Century French Thought.* Berkeley: U of California P, 1993.

Kant, Immanuel. *Critique of Pure Reason.* Trans. J. M. D. Meiklejohn. Mineola: Dover, 2003.

Lacan, Jacques. *The Four Fundamental Concepts of Psycho-Analysis.* Trans. Alan Sheridan. London: Hogarth, 1977.

Manovich, Lev. *The Language of New Media.* Cambridge: MIT P, 2002.

"NielsenNet Ratings for September 2003." *USA Today.* 23 Oct. 2003: 8D.

Panofsky, Erwin. *Perspective as Symbolic Form.* New York: Zone, 1991.

Romanyshyn, Robert D. *Technology as Symptom and Dream.* London: Routledge, 1989.

Rose, Jacqueline S. "The Case of Peter Pan: The Impossibility of Children's Fiction." *The Children's Culture Reader.* Ed. Henry Jenkins. New York: New York UP, 1998. 58–66.

Silverman, Kaja. "Fassbinder and Lacan: A Reconsideration of Gaze, Look, and Image." *Visual Culture: Images and Interpretations.* Ed. Norman Bryson, Michael Ann Holly, and Keith Moxey. Hanover, NH: Wesleyan UP, 1994. 272–301.

—. *The Threshold of the Visible World.* New York: Routledge, 1996.

Sobchack, Vivian. *Screening Space: The American Science Fiction Film.* New Brunswick: Rutgers UP, 1998.

"Stitch: Master of Disguise. 2003. (29 August 2003). <http://disney.go.com/blast/content/games/master_disguise/index.html>.

Watts, Steven. "Walt Disney: Art and Politics in the American Century." *The Journal of American History* 82 (June 1995): 84–110.

Wigley, Mark. "Untitled: The Housing of Gender." *Sexuality & Space.* Ed. B. Colomina. New York: Princeton Architectural P, 1992. 327–89.

Wysocki, Anne Frances. "A Bookling Monument." *Kairos* 7.3. 2002. <http://english.ttu.edu/kairos/7.3/binder2.html?coverweb/wysocki/index.html.

Young, Iris Marion. *Intersecting Voices: Dilemmas of Gender, Political Philosophy, and Policy.* Princeton: Princeton UP, 1997.

5 The Racialized Gaze: Authenticity and Universality in Disney's *Mulan*

Sue Hum

Disney's animated feature film, *Mulan,* establishes that the audience should trust what they see, privileging images over words, graphic imagery over verbal imagery. Unlike the characters in the film who have yet to discover her heroic mettle, the audience witnesses Mulan's real personality when her unconventional behaviors are juxtaposed with the traditional imperatives and cultural customs of an imagined China. By "showing not telling," Disney reveals Mulan's "true" character and her distinct, unavoidably American sensibility. With the persistent chorus, "Bring Honor to Us All," in the background, the audience comprehends how Mulan cannot and will not accept her role as a perfect Chinese bride and perfect Chinese daughter, described as dignified, refined, poised, and silent. The traditional Chinese female role is not Mulan's way to honor. The audience agrees with the matchmaker's prediction, "You may look like a bride, but you will never bring your family honor." No, not as the perfect bride or perfect daughter, but, as the film unfolds, Mulan becomes the gender-crossing heroine who achieves honor through her unconventional ingenuity and tradition-resisting conduct, single-handedly saving China from the invading Huns. Throughout this narrative, Disney sets up the primacy of the racialized gaze.

This chapter addresses the complicated issue of the reception and interpretation of racial identity in popular films, in particular the construction of Chinese subjectivity in Disney's *Mulan*. My analysis of Disney's *Mulan* demonstrates the existence of what Christian Metz calls the "scopic regime of the cinema," a dominant way of seeing promulgated by the very nature of films that contributes to the constitution of a racist cultural order (161). According to Metz, each scopic regime—culturally specific ways of interpreting what we see—seeks to organize reality into one essential socio-historical construct, reinscribing the values and beliefs of the dominant group through the production of sanctioned and oppositional subjectivities. I expand on Metz's model, arguing that issues of race and ethnicity in hegemonic, white America, as reflected in its popular films, are organized and reinforced by the scopic regime of the racialized gaze.[1] Simply, *Mulan* is simultaneously an invitation to and a validation of the racialized gaze.

The racialized gaze configures images of racial and ethnic identity as inconsequential in two ways. First, the racialized gaze operates through the dynamic of authenticity, the politics of judging whether individuals from a culture fulfill certain "correct" and even "native" race-related characteristics. This dynamic of authenticity reduces racial difference to a compendium of aesthetic and surface markers, such as those reflected in popular iconography and tourist stereotypes. This process denies the existence of deep differences that result from historical oppressions and exclusions. The dynamic of authenticity trivializes race, treating it as an aesthetic that simulates a "real" experience for the spectator. Second, the racialized gaze through the dynamic of universality superimposes the assumption of sameness, that is the doctrine that all humans beings are essentially alike in needs, desires, and aspirations. This dynamic of universality highlights how the tale of Mulan, despite its ancient Chinese origins, has been transformed into an American coming-of-age saga, a journey of innocence and high adventure that chronicles the heroine's enterprising "American" grit as she seeks to be true to herself and thus be validated for who she "really" is. In short, the racialized gaze trivializes and erases racial identity.

THE SCOPIC REGIME OF THE RACIALIZED GAZE

The area of vision and visuality studies, conducted in various disciplines such as art history, film studies, philosophy, cognitive biology, anthropology, and so forth, identifies our ways of seeing not only as a physical, biological ability—that is "natural"—but also as a socio-cultural phenomenon—that is "cultural" (Foster, *Vision* ix). The biological act of *how* we see, then, is always entangled with the learned, historical, cultural act of making sense of *what* we see. As philosopher Marx Wartofsky argues, all visual experience is "itself an artifact, produced by other artifacts, namely pictures," contending that *all* perception—how we make sense of what we see—is the result of historical changes in representation (qtd. in Jay, *Downcast* 4–5). Thus, perceptions of racial identity are tied to culture and technology, both of which contribute to and are manifested in the racialized gaze. I begin my exploration of the racialized gaze and *Mulan* by discussing the relationship between a scopic regime and ideology, describing how the dominant way of seeing in the West—Cartesian perspectivalism—is a manifestation and dissemination of bourgeois ideology. Next, I describe the symbiotic relationship between Cartesian perspectivalism and the racialized gaze, the latter deriving from, perpetuating, and reinscribing the former, in the process maintaining the hegemony of bourgeois ideology.

In "Scopic Regimes of Modernity," historian Martin Jay identifies three separate, competing scopic regimes that consist of complex socio-cultural visual practices, habits, and theories: Cartesian perspectivalism, Baconian empiricism, and baroque. Each scopic regime organizes visual stimuli into culturally approved perceptual patterns so that *how* we see becomes *what* we see. Each scopic regime maintains and perpetuates an ideology, functioning as what French cultural critic Roland Barthes calls "mythologies." Each mythology represents a body of beliefs, knowledges, and practices which preserve and actively promote the values and interests of the dominant group in society: "Myth does not deny things, on the contrary, its function is to talk about them; simply, it purifies them, it makes them innocent, it gives them a natural and eternal justification, it gives them a clarity which is not that of an explanation but that of a *statement of fact*" (*Mythologies* 156, emphasis added). According to Barthes, mythologies translate ideology into a transparent, taken-for-granted reality. Normative ways of interpreting visual stimuli, particularly images, evidence a given culture's mythology. A scopic regime, then, naturalizes and promotes the social, economic, and power relations of the dominant group.

The prevailing scopic regime of modernity, Jay among others has argued, is Cartesian perspectivalism, where the seeing subject is a detached observer and the seeing stance is a "view from nowhere." When the observer remains ostensibly disinterested, how she or he sees becomes simply a "natural" experience; the eyes become a neutral tool for recording natural phenomena and transmitting that information objectively. This detached, disinterested observer and the "view from nowhere" are the primary characteristics of what is considered the "dominant, even totally hegemonic, visual model of the modern era, that which we can identify with Renaissance notions of perspective in the visual arts and Cartesian ideas of subjective rationality in philosophy" (Jay, "Scopic" 4). Cartesian perspectivalism presents vision and visuality as unmediated by the observer, technology, and culture.

Cartesian perspectivalism is characterized by three interrelated ways of seeing that obscure the observer's role in producing the observed. First, the eye is like a flat mirror, reducing a three dimensional scene to an "artificial" two-dimensional surface (Jay, "Scopic" 6). This mirror-reflected image supposedly corresponds directly to naked reality. Second, a singular, unblinking eye, not unlike the eye of the camera, produces a "visual take" that is fixed, decontextualized, and de-eroticized (7). That which is captured in a photograph is that which we assume to be a "pure image," a perfect, static, life-like record of reality (Barthes, "Photographic" 19). Third, a reality-effect of the representations fosters de-narrativization and de-textualization, eliminating the discursive role of images (Jay, "Scopic" 8–9). Images, then, no longer recount stories, but are conflated with reality: "the *reality effect* is produced, the basis of that unavowed verisimilitude which forms the aesthetic of all the standard works of modernity" (Barthes, *Rustle* 148). Not only are observers "outside the object of inquiry," there is a "distance between the disincarnated eye and the depicted scene" (Jay, "Scopic" 26–7). Because we are distanced from what we see, *how* we see comes to represent rather than resemble reality. When imagistic representations are coterminous with reality, the ocularcentric cliché, "seeing is believing" gains robustness.

Each scopic regime trains our vision to maintain that ideology through systematic, agreed-upon acts of perceiving and interpreting images. However, Barthes seeks to undermine the popular tendency of reading images with an acceptance of *"one and the same time* the perceptual message and the cultural message" ("Rhetoric" 36). This common inclination, which Barthes equates with the "function of the mass image," proliferates through popular culture mechanisms, including advertisements and movies ("Rhetoric" 37). In short, the hegemony of a mythology is maintained by its transmission and transformation of an ideology as invisible and natural. Cartesian perspectivalism, many contend, is complicitous with bourgeois ideology, transforming imagistic products—paintings, photographs, and films—into portable commodities circulating within a capitalist exchange (Jay, "Scopic" 9). Gaining prominence during the Victorian era, bourgeois ideology encouraged the transformation of images of English domestic life into commodities, objects that were exported to its colonies, particularly Africa (McClintock 34). At the same time, the Victorian middle-class homes were filled with bric-a-brac from foreign, faraway lands—ashtrays made from gorilla's hands, shrunken heads, delicate porcelains, fine silks, and so forth—souvenirs gathered during the British Empire's imperialistic projects. Bourgeois ideology's project of cultural imperialism, aided by the spread of commodities, is intertwined with its system of representation. Speaking from an ethical perspective, Barthes finds myths "sickening" because they resort to a "false nature, a superabundance of significant forms, as in these objects, which decorate their usefulness with a *natural* appearance" (*Mythologies* 126n, emphasis added). The hegemony of an ideology depends on the ways in which it influences how and what we see, transforming the process of seeing (visuality) into the content of that which is seen (vision).

Emphasizing the situatedness of vision and visuality, Jay proclaims in *Downcast Eyes* that observation "means observing the tacit cultural rules of different scopic regimes" (9). What and how we see are sited in a specific socio-historical ideology. Because each scopic regime manifests and reinscribes an ideology, *how* we see influences *what* we see; visuality is *always* a "view from somewhere." By contrast, the Cartesian observer inhabits a subject position that "fails to recognize its corporeality, its intersubjectivity, its embeddedness in the flesh of the world" (Jay, "Scopic" 24). Cartesian perspectivalism brackets out materiality, and by so doing also eliminates deep differences, such as race, gender, class, and sexual-orientation. Without those differences, the subject becomes an "Everyman" whose vision, an ability human beings have in common, is universal and transcendental. If we are all the same, then we also see the same way: "exactly the same for any human viewer occupying the same point in time and space" (11).

The Cartesian spectator takes on the unmarked, normative subject position of Western civilization: a white, Eurocentric, middle-class heterosexual male. bell hooks notes, "mass media was a system of knowledge and power reproducing and maintaining white supremacy. To stare at the television, or mainstream movies, to engage its images, was to engage its negation of black representation" ("Oppositional" 117). Evolving from as well as feeding back into Cartesian perspectivalism, the racialized gaze selects and organizes race-related stimuli to fit the normative subject position in bourgeois ideology. Pointing to representations of blacks in *Amos 'n' Andy,* hooks observes that blacks are portrayed as what they represent for whites (117).[2] Thus, Cartesian perspectivalism maintains a symbiotic relationship with the racialized gaze, which transmits and transforms representations of racial identity according to the cultural value systems of the status quo *and* encourages spectators to accept that dominant interpretation as "real" and "natural."[3]

Jay argues that "it is difficult to deny that the visual has been dominant in modern Western culture in a wide variety of ways" ("Scopic" 3), and Disney exploits this visual imperative. Disney reminds the audience that we should trust our eyes first, a message that is subtle, implicit, yet palpable. The audience ascertains Mulan's true character through three telling, visual moments, portraying her intelligence, fairness, and uniqueness. En route to the matchmaker's, an appointment for which she arrives late, Mulan is distracted by a game of Chinese chess. Her astuteness is evident when she stops, peruses the game pieces, and then moves a piece to the joy of one player and the annoyance of the other. Beyond her intellectual acumen, Mulan's sense of justice leads her to intercede with two boisterous bullies, returning a doll to a young girl. As she gazes into the mirror to examine her "perfect" Chinese bride make-up, Mulan adds a touch of individuality to an otherwise perfect albeit generic hairdo: a defiant curl on the front of her forehead. Contrasted against the four brides-to-be who look alike in makeup, hairdo, dress, and comportment, Mulan, the audience learns from the graphic imagery, will bring honor by unconventional means. The redundant cliché, "to see with one's own eyes," foregrounds perception as a way of bringing order to the uncertain terrain of reality.[4] Not only does Disney reinforce our already existing tendencies to privilege vision as the most reliable and legitimate way of knowing, it also wants us to treat its representations as direct, unmediated experiences.

Traditionally defined as the class interests of the bourgeoisie, bourgeois ideology plays a role in systematically constructing for its subjects normative positions of identification. In the American context, the audience recognizes and closely identifies with the mythos of rugged individualism. The audience, like the neutral researcher, observes how Mulan's conduct, through tangible behaviors serve as transcripts of her disposition as a rugged individual. The above three incidents that exemplify Mulan's intelligence, sense of justice, and defiant distinctiveness, coupled with her spirited inventiveness at the very beginning of the film—when she has the puppy, Little Brother, perform her chore in a modified "carrot approach," by tying a bag of feed to his tail and a bone on a stick so he will spread the chicken feed—provide the audience with observable phenomena from which dependable conclusions can be drawn about her character. The audience must suspect—and how could they not—that Mulan will fulfill the Emperor's prediction at the beginning of the film: "single grain of rice can tip the scale; one [wo]man may mean the difference between victory and defeat." All this the audience learns, not by being told but by seeing for themselves. While they may assume that their vision is "natural," their perception—the process of interpreting and making judgments about Mulan's personality—is already habituated to the racialized gaze. What the audience fails to recognize is how bourgeois ideology interpolates their formulation of Mulan as well as their perception of her behavior.

Both Cartesian perspectivalism and the racialized gaze co-exist in a symbiotic relationship, perpetuating existing, entrenched (racist) power arrangements of the status quo.[5] The scopic regime of the racialized gaze, sedimented with hegemonic interpretation and reception traditions, enables historically determined ideological power structures, inspiring a belief that there is only one way to see (and represent and interpret) race and racial identity. Therefore, the racialized gaze—in its capacity to define and to construct—foregrounds a certain interpretation of race-related images and those composed images reinforce the veracity of that interpretation. The racialized gaze reinscribes the supremacy of bourgeois ideology, relying on two paradoxical dynamics—processes of interpretation and reception—of authenticity, which trivializes racial differences and universality, which erases race. A product and producer of existing (racist) power arrangements, the racialized gaze, through its twin processes of authenticity and universality, also anticipates and manages accusations of racism. Next, I turn to the dynamic of authenticity, exploring how the scopic regime of the racialized gaze treats race as a product and a commodity. I illustrate how images of race in *Mulan* are the result of habits of seeing influenced by bourgeois ideology. My examination demonstrates how the encouraged interpretation of racial identity invokes ritualized, agreed-upon ways of seeing that manifest in and is manifested by the scopic regime of the racialized gaze.

AUTHENTICITY AND THE RACIALIZED GAZE

As I explain above, the racialized gaze serves to construct a racial identity that replicates the cultural value systems of the status quo; as a result of the racialized gaze, spectators accept this racial configuration as "real" and "natural." Central to that racialized gaze is the dynamic of authenticity—the compulsion to accept what one sees as pure and truthful—which derives its power from a symbiotic relationship to Cartesian perspectivalism. Cartesian perspectivalism endorses a way of seeing that underscores the importance of realism—what we see accurately mirrors, or, at the very least imitates, the outside world: "That 'realism' is dominant as an epistemology and aesthetic goal since the Renaissance seems to be an inevitable part of materialist history in so far as we are seeking to free ourselves from superstition, religion, idealism in order to gain control over our material, social, and psychological word" (Gledhill 98). Furthermore, realism presupposes that objects that are represented in film and art exist independently and outside the processes of representation, that is, the "view from nowhere." This same expectation of realism is extended to the camera, which captures a high degree of resemblance or verisimilitude between the work of art and that which it seeks to represent.[6] However, laws of verisimilitude imply consonance with what is generally accepted by a particular society to be true (Gledhill 96). So it is not reality that is mirrored; it is a culture's interpretation of reality that is mirrored. Although it is a mythification to believe that the real can be captured by the camera or that the camera and the conditions of a film's production are insignificant, realism is an expectation of the dominant ideology. Within the capitalist circuit, the authentic products of a culture—artifacts or souvenirs that maintain that culture's integrity of tradition, experience, and imagination—fetch more as commodities. In other words, authenticity is a bourgeois ideal, both for commodities and signifying practices. In this section, I describe how the racialized gaze utilizes the dynamic of authenticity, resulting in a cosmetic, commodified understanding of racial identity. Authenticity relies on verisimilitude so that a lack of authenticity is perceived as purposeful distortion. By enacting the values of bourgeois ideology, the dynamic of authenticity treats race as a commodity through three strategies: use of tourist stereotypes, metonymy, and popular film conventions.

Unlike cartoons, animation, although not life-like, convinces the spectator of its success based on the verisimilitude between the representation and the world it seeks to capture. Because the audience believes that animation is based on *and* resembles reality, viewers willingly accept that the "real" world can be accurately reproduced if the artist tries hard enough. Through meticulous and painstaking craftsmanship, animation must achieve factual authenticity, which is itself a bourgeois ideal. Disney has purposefully cultivated the "facticity of race," a phrase I use to highlight the meticulous verisimilitude in *Mulan,* downplaying the constructedness of its cultural scene. *Cinefantastique* reports the painstaking, fastidious steps Disney took to achieve an accuracy of "real life" Chinese experience in *Mulan,* sending over 30 animators and filmmakers to visit China so they could familiarize themselves with the "culture, landscape, and architecture" (Lyons, "Times" 7). In addition, the creative team deferred to *authenticity* consultants and cultural specialists, including artists from Taiwan ("Effects" 25). Such conscientious research and thorough attention to cultural minutiae only bolsters Disney's credibility as a reliable delivery agent of cultural knowledge. Disney's efforts may be the result of lessons learned from the negative publicity incurred from racial and ethnic stereotyping with the 1992 release of *Aladdin* and the 1995 *Pocahontas.* Disney carefully produced, marketed, and advertised *Mulan* to demonstrate its responsibility and cultural sensitivity in handling race and ethnic issues. Disney was successful at the box office, earning $120 million during *Mulan's* theatrical run (Scally 41; Alaimo 71). The *World Almanac* lists Disney's lucrative cash cow as first in the top ten video sales for 1999 and in the top twenty children's videos of 2000. Imaged in immediately recognizable, formulaic, and naturalized ways, *Mulan* and its commercial success testify not only to the effectiveness of its cultural "realism" among a largely white, middle class American audience, but also to its effectiveness as the purveyor of bourgeois ideology.

The myth of authenticity, then, represents both a way of knowing and a way of seeing. The cultural capital in "getting-it-right" underscores a perceived realism that reinforces the value of authenticity in racial identity, purposefully negating the artist's role and the conventions that govern the production, circulation, and consumption of its artistic images. In addition to an overwhelmingly positive response from the American audience, native Chinese scholars published accolades for treating Chinese culture with respect (see Zhu; He). Zhu Yi claims that "*Mulan* was the only foreign film to have ever depicted China with such elegant brush strokes and to have used majestic symphony music to accompany a marching Chinese army [. . .]. It is probably a sensation felt only by people who have experienced what it is to be Chinese in the United States" (20–21). He observes that "the scenes in the film are designed to have a Chinese poetic flavor" (24). Underlying the Chinese scholars' stamp of approval is the belief that there exists a tangible, authentic Chinese culture that can be reproduced and represented, if enough care is exercised. Simply, authenticity exists; artists must work to achieve it; audiences expect it and will pay for it.

A lack of authenticity, then, occurs when verisimilitude is undermined. Inaccuracy, distortions, and corruptions—purposeful or accidental—result in inauthenticity and stereotypes. Some Asian American educators criticize Disney for depicting Orientalist characterizations, but even more detrimentally, for representing Chinese culture inauthentically: "The filmmakers have every right to recreate the image of Mulan so long as it doesn't violate its *cultural authenticity*"(Mo and Shen 131, emphasis added). Disney's portrayal of Chinese culture is full of egregious inaccuracies, stereotypes, and transmutations, interpreted by Weimin Mo and Wenju Shen as "cultural blasphemy" and disrespect (137). Sheng-mei Ma observes that Disney's Mulan is "presented as exotic dresses" (140), exploiting "Orientalist images as racial markers" (141). In addition, Ma condemns Disney for relying too heavily on familiar Chinese iconography in a clumsy attempt to convey culture (130). Concerned with how mass media shapes children's understanding of culture, Mo and Shen advocate a critical, interpretive stance in the classroom, recommending that teachers "discuss the stereotypes and cultural distortions in the films" (141). Both the praise for *Mulan*'s cultural sensitivity and the criticism of *Mulan*'s inaccuracies are predicated on the existence of authenticity, the deterministic, essentialist, fixed view of racial identity.

The racialized gaze is the master sense by which we judge and evaluate authenticity. Despite their negative responses to *Mulan,* Mo, Shen, and Ma share with Disney the same epistemological notions of culture: an authentic, essentialized, pure Chinese culture exists, one that can be accurately depicted. Disney's efforts (and failures) at rendering Chinese culture in a "true-to-life" fashion underscore the belief that racial identity can be accurately and precisely determined, hence a preoccupation with authoritative and realistic representations. Notions of authenticity are accompanied by a network of social and literary narratives of homogeneity and uniformity, delineating a complex set of racial injunctions and truth claims. Both positive and negative reactions to *Mulan* coalesce around "authenticity" because both share the same bourgeois ideal. The struggle for authenticity is the struggle to control processes and products of signification, to establish coherent systems of racial subjectivity while resisting new, sometimes oppositional, cultural alignments.

In the scopic regime of the racialized gaze, racial identity is not only characterized in essentialist, reproducible terms, it is also reduced to a compendium of static, essentialist, yet "authentic" images, circulating as assimilated, consumable commodities, easily recognizable by American audiences. Cartesian perspectivalism's focus on images as commodities in a capitalist exchange translates into the racialized gaze's fetish for consumable, exotic iconography and tourist stereotypes, which compound the problems of authenticity even further. The desire for verisimilitude, which marks the dynamic of authenticity, leads to a "racial shorthand" that flattens the complexity of race into easily recognized stock representation. For Barthes, an image is a "re-presentation," observing in his analysis how a French advertisement uses "a stock of stereotypes" to create Italianicity ("Photographic" 18): "*Italianicity* is not Italy, it is the condensed essence of everything that could be Italian, from spaghetti to painting" ("Rhetoric" 48). Barthes notes that "it is a specifically 'French' knowledge [. . .] the knowledge on which this [Italianicity] sign depends is heavily cultural" (34–35). Just as the French notion of "Italianicity" relies on observable, consumable, culturally selected phenomena, the racialized gaze highlights surface differences of simplified, reductive representations, which take the place of material, historical, deep differences. Spectators assume that these immediately recognizable stock characteristics, tourist stereotypes, and exotic iconography *are* authentic or realistic representations; these "re-presentations" or images are not only confused with, but also replace "reality." The ideology on which authenticity rests is "a system of values; now, the myth-consumer takes the signification as a system of facts: myth is read as a factual system, whereas it is but a semiological system" (Barthes, "Mythologies" 142).

What enables this system of "facts" is a cultural repertoire, a shared lexicon of social knowledge, conscious and unconscious, relying primarily on stereotypes. The facticity of race in these dehistoricized and decontextualized images, then, anchors the myth of authenticity, "racializing" the visitors' gaze and perception. Millions of American and international visitors acquire ahistorical "facts" about China, Japan, Norway, and other countries when they visit Disney's Epcot Center in Florida, oblivious that these "facts" are constructed, organized, and mediated through an American interpretive framework and condensed to a monologic, static image. Epcot Center represents an unexamined celebration of diversity, relying merely on the display ethnic costumes and stereotypical racial markers, laying them out for easy consumption in exotic configurations. According to hooks, "stereotypes abound when there is distance. They are an invention, a pretense that one knows when the steps that would make real knowing possible cannot be taken or are not allowed" ("Representations" 170). Epcot's images and exhibits endure, their authority derived from the visitors' immediate recognition, consequently enabling visitors to remember what they see. To see is to believe; to believe is to know as real. These superficial, aesthetic markers of racial identity and culture, what Barthes calls "condensed essence," become what Americans *see* as "authentic" about each culture; their understanding of culture, then, "is subject to the physical constraints of vision" ("Rhetoric" 49). The consistent repetition of tourist stereotypes, not only at the hands of Disney but also across other media, manifests an authority, which in turn represents authenticity.

Disney's reliance on the "condensed essence" of tourist stereotypes is most obvious in its images of Chinese physiology. In their efforts to represent a distinct Chinese sensibility, Disney artists depend on the inevitable logic of visibility, relying on familiar, widely known, accepted, albeit Orientalist visual markers that are clearly distinguishable by Americans. While Mulan's almond-shaped eyes are at a slight angle to achieve a Chinese look, her eyes are too big, too rounded, too wide-set, a characteristic of more European facial features. She is an amalgam of heterogeneous Asian cultures, her clothing highlighting how Disney's animators have blurred historically defined cultural boundaries. When she meets the match-maker, Mulan is clad in a Japanese kimono and clogs, her makeup is more reminiscent of a geisha. Mulan's Korean-styled hair is tamed by Chinese hair-combs. Disney artists' reductive approach to racial realism depends on a superficial understanding of difference located on the surface, the skin, the facial features. Racial identity, it would seem, is constrained by fixed, knowable biological details. The realistic emphasis presupposes that the object of observation—in this case, Chineseness—can and does exist independently of the processes of observation and the mediating, interpretive role of its observers. Disney's realism naturalizes tourist stereotypes as authentic racial identity to an American audience, and at the same time fails to acknowledge or reflect upon a film's constructedness and the invisibility of its editing processes.

To signify and authenticate Chineseness further, Disney also relies on metonomy which "furnishes the image with the greatest number of connotators," (Barthes, "Rhetoric" 50). A rhetorical figure or trope, metonymy constitutes the action of substituting a word or phrase denoting an object, action, institution, and so forth to connote something so that the thing used is regarded as a symbol of or substitute for something else. The associative relationship in metonymy depends more on contiguity rather than similarity (50). Barthes warns that the "most important thing, however, at least for the moment, is not to inventorize the connotators but to understand that in the total image they constitute *discontinuous* or better still *scattered traits*" (50). *Mulan* opens with the most recognizable and familiar of Chinese icons, the Great Wall of China. As the Wall emerges from a Chinese calligraphy brush, the audience views more images of Chinese culture: dragons, incense sticks, pink blossoms, calligraphy, gongs, cemetery stones, and so forth. Individually and as a group, these icons symbolize, represent, and substitute for a coherent and authentic Chinese racial identity. Through a monologic construction of Chinese culture, Disney assumes mistakenly that authentic racial identity resides in iconography, thus reducing race to commodities that are easily reproduced. Metonymy becomes Disney's tool to represent culture, condensing thousands of years of Chinese history, values, and beliefs to the most recognizable symbols. Disney's audience encounters Chineseness through aesthetic differences, that is, through tourist stereotypes and iconography, so that racial difference is contained and fixed. Such representations of racial identity neither challenge nor expose the ways in which difference is constituted historically and operates currently as mechanisms of power and oppression.

Most viewers are not privy to Disney's creating and editing processes; the success of its featured animations depends on uncritical
and unreflective viewing: "the more technology develops the diffusion of information (and notably of images), the more it provides the
means of masking the constructed meaning under the appearance of
the given meaning" (Barthes, "Rhetoric" 46). One way of masking the
construction of images is to rely on accepted American film conventions, particularly those easily recognizable moments in popular film.
As Barthes explains, signifiers from a previous system are recycled and
adapted to a culture's myths, in this case from Chinese material to
American mythos. Despite her Chinese origins, Disney's Mulan cannot pass for Chinese; the film's exotic appeal inadvertently reveals the
protagonist's hybrid subjectivity, underscoring an American articulation that stabilizes and reaffirms that American identity. Disney animators depict those entertaining moments of Mulan in drag, providing specific interpretive frameworks for the American audience's
viewing/reading practices. For example, Mulan must start a fight to
"prove" she is a man, leading Disney into a humorous rendition of
the rag-tag, undisciplined soldiers Captain Li Shang must train. The
three soldiers, not unlike the Three Stooges, provide a comic foil for
Mulan's inventiveness and self-reliance. These same soldiers disguise
themselves as "geishas" to enter the palace unnoticed in an effort to
rescue the Emperor from the evil Khan. Reminiscent of a scene from
Some Like it Hot, these "ugly concubines," wondering if their dresses
make them look fat, a predictable Western concern, distract Khan's
soldiers so that Li Shang can rescue the Emperor. Echoing other popular movies, these scenes provide an intertextual framework that ac-
tivates a particular racialized gaze so that the audience, cued to pay
attention to the exotic Chinese setting, consume the mysterious differences and cultural iconography. The myth of authenticity naturalizes
the procedures, operations, and alignments that construct it.

Both Disney and its critics share the same epistemology regarding
the importance of racial and cultural authenticity. What is not apparent is how *Mulan* functions as part of a larger system of signification in
which the dynamic of authenticity promotes the racialized gaze, which
reduces racial difference to aesthetic markers including tourist stereotypes and iconography. The scopic regime of the racialized gaze, itself
naturalizing bourgeois ideology, treats race as a stable commodity, one
that can be mass-produced and sold.

UNIVERSALITY AND THE RACIALIZED GAZE

Even the trivial, cosmetic differences highlighted by the dynamic of authenticity are stripped away to reveal a universal (white/western) identity that is held in common by all (white) people. The racialized gaze blinds us to the differences that matter. Because Cartesian perspectivalism discounts or brackets out the body in order to achieve a "view from nowhere," this ahistorical, disembodied, decontextualized way of seeing also extends to racial identity. Bourgeois ideology transforms complex historical and cultural processes into natural, static, and essential ones. The racialized gaze "de-fangs" the category of race, eliminating histories of oppression and exclusion. In keeping with bourgeois ideology's emphasis on transcendental universal humanism, the racialized gaze reinscribes an ahistorical, color-blind notion of subjectivity, focusing specifically on that which all human beings share in common. Through the dynamic of universality, racial identity not only transcends history, place, and materiality, it becomes an uncritical, monologic construction that, according to Barthes, transforms history into nature (*Mythologies* 110; 118). In the same way that Cartesian perspectivalism underscores the perspective of the "Everyman," the racialized gaze builds off that unmarked normative subjectivity to erase race. In her analysis of Julie Dash's film *Illusions,* hooks maintains, "White people in the film are unable to 'see' that race informs their looking relations" ("Oppositional" 129). By seeing race through the lens of similarity, racial differences are rendered inconsequential: "They [whites] have a deep emotional investment in the myth of 'sameness,' even as their actions reflect the primacy of whiteness as a sign informing who they are and how they think" ("Representations" 167). hooks observes that "the discourse of race is increasingly divorced from any recognition of the politics of racism" ("Representations" 176). After all, those who do not see the category of race, those who believe themselves to be color-blind cannot, by definition, be racist. And, if they are not racist, how, then, can they participate in or enact histories of oppression and exclusion?

In this section, I describe how the racialized gaze utilizes the dynamic of universality, resulting in the erasure of deep differences in racial subjectivity. Universality relies on naturalism so that differences produced by history can be overlooked by using the lens of sameness. By enacting the values of bourgeois ideology, the dynamic of universality highlights the intimacy of what Barthes calls "being-there" to le-

gitimize and substantiate the discourse of commonality, while rendering bourgeois ideology transparent. Echoed in Barthes's description of
film-watching, the spectator is "hypnotized," unaware that *how* s/he
sees is ideological in nature:

> In the movie theater, however far away I am sitting,
> I press my nose against the screen's mirror, against
> that "other" image-repertoire with which I narcissis-
> tically identify myself [. . .] the image captivates me,
> captures me: I am *glued* to the representation, and
> it is this glue which established the *naturalness* (the
> pseudo-nature) of the filmed scene [. . .]. Has not the
> image, statutorily, all the characteristics of the *ideo-*
> *logical?* (qtd. in Jay, *Downcast* 457)

Not only does Barthes highlight the ideological nature of images, but
he also recognizes how the dominant gaze operates, pointing to the
dynamics of universality which depend on "naturalness." According to
Barthes, naturalness, or naturalism, remains the dominant expectation
of representation in popular film, playing a crucial role in reinforcing
the dominant ideology.[7] Although closely related but not synonymous
with realism, naturalism, like realism, presupposes an objective, detached mode of representation. Naturalism is not a natural or given
state, but is produced through a complex interplay of techniques and
devices. What is dangerous about naturalism, however, is that the me-
chanics of its production are hidden from the viewer so that phenomena are perceived as "natural." When socio-cultural relations and events
are professed to be natural rather than a product of human or political
intervention, they remain unchallenged. Naturalism, then, reinforces
bourgeois ideology, which has everything to gain from the erasure of
history. What results is the simultaneous erasure of deep, material differences within a cultural context that forms it and is formed by it.

    The mechanics of naturalism rest in myth, the method by which
ideology derives a "natural justification" for its purpose: "What the
world supplies to myth is an historical reality, defined, even if this
goes back quite a while, by the way in which men have produced or
used it; what myth gives back in return is a *natural* image of this reality" (Barthes, *Mythologies* 155). In effect, myth "naturalizes" images
and words, transforming the products and processes of society into
something that is taken-for-granted, innocent, and essential, that is,

something that is "natural." As we have seen above, myth not only "purifies" by depoliticizing and dehistoricizing modes of representation, it offers those constructed signifying practices as statements of fact. Rather than concealing ideology, myth provides ideology with a universal, factual, true-life ethos.

According to Barthes, a film's success in articulating the dominant myths of a culture depends on the creation of a "'magical' fictional consciousness" of "being-there" ("Rhetoric" 44–45). The film simulates for the audience the immediacy and intimacy of experience, a way in which naturalism is achieved. The angst Mulan expresses seems to be a universal predicament faced by most, if not all, teenagers. Part of the challenge of coming-of-age is the definition of self against the dictates of family, community, and culture. Because this trope of individualism is so familiar, the American audience can transcend time, space, and culture to identify with the alienated, isolated Mulan. In the animated feature's second song, "Reflection," Mulan frets that she will "never pass for a perfect bride or perfect daughter," and if she were truly to be herself, she would break her family's heart. Who in the audience, at some point in their lives, has not felt misunderstood by their family? Suffocated by their culture? Mulan wonders in the song's touching refrain, "When will my reflection show who I am inside?" Having to pretend for the sake of family and tradition may be a timeless, universal, human conundrum.

Even as Mulan asks, "who is that girl I see staring straight back at me; why is my reflection someone I don't know?" the American audience is familiar with this clichéd tension between individual desires and cultural imperatives. The audience sees how that white-faced mask may represent who her parents and culture want her to be. Mulan verbalizes for the audience a foregone conclusion—"somehow I cannot hide who I am though I've tried"—as she kow-tows her respect to her ancestors. In a poignant moment, as she is reflected in many ancestral cemetery stones, she asks, "When will my reflection show who I am inside," as she wipes the make-up (and the pretense) off her face, so that, with the mask discarded, at last, the outside matches the inside, consistent with the song's metaphor, "reflection." What we see is what we get: a teenaged girl trying to chart her own course in a tradition-bound culture, not unlike the American children in the audience. The myth of individualism is so ingrained in the American psyche that Mulan's plight is not only a familiar one, but also as the audience assume a "natural" affinity with her, they come to believe they are color-blind. If we can see beyond race, beyond difference, then we really cannot be racist. Color-blindness then becomes a tool Disney uses for anticipating and managing accusations of racism. By seeing past racial difference, however, the audience's gaze reduces everything to the dominant system already in place, one that is most definitely white.

The above example demonstrates the importance of the American audience's identification with Mulan and her problem without their transformation, that is, a recognition of material history, particularly the Chinese gender roles and cultural expectations that circumscribe Mulan's choices. To understand Mulan's grief does not necessitate an understanding of the role race and culture play in constructing and maintaining that grief. As Barthes has pointed out, history becomes naturalized and detemporalized. This phenomenon, which I identify as the myth of human sameness, represents the belief that underlying all the outward trappings, whether it is culture, race, gender, class, age, and/or sexual-orientation, we are all ultimately the same: human-ness is an unquestioningly universal subjectivity. Because we're all just people, the dynamic of universality erases history and difference, rendering them moot in our discussions. Within the paradigm of universal subjectivity, racial differences, which are evidenced by surface and aesthetic difference alone, become irrelevant. By bracketing racial matters (so that it does not matter), history and geography are also bracketed out as contributing factors in our consideration of subjectivity. According to hooks, the liberal belief in sameness is one way to "make racism disappear. They [whites] have a deep emotional investment in the myth of 'sameness,' even as their actions reflect the primacy of whiteness as a sign informing how they are and how they think" ("Representations" 167). The result, then, is that Disney's audience, trained in and enacting the racialized gaze, are unable to "see" that race does inform our looking relations. Influenced by the naturalized images, the audience does not see how race is already always sedimented with systematic mechanisms and power structures that enable institutional inequalities. Thus, the myth of human sameness disguises the (racist) machinery of cultural production.

The dynamic of universality also reduces cultural differences to empty signifiers, thus emptying deep differences of its meaningfulness. For example, in the breakfast that Mushu hands Mulan on her first morning at the soldier camp, the audience sees a bowl of rice gruel, a common traditional Chinese breakfast, topped with eggs and bacon, a common traditional American breakfast. The purposeful layering of Chinese and American breakfasts may be Disney's attempt at humor, but this mode of representation demonstrates that cultural differences that result from history are emptied of their significance and meaning. The conflation of traditional Chinese and American breakfasts, signifiers from two previous systems, creates a new signified: breakfast, whether in China or America, is the same. Any cultural differences are only details that can be ignored. In addition, although Mulan eats with chopsticks, demonstrating she is "authentically Chinese," Ma points out, "no Chinese would be so ill-mannered as to thrust the chopsticks upright in the rice bowl" (130), a behavioral marker of inauthenticity. In Disney's representations, differences across cultures do not matter: they are empty signifiers that merely gesture toward race. What the dynamic of universality obscures is the way in which race is a lived experience: "the image is re-presentation, which is to say ultimately resurrection, and as we know, the intelligible is reputed antipathetic to live experience" (Barthes, "Rhetoric" 32).

The racialized gaze relies on a one-dimensional understanding of race, conflating cultures, differences, and histories under the rubric of commonality. Barthes explains, "text (most often a snatch of dialogue) and image stand in a complementary relationship; the words, in the same way as the images, are fragments of a more general syntagm and the unity of the message is realized at a higher level [. . .] dialogue functions not simply as elucidation but really does advance the action by setting out, in the sequence of messages, meanings that are not to be found in the image itself" ("Rhetoric" 41). For example, although *Mulan* is a tale set in ancient China, Disney purposefully creates a "side-kick" in the form of the pint-sized dragon, Mushu, whose voice is that of a black, urban male. Expressing himself in the cadence, rhythm, pronunciation, and verve of black male talk, Mushu is irreverent, disrespectful, informal, crude, and, worst of all, loud. Mushu's talk and behavior, his manner and comportment create a recognizable cultural reference to American audiences. The audience can identify with Mushu even though dragon-lizards are unfamiliar for American culture because he sounds like people we "know," whether in popular media or in real life. Like Mulan, Mushu is a product of the racialized gaze as his image, especially his sound, is stereotypically essentialized to exaggerated and simplified rhythms. While many may dismiss the blending of Chinese and African-American speech patterns as poetic license, such conflation highlights how racial difference, as seen through the lens of human sameness, can become a large, amorphous, undifferentiated mass. George Lipsitz notes that commercial motion pictures "are historical in the sense of being cultural artifacts and social-history evidence about the times in which they are made. But films are historical in another way as well: they reposition us for the future by reshaping our memories of the past" (164). What Disney ignores is the fact that such cultures and their differences are produced and shaped by historical, contextual, and economic forces, all of which are erased by the dynamic of universality. The racialized gaze strips away process and context, reducing all racial identity and difference to similarity. Furthermore, minorities—both Chinese and African American—are not treated in the same ways by American institutions.

By rendering ideology transparent and innocent, the racialized gaze through the dynamic of universality erases the ways in which history must be reckoned with. When history becomes nature, naturalism "second natures" the racialized gaze. In other words, the racialized gaze has become so intertwined with our ways of seeing that it is like second nature: an unconscious, taken-for-granted process of seeing and perceiving racial difference as both aesthetic and universal. However, racial identity is constituted within and in response to representation: "You are the only one who can never see yourself except as an image; you never see your eyes unless they are dulled by the gaze they rest upon the mirror or the lens [. . .] even and especially for your own body, you are condemned to the repertoire of its images" (Barthes, qtd. in Jay, *Downcast* 448). In addition, as Stuart Hall observes, "identity as a 'production,' which is never complete, always in process, and always constituted within, not outside, representation" (704). Although we can never have the "right" representation, we can have better representations that highlight the fluid, shifting, contextual, performative nature of racial identity.

CONCLUSION

How could we deal with the native in an age when there is no possibility of avoiding the reduction/abstraction of the native as image? How can we write about the native by not ignoring the defiled, degrad-

ed image that is an inerasable part of her status—i.e.,
by not resorting to the idealist belief that everything
would be alright if the inner truth of the native is
restored because the inner truth would lead to the
"correct" image? (Chow 29–30)

In *Writing Diaspora,* Rey Chow highlights the tendency of treating
Chinese as natives, particularly within the context of colonial discourse. To demand cultural authenticity is to freeze race within a tidy,
closed, hermetically sealed system; to emphasize human sameness is
to bracket history by naturalizing ideology. Thus, the quest for an authentic and exact imagistic representation of the native, like the quest
for the holy grail, is a hopeless one. As Homi Bhabha notes, the stereotype "is a simplification because it is an arrested, fixated form of
representation that, in denying the play of difference, [. . .] constitutes
a problem for the *representation* of the subject in signification of psychic and social relations" (75). In short, it is this fixity, this stability of
stereotypes that feeds the scopic regime of the racialized gaze. It is this
fixity that undergirds the belief that Mulan (and Chinese subjectivity)
can be represented accurately, the belief that inner truths exist; and, if
we are careful and meticulous enough, racial identity can be realistically depicted. However, as Hall points out, "cultural identity is not a
fixed essence at all, lying unchanged outside history and culture [. . .]
it is always constructed through memory, fantasy, narrative and myth.
Cultural identities are the points of identification, the unstable points
of identification or suture, which are made, within the discourses of
history and culture" (707). Through my description and critique of the
racialized gaze, I demonstrate how the dynamics of authenticity and
universality prevent an audience from grasping how Chinese history
and material culture contribute to deep racial differences, blinding us
to the adaptive, improvisational, and contextual nature of racial identity. Representations of Mulan—and representations of racial identity,
in general—can never achieve positivistic perfection or essentialist ex-
actness because racial identity is contingent.[8]

NOTES

[1] The consensus is that "to gaze implies more than to look at—it signi-
fies a psychological relationship of power, in which the gazer is superior to
the object of the gaze" (Schroeder 208). Distinguishing between the look
and the gaze, Evans and Gamman define the look as a perceptual mode open

to all while the gaze is a mode of viewing reflecting on a gendered code of desire (16).

[2] According to Claire Johnston, "myth transmits and transforms the ideology of sexism and renders it invisible—when it is made visible it evaporates—and therefore natural" (210). To extend the same logic, within a racist ideology and white-dominated cinema, people of color are presented as what they represent to the Anglo community.

[3] See also Diawara where the black spectator resists the dominant interpretation of blackness.

[4] Kennedy translates Aristotle's definition of rhetoric as *seeing* the available means of persuasion in each case (35); "*to see* translates to *theorēsai*" and the English word, theory, comes from the related noun, *theoria* (n34; 37).

[5] hooks explains, "many black women do not 'see differently' precisely because their perceptions of reality are so profoundly colonized, shaped by dominant ways of knowing" ("Oppositional" 135).

[6] Claire Johnston argues that the "camera was developed in order to accurately reproduce reality and safeguard the bourgeois notion of realism which was being replaced in painting" (214).

[7] Barthes's use of the natural is not akin to the naturalist literary movement. In American and British literature, naturalism refers to a type of "realistic" fiction in the late nineteenth and early twentieth centuries where humans have little control over their destinies, where artists and writers stress either biological or social determinism.

[8] Thanks to Carlos Salinas, Elissa Foster, Kristie Sealy Fleckenstein, Mona Narain, Bernadette Andrea, and Nancy Myers for helping birth this essay.

Works Cited

Alaimo, Dan. "'Mulan' Leads Disney Video Slate." *Supermarket News* 9 November 1998. 71.

Aristotle. *On Rhetoric*. Trans. George A. Kennedy. New York: Oxford UP, 1991.

Barthes, Roland. *Mythologies*. Paris: Editions du Seuil, 1957.

—. "Photographic Image." *Image, Music, Text*. Trans. Stephen Heath. New York: Hill and Wang, 1977. 15–31.

—. "Rhetoric of the Image." *Image, Music, Text*. Trans. Stephen Heath. New York: Hill and Wang, 1977. 32–51.

—. *Rustle of Language*. Trans. Richard Howard. New York: Hill and Wang, 1986.

Bhabha, Homi. "The Other Question: Stereotype, Discrimination and the Discourse of Colonialism." *The Location of Culture*. New York: Routledge, 1994. 66-84.

Chow, Rey. "Where Have All the Natives Gone?" *Writing Diaspora: Tactics of Intervention in Contemporary Cultural Studies.* Bloomington: Indiana UP, 1993. 27–54.

Diawara, Manthia. "Black Spectatorship: Problems of Identification and Resistance." *Screen* 29.4 (1988): 66–76.

Evans, Caroline, and Lorraine Gamman. "The Gaze Revisited, Or Reviewing Queer Viewing." *A Queer Romance: Lesbians, Gay Men, and Popular Culture.* Ed. Paul Burston and Colin Richardson. London: Routledge, 1995. 13–56.

Foster, Hal. "Preface." *Vision and Visuality: Discussions in Contemporary Culture.* Ed. Hal Foster. New York: New P, 1988. ix–xiv.

Gledhill, Christine. "Recent Developments in Feminist Criticism." *Film Theory and Criticism: Introductory Readings.* 4th ed. Ed. Gerald Mast, Marshall Cohen, and Leo Braudy. New York: Oxford UP, 1992. 93–114.

Hall, Stuart. "Cultural Identity and Cinematic Representation." *Film and Theory: An Anthology.* Ed. Robert Stam and Toby Miller. Malden: Blackwell, 2000. 704–14.

He, Zhongshun. "What Does the American *Mulan* Look Like?" *Chinese Sociology and Anthropology* 32.2 (1999–2000): 23–24.

hooks, bell. "Representations of Whiteness in the Black Imagination." *Black Looks: Race and Representation.* Boston: South End, 1992. 165–78.

—. "The Oppositional Gaze: Black Female Spectators." *Black Looks: Race and Representation.* Boston: South End, 1992. 115–31.

Jay, Martin. "Scopic Regimes of Modernity." *Vision and Visuality: Discussions in Contemporary Culture.* Ed. Hal Foster. New York: New P, 1988. 3–23.

—. *Downcast Eyes: The Denigration of Vision in Twentieth-Century French Thought.* Berkeley: U of California P, 1993.

Johnston, Claire. "Women's Cinema s Counter-Cinema." *Movies and Methods: An Anthology.* Ed. Bill Nichols. Berkeley: U of California Berkeley P, 1976. 208–17.

Lipsitz, George. "The Meaning of Memory: Family, Class, and Ethnicity in Early Network Television Programs." *Time Passages: Collective Memory and American Popular Culture.* Minneapolis: U of Minnesota P, 1990.

Lyons, Mike. "Mulan: Effects Animation, Finding a Balance Between Art and Realism." *Cinefantastique* 30.2 (1998): 25–26.

—. "Mulan: Times are Changing for Disney Heroines." *Cinefantastique* 30.2 (1998): 7.

Ma, Sheng-mei. "Mulan Disney, It's Like, Re-Orients: Consuming China and Animating Teen Dreams." *The Deathly Embrace: Orientalism and Asian American Identity.* Minneapolis: U of Minnesota P, 2000. 126–43.

McClintock, Anne. *Imperial Leather.* London: Routledge, 1995.

Metz, Christian. *The Imaginary Signifier: Psychoanalysis and the Cinema.* Trans. Celia Britton et al. Bloomington: Indiana UP, 1982.

Mo, Weimin, and Wenju Shen. "A Mean Wink at Authenticity: Chinese Images in Disney's *Mulan.*" *New Advocate* 13.2 (2000): 129–42.

Mulan. Dir. Barry Cook. Prod. Pam Coats. Screenplay by Rita Hsiao and others. Videocassette. Buena Vista Home Entertainment, Walt Disney Home Video, 1998.

Scally, Robert. "4Q Rollouts Spill into '99." *Discount Store News* 37 (21) 9 November 1998. 41+.

Schroeder, Jonathan. "Consuming Representation: A Visual Approach to Consumer Research. *Representing Consumers: Voices, Views, and Visions.* Ed. Barbara B. Stern. London: Routledge, 1998. 193–230.

Zhu, Yi. "Seeing *Mulan* in the United States." *Chinese Sociology and Anthropology* 32.2 (1999–2000): 20–22.

6 Making Meaning in "School Science": The Role of Image and Writing in the (Multimodal) Production of "Scientificness"

Gunther Kress

"School Science" has undergone profound changes in the last few decades, yet one of its tasks remains that of inducting the young into particular ways of thinking, into particular orientations to the world, and into particular ways of thinking about (the production of) knowledge. One profoundly significant factor in this complex of changes that the subject has experienced is that of representation. The visual—here as elsewhere—has become enormously more significant than it had been before. So at one level the issue is quite simple: what is the role of the visual in the constitution, representation, and communication of School Science as part of a wider interest in the role of the visual in contemporary multimodal communication?

In order to explore this overarching theme, I ask further questions. For instance, what are these newer multimodal message-entities actually like, and what roles are played by the visual and the written modes in them? For my purposes, chief among the questions are how is knowledge realized in a specific mode, and how is it configured differently in different modes, or reconfigured in the change from one mode to another, say, in the shift from the mode of writing to the mode of image? How is human engagement with the world shaped by specific modal representations, and reconfigured in the transduction from one mode to another? In what ways, I want to ask, is our engagement with the world shaped differently in the use of different modes, as for instance through image and through writing?

I will explore that in relation to an example from secondary school-ing.[1] The knowledge at issue in this bit of the science curriculum is "What is an onion cell like?" It is an instance of the more general question "What are plant cells like?" However, the matter at issue is broader still, and it affects all of the science curriculum. It is "what is it to be scientific and to act scientifically?" and "how do I demonstrate scientificness?"

The theoretical approach taken in this chapter is that of multimod-al social semiotics. I do not wish to say much about social semiotics (Hodge and Kress; Kress, "Against," *Before*) except that it treats signs as always newly made, and as apt, motivated relations of signifier and signified, and sees them as the consequence of the result of real ac-tion arising out of the interest of sign-makers. That much is essential if we wish to read back from (signs in the) text to the meanings of the meaning-maker.

I will, however, say three things about a multimodal approach to representation and meaning making. First, it assumes that in principle all modes have the capacity to be developed into fully articulated, fully functioning resources for representation and communication. Second, it assumes that the materiality of modes—sound, graphic substance, stone, and so forth—provides affordances of certain kinds, which are shaped in particular ways by the work of humans in culture over time. These two factors together produce the semiotic resources of a specific mode, from which signs are constantly newly fashioned by socially situated sign-makers. Third, a multimodal approach assumes that all texts are always constituted multimodally. Over the last three or four decades, public communication has become more intensely multimodal, so that in many domains image is beginning to displace writing partly or wholly. Hence, it is now essential to develop new ap-proaches to text-production, to reading, and to theories of meaning and learning.

The three assumptions are each essential, each for different reasons. The first requires that we attend to all modes present in a text-mes-sage and to the meanings of them all. The second assumption forces us to attend to the specificity of meanings made in distinct modes due to the different meaning potentials of each mode. That makes it impossible to think of meaning in a generalized way; it is now neces-sary to be precise about the kinds of meanings made in and through particular kinds of modes. Lastly, the third assumption insists that if all texts are multimodal, then the meaning of any text always exists in the totality of meanings made in all the modes of the text and not just in the meanings made in one mode. Texts must be read multimodally, that is, as the overall meaning derived from all meanings in all modes. Further, the meaning contribution of each modal constituent can never be understood by itself; its meaning is always both the effect of the meaning of the modal element itself and of its interaction with other modal elements. In other words, an image element in a multimodal text means both as image and as image together with other, say written, elements.

These assumptions lead to a particular methodology of reading, namely one which requires that all modes be read with equal attention, that the different meanings of all the modes be carefully attended to, and that the meaning of a text can never be derived from reading the meanings of one mode alone. As an example, in the case of texts constituted largely in image and writing, the first task is to establish what the textual units are at each level; which mode might be communicationally foregrounded or backgrounded, or whether both have equal communicational status, and what types of meaning each carries. Once this distribution of meaning is established at the largest textual level, it is then possible to consider the meanings of the units of the text—in the different modes—at the next level "down."

So, while my interest in this chapter is first and foremost with the representational and communicational role of the visual, given what I have said, it makes no sense to focus on image alone—just as I would now regard it as impossible to focus on the written components of a multimodally constituted text, paying scant or no regard to image components. I assume that I cannot discover the meanings of the examples that I discuss below other than by dealing with all aspects of the text entity.

My example comes from a science classroom in a secondary school in inner London. The students—all young women—are between 13 and 14 years old; in the English school system they are in Year 8. Knowledge, we know, is a social category; here it is (re-)produced in the social context of a school, itself part of wider social institutions—of education and of science. "Scientificness" signals belonging to a community and its practices. If we introduce the term meaning to indicate the semiotic aspects of social practices, then we can say that to be able to act in certain ways is to be able to mean certain things, or vice versa.

The question now becomes: "what is it that we want to mean, and what modes (and genres) are best for realizing that meaning?" And here, specifically, "how can we mean as scientists mean?"

At the end of the series of lessons in which my example texts were produced—its topic being plant cells—four students worked together in a group, first preparing a slide with the epidermis of an onion, then each looking at this one slide through the microscope, and afterwards carrying out the task given by the teacher (writing a report). Each had to "record" the experiment: "draw what you have seen" and "write what you did" in conducting the experiment. Beyond this, the teacher had given just two instructions: "put your writing at the top of the page" (he was anxious that the drawing should not take up too much of the space on the page, so as to leave enough room for writing), and "use your lead pencil—do not use colored pencils in your drawings," in which his implicit aim had been to mark off one distinguishing feature of scientificness (indicated through black and white drawing) from artisticness (indicated through using colored pencils), or from everyday realism.

Description/Analysis: Genre and Discourse

I will look at just two of the four texts that were produced. I treat the first one, Figure 1, as a single textual entity, consisting at the first level of description/analysis of two larger semiotic elements of equal (representational) status, a visual and a written element (though there are also headings). I first analyze each of the two elements separately. My purpose is to establish what representational and communicational contribution each makes to the whole and how they might differ from each other. This will allow me to focus on the specific role of the visual as such and in the overall text.

Contrary to the teacher's instruction, the first example has the drawing at the top of the page and the written part at the bottom. Image and writing are clearly separated on the page; each has its own, slightly differing heading. The written text is in the generic form of a recount, that is, a temporally ordered/sequenced presentation of events, reported in sentences. The image part has the form of a line drawing; it is not clear what generic label is available to name it—something analogous, say, to diagram (the label which the teacher used in comments on the second example) or flowchart, for instance.

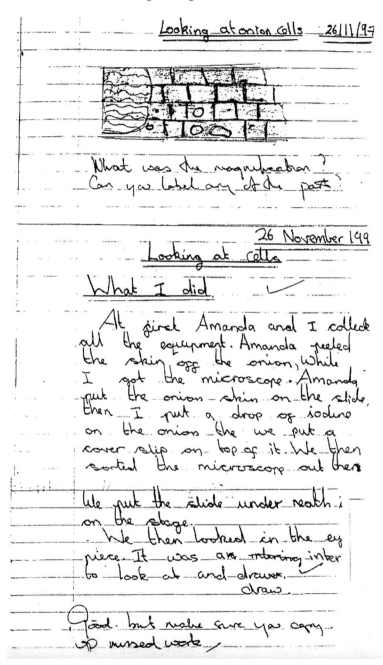

Fig. 1. First Student Example.

I will say something briefly about the meaning of the genre of recount, and then make a comment about what is recounted, seeing that
as the discursive aspect of the text. After that I will comment on the
visual part and attempt to describe its generic form. That might allow
me to attempt an answer to my question: "how is scientificness produced multimodally?"

I use *genre* as that social-textual category which realizes, as textual
sign, the social relations of the participants involved in the interaction
which produces the text. The social roles and relations established and
implied by the genre of recount are those of *recounter*—I am someone
who knows what is to be recounted—and *recountee*—you are someone
whom I regard as wishing to have the events recounted to. There is, as
the third participant, the recounted. If I am receiving the recount, my
role is that of being someone who is interested in having these events
recounted to myself, in being the recountee, and in accepting you as
the recounter. The recount presents a social world of action/event,
temporally ordered and complete.

Two kinds of matter form the content, the recounted, of this recount. With this we move into the realm of discourse (in the sense of
Foucault). One is the entities and their relations expressed in the recount, of actors acting in events with and on objects, either singly ("at
first Amanda collected all the equipment") or jointly ("We then sorted
the microscope out"). This is recounted realistically; that is, it is presented as being a recount of what actually happened, of the significant
events in the temporal sequence in which they happened. There is a
clear implication that no other relevant events occurred.

The second kind of matter concerns the epistemological character
of the recount. It makes an implicit claim about the form of the relation of the events and practices which are recounted in the text to the
practices in the world which is recounted and of the relation of the
domain of the practices to other domains. It is the claim of everyday realism, in the everyday world: "this, simply, is how it was; these
were the main participants, the main events, and they occurred in this
order."[1] Significantly from the perspective of types of scientificness
constructed, this particular recount also claims that "practices in the
science classroom are (like) practices in the everyday world."

As for the visual element, there are no existing and apt genre-labels
for the drawing. The teacher's use of the term *diagram* strikes me as
not apt; his instructions seemed to point more to something like visual

report. In the drawing, there are no actions or events, and there is no temporal sequence; we are not in a (social) world of actors and actions. We are not told about this world; we are shown it. We are in a (social) world in which there are entities in spatially represented relations to each other. What is the social relation among the participants who are present or implied in the act of communication? Here it is an objective one. This visual text-element, the displayed entity, is presented as objectively there; it is presented to the viewer front on, leading to maximal involvement of the viewer. The viewer is positioned as confronting this image straight on, at eye-level; neither to the side, a positioning that would indicate a lesser degree of involvement, nor below or above the element shown, a positioning that would indicate differences in power between the entity displayed and the viewer. The entity is presented in a maximally neutral manner: it is simply there, objectively. Instead of the relations of recounter and recountee, we have the relation of (visual) reporter (displayer) and beholder (I avoid the term "viewer," as it implies a greater degree of agency than that which the display assumes or demands) of that which is displayed.

This manner of presentation is ambiguous: it can be read either as maximal involvement of the beholder, engaging with the object front on, directly, fully; or as minimal involvement. If I take the latter reading, I focus on the absence of the social: the object is simply there, as though there were neither a reporter/presenter, nor a beholder. It is the visual means of avoiding or denying human involvement and agency. In some of its effects, (though not all) it is akin to a visual equivalent of the agentless passive of scientific writing: " . . . as has been demonstrated." Generically, I will call it a visual report.

The question then is: what is reported? What are the entities which are visually reported, and in what relation do they stand to each other? What is shown in the drawing (analogous to what is told in the recount) and by the drawing as a whole? And we can ask: what is the social world that is represented in this part of the message?

The drawing shows a rectangular block, strongly framed horizontally along the top and the bottom, with clearly distinct components. The block is open, horizontally, at each end, suggesting that it is a part of, an extract from, a larger entity. So while this drawing is not textually complete, it is conceptually complete: were you to extend the drawing to the left or to the right, then all other parts of that larger entity would be just like this extract. The elements of which the block

is composed are drawn as broadly uniform in shape and size. One
of the handouts used in a lead-up lesson had a sentence telling students that, in looking into the microscope, "It should look like a brick
wall—each brick is a cell." Quite clearly that metaphor has guided this
student's seeing. On the left-most edge of the block there is a large irregularity—the semi-circular shape—and there are also small bubble-
like elements within several of the bricks (these are likely to have been
air-bubbles on the slide).

Overall, it is a structure of relatively uniform elements in a regular
arrangement: the bricks are roughly equal in size, arranged in horizontal layers. It is a world of regularity, produced by the theory inferred
by this student from, among many other things, the metaphor in the
handout. The regularity is disturbed by the irregularity of the circular shapes. In other words, the drawing represents the truth of theory,
though the empirical reality seen through the microscope is to some
extent allowed into this representation. The large air-bubble as well as
the smaller ones appear in the visual representations of all four students, though in different ways; clearly it was too large a feature not to
recognize, not to see it.

What is shown is a world of objects as they are: static, stable elements in a regular arrangement. While the world of the recount is
complete in that it represents all that there is to recount, the world of
this visual report is complete in that it represents all there is to know;
to show more would be to show more of the same. And while the world
of the recount is set in the social world, in time, and is complete in
that it has happened, the world of this visual report is in the world of
theory, out of time—it just is—and it is complete in being.

In terms of the social effect of this representation, we can say that
the point of view of the visual report—realized through the affordance
of spatial representation—is maximally objective, and positions the
object for the viewer as simply there. The point of recounting by contrast is realized through the temporal affordance of writing: from the
present, a series of past events is recounted. The formal feature used
in the visual report is the spatial means of horizontal angle formed by
beholder and object, used as a signifier of involvement; in the recount
the formal feature used is that of (past) tense, from an implied present standpoint, also used as a signifier of involvement. It positions
the recountee as somewhat distanced, as not fully involved. Fuller involvement would be, for instance, a report in the present tense: "first

we go and collect the equipment; now we place the slide. . . ." These contrasting kinds of involvement realize differing social relations in the act of communication. Generically speaking, the recount and the display not only use different modes—writing and image—but they differ in the projected social relations of the participants in the process of communication.

We can make a further comment on the relation between the world represented here and that of the everyday world. The drawing in Figure 1 is not a realist one: it is generalized away from everyday realism (Kress and van Leeuwen 163), both through the means of using the soft black pencil on the white page (rather than the use of color, as in one of the other pieces of work) and the abstracting, generalizing, diagrammatic form of representation. The former tells us that certain aspects of the everyday world, such as the color of the viewed entity, are not relevant or desired here. Similarly other aspects, such as the real boundaries of the object, are not indicated. The represented object does not have real boundaries, it is not (clearly) framed on the left and the right side: it is, after all, a theoretical object, not a natural, realist, everyday one.

These are all pointers to the kind of world into which we are invited. The visual report suggests a particular coding-orientation[2]: not the realism of the everyday world, but the realism of the scientific-technological world.

The Question of Genre

Is this a coherent textual entity? Clearly it is a single text/message entity, namely the in-class work demanded by the teacher. We might defer the question of whether we want to call this complex of image and writing a (single) text, or whether we should invent another term for it; it is, however, unified, a coherent response to a specific communicational demand. The genre of the written part is clear, as indeed—even though we struggle with an appropriate label—is the generic organization of the image part. Each of the two genre-elements realizes different social relations, different social arrangements, structures and processes, a different stance in and towards the wider social world. And each represents different aspects of the world.

So what is the genre of this text-entity overall? And what consequences do answers to such questions have for likely changes to the uses, forms, and values of technologies of multimodal text-making?

To answer the first question, we can say that there is a clear difference between the naturalism (established within the realism of everyday life) of the recount, located in the world of the everyday, and the abstraction (within the world of scientific theorizing) of the visual report, located in the world of scientific/technological practices. The first positions me as someone who hears an account of a completed, ordered, sequence of events, somewhat distanced by the tense used; these are events that happened in a past relative to my present. The sense of everydayness is reinforced by the syntax of the writing, which is close to the clausal structures of everyday speech, as is its use of words—"we then sorted the microscope out"—coming from a quite casual register. In this account, doing science is like doing cooking, or doing the dishes. The genre of the recount treats them all equally. Scientificness, as it is presented here, is very much like the everyday.

The visual report positions me as someone who is given a view of part of an entity, but who understands that it stands for the structure of the whole; it is not part of my everyday world. I am shown a theoretical object, not one that I know from my everyday. I am positioned, by this example of the genre of the display in a different domain, out of time, in a world of regularity produced by the theory through which I am seeing.

The recount locates me in a social world of events, of actors and objects related through actions; the visual report locates me in a theoretical world without action, of object-entities related through highly regularized and recurring spatial arrangements. This difference would be reinforced were we to move to the next descriptive/analytical level down and engage in a syntactic analysis of the writing and the image. In the case of the former, we would be firmly in the world of transitive actions, whereas in the latter, we would be equally firmly in the world of classification.

The task of the science curriculum is, still, to induct young people into the practices that constitute doing science. That practice is presented in two distinct ways here: in the recount, doing science presents me with a world of ordered actions/events which are like actions/events in the everyday world. In the visual report, doing science presents me with another world: not of actions and events, but of classifications of objects in states of regular arrangement, abstracted away from the everyday world. The drawing style does not belong to the everyday, neither in its abstraction away from color nor in its regularity of representation. The regularity is the regularity of theory, not that of the everyday world. If the recount distances me somewhat from its world through time/tense, the visual report ambiguously either ignores me totally—I am so neutral as not even to exist—or it involves me fully, though so objectively and neutrally that my presence has no effect on the displayed world.

If this multimodal text-entity overall has a genre, then it is, quite simply, a mixed genre in which differently organized worlds appear differently: one a world of actions where the actors are like you and me, involved in events which are those of our everyday, the other a world without actors, a world of things as they are, things which do not belong to the world of the everyday. If one is the world of the everyday, then the other is the world of theory, of abstraction. One draws me in by suggesting that I am like the actors in a world that is familiar to me. The other positions me as a neutral observer of an objectively present world, but an observer with a special status and a special lens.

The contradiction inherent in this position is made relatively invisible and therefore not overtly problematic because the two distinct positions are realized in distinctly different modes, with absolutely distinct logics: one the logic of time and sequentiality, the other the logic of space and simultaneity. If both positions were realized in the one mode, then this young woman might have found it much more difficult to have brought them together, with their un-reconciled contradiction.

That, then, is the meaning of this genre overall; these are the social relations and the social roles of the participants projected by the combined genre. If this mixed genre contains un-reconciled contradictions, then seen from the point of view of School Science and of this sign-maker, so be it. Of course, it is a genre produced by a non-expert. The fact that she mixes the social relations of the world of the everyday with (a-)social relations of the world of scientific work is what she has taken from the teaching she has had. She is able to form her own generic response, able to see science in her way and to represent it in her way.

DESIGN

Before considering the second example, I will reflect briefly on how the student has constructed this text and this world with the notion of design in mind. Design brings together the interest and purposes of the designer with an awareness of the needs and requirements of the audience of the design, in the environment in which the design is to be realized, fully aware of the potentials and limitations of the resources which are available for implementing the design. Design focuses on the interest of the designer, on the constraints of the resources and the environment, and on the choices which can be and are made in that environment.

This student has made a range of choices, some of which will become clearer in the comparison with the next example. For instance, she chose to put the image at the top of the page; she chose to use the genres of visual report and of recount; she chose to use the framework of theory to see/understand what appeared in the microscope. In choosing the genre of recount, she has represented scientific procedures and actions as being like those of the everyday world but in relation to a world which is very differently constituted. She has described these actions precisely. In this text we see design at work. This young woman has made a number of design decisions in her multimodal representation: a decision about layout (in the decision of where to place which element); a decision about generic (and thereby epistemological) form (everyday or scientific) for each of the two elements; a decision about which mode to use for the realization of the knowledge represented here, and for each of the distinct epistemological positions; and decisions about other issues, as well.

If we see the text like this, then the generic position would become clearer: overall she positions herself between the everyday and the world of theoretical endeavor. Epistemologically, the mixed genre says, "Being scientific means that you look at things which do not belong to the everyday world through the lens of scientific theory; and, while your actions are entirely like those in the everyday, you record them precisely and fully."

Now we have a somewhat different means of seeing this text and thinking about the initial question. What, we might ask, had been the interest of this young woman? What guided the processes of her selection from all the material that she had received over the course of four lessons? Which mode had she been most attentive to, writing or image? We know that some scientific knowledge is presented in canonical form as images: magnetic fields, springs, wave-forms, and so forth. This young woman's drawing approaches canonicity; her writing does not. Was she, therefore, much more focused on image-representation than on writing? In both writing and image she is concerned to present the truth: the truth of what happened and the truth of what is. The problem—from the point of view of science—is that these truths come from different social domains.

Mixed genres are commonplace; indeed we might say that all genres are mixed, that there are no pure genres. Nevertheless, the kind of mixing presented here (a disjunction really) would be a severe problem if both text-elements were in written mode (or if this was the text of an expert). Because the two generic positions are realized in different modes, the disjunction is not readily apparent, or does not become a problem: it does not appear as a contradiction. In fact, it may well be a very good representation of the social relations as they exist in the science teaching that she is experiencing. Is it a problem that we do not have labels for these mixes, or indeed do not have labels for many kinds of generic organization? I think that this is not the main issue at all; if we find that we need labels, we will surely make them up. What is important is to recognize that texts realize, among other things, the kinds of social relations pointed to here, and do so in complex ways, which themselves realize the affective and social positions of their makers.

Another Example: The World Designed Differently

Several differences are immediately apparent in Figure 2: the diagram (the teacher's written comment is "Diagram needs to be much larger") is below the written text, as indeed the teacher had requested. There is a clear separation/division between the written part and the visual; they are separated by the heading "what we saw." The image partly protrudes into that heading, and the heading is tightly linked to the written text, visually—in terms of layout—insisting, as it were, on a connectedness, even a unity, of writing and image. Where in the first example they had been clearly separate, here there is a material, semiotic/visual integration of both.

The genre of the written text is that of procedure: a sequence of distinct (in this case numbered) steps, which, when followed, will lead to the achievement of the intended aim. The social relations expressed in the procedure differ from those in the recount. The recount tells what has happened; there might be a weakly present, implicit assumption that others will follow these actions. In the procedure the social relations are entirely different. Here we have those with the power/au-

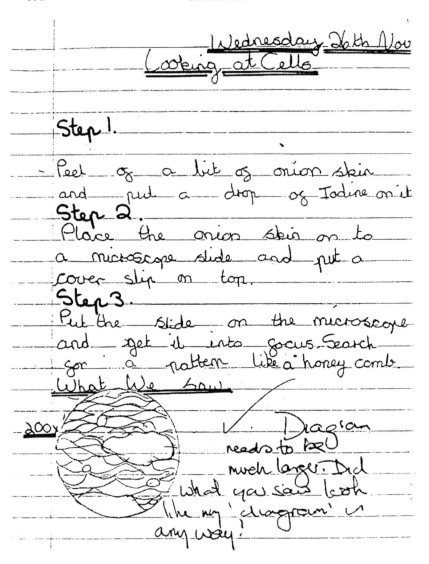

Fig. 2. Second Student Example.

thority to order actions to be followed in the sequence indicated, and there will be those who are assumed to carry out those actions. This is very different from the recount. It is no longer the informal telling of what happened (so that you might perhaps do the same); this is being told what to do. The claim made implicitly by the user of the genre of procedure is one of power, of actions commanded to be done, and of intended outcomes. If the recount is a kind of textual statement, the procedure is a kind of textual command.

As in the first example, the written part is generically complete. Its relation to the world of the everyday is different; it is not the world of everyday happenings. This is a world in which power enables predictions to be enacted where those with power can insist on actions being taken in a specific way and in a certain sequence. In the recount, sequence has the function of telling in what order things happened; here, however, sequence predicts the order in which events will be performed: things are controlled ahead of their happening. In the procedure we have only those (potential) actions (as commands) which are essential to the carrying out of a task which already exists as a pre-structured schema. If it mattered that the drawing should be interesting to look at and draw, then these would become imperatives, integrated appropriately in the sequence.

In terms of communicational roles, the difference is that the written text is a set of instructions, and the individual segments are commands to carry out the instructions in the sequence indicated. Consequently, the roles here are of a different kind: to act in a world in accord with the commands of some other who has power, with clear procedure, and in accordance with those procedures.

There is a difference between the world projected by this written text and the everyday world. In the world of the procedure, I have less power than others, or less than I might have in my everyday world. The manner in which I am drawn into the text is by means of power and not by the pleasure or interest of the recount. Hence, involvement differs from that of the recount. Here I am positioned as someone who is expected to act. Unlike in the recount, there is no claim that the world of scientific practices is like the world of everyday practices.

There is an equally marked difference in the drawing compared to the first example. One clue comes from the teacher's talk; in it he had used several metaphors, for instance: "It might look like a honeycomb." In both texts a metaphor given in language—in writing in the one instance and in talk in the other—has been transducted by the pupils into visual form.

The drawing shows a strongly delineated circle. The entities here are very different to those in the previous drawing. Like her fellow students, this young woman had seen air-bubbles, larger and smaller. However, the cell-entities which she saw are less regular in shape, and their arrangement is not as orderly as in the brick wall example. Regularity of elements or of arrangements is not a feature of this image. The drawing differs from the first example in that what it shows is complete: we are shown everything that was seen. Everything that was there to see is in the drawing. It is complete textually as well as conceptually. What she saw was not a theoretical entity, but actual, empirical reality—which is not to say that the drawing represents the reality. Rather the claim of this visual representation is that this is what was actually there—rather than this is what was (by theory) supposed to be there.

Like the first example, this drawing is presented objectively, neutrally, front on, with the full involvement of the viewer. It is an objective view of the real world. The form of realism, the coding-orientation, is that of the everyday. Involvement suggested by the drawing differs from that of the writing. To restate: here the writing relates to the world of theory, as "ought," and the drawing to the world of "is," an exact inversion of the first example, where the drawing related to the world of "ought" and the writing to the world of "what was."

In the drawing in the first example, scientificness resides in abstraction away from what was on view in the microscope, abstraction guided by theory. There is no representation of the machinery of viewing, the eye-piece/lens of the microscope, and in fact no pretence that the drawing represents what the physical eye had seen. What is represented is what had been seen by the eye of theory. In the second example, by contrast, scientificness lies in the accuracy of representing that which is there in view, the world which the human eye can see, the empirical real in its messiness. In the first example, truth is the truth of abstraction, the truth of theory; in the second, truth is the truth of the concrete, of that which is there, the truth of the empirically real world. We are shown not only what the young woman saw, but also the means by which she saw what she saw. Hence we see the eyepiece through which the young woman looked: we see everything that she saw. For this student, being scientific, when represented through the visual mode, resides in the accuracy of observation and representation.

Compared to the first example, the meaning functions of the written text and the image are inverted. In one the written text was broadly realistic/empirical, and the visual broadly non-realistic, theoretical. Here the written text is hypothetical/theoretical; the visual part, by contrast, is realistic/empirical. Together, the two parts of the text suggest (through writing) that scientificness is defined by schemata for action which underlie and organize action and that the essential task is to provide (in image) an accurate account of the empirically real.

Although scientificness is carried in distinctively different ways in the two cases, what unites them is a concern for truth through accuracy: in the first case the concern for accuracy of what happened is matched with accuracy of depiction of what is the case in theory. In the second case, accuracy about hypothetical actions is matched with accuracy in the depiction of the empirical world. Underlying both are design decisions of great precision and subtlety: in choice of mode for contents, for (local) epistemology, and for the combination of the message complex.

What are the roles of the two modes of writing and image in these multimodal ensembles? Even though the written parts of the two ensembles are generically different from each other, they share a fundamentally common feature. Both focus on action and event, even if differently; both the visual elements by contrast focus on what is, the visual display of the world that is in focus. In each of the two texts as a whole, the component parts are incomplete without the other. Each mode, writing and image, does distinctly different and specific things: the logic of time governs writing, and the logic of space governs the image. Within each logic there is the possibility of variation of genre. The generic variation of the ensembles in each case produces a specific stance towards the notion of scientificness. That stance represents the learning that has been achieved by each young woman for herself.

PRACTICING DESIGNS

The two texts here are of ensembles of modes, brought together to realize particular meanings. The fact that they are made by unpracticed designers is, from an analytical perspective, an advantage: it shows how an untutored (naïve?) maker of such ensembles uses the affordances of the modes for their ends. The purpose of the science curriculum is to induct young people into practices of scientificness. Here we see the response of two students to this demand, expressed through design decisions made in the realization of that meaning. Both were faced with the question: "What is it to act or be scientific?" and each gives a distinct answer, expressed through choice of modes and choice of genres, much more profoundly than through curriculum content.

Both students understand the affordances of writing and of image. Writing best of all does the job of representing action and event; image is best at showing the world of objects and their relations, the world as it is. The teacher's inexplicit—or open—framing of the task leaves much of the design decision to the students: interpreting the relatively open request "write what you did" in generically specific terms and doing the same for the request "draw what you saw."

In the first of the two examples, to be truthful to science means that I am expected to report things as they were (in writing). I have to stay true to the empirically real. But this student also knows that science is about constructing general accounts of the world, and she does that in her drawing: the truth of this world lies in this abstraction, which generalizes away from the messiness of the empirical to a general truth. The truth of actions is reached via the mode of writing, and the truth of how the world looks is reached via the mode of image.

For the second student the question is the same, though she answers it differently: the truth of science lies in the generality of the procedures, in the generality of the practices, which must be the same each time they are performed and is not open to the chance of contingent event. This truth is reached via the mode of writing. The truth of what the world is like is reached via the mode of image, the precise recording of what there actually is in that world with no concession to anything but strict observation. These are epistemological matters, but they are realized through design decisions focused on the use of modes, on the truth they harbor, on the use of genres and the truths that they contain.

On the face of it, these decisions have nothing to do with the existence of the new information and communication media. In reality they absolutely do. The manner in which these young people encounter School Science owes much to the revolution in representation which has already in their world altered the status, the function, the uses, and the forms of writing. The books which they use are already transformed by the joint effects of the use of the mode of image and the effect on the page of the organizations of the screens of the new media. The fact that there are now design decisions to be made and that decisions about genre are now relatively open are both a direct effect of the new media via their effect on the look of the page. These decisions are also an indirect effect of the new media in that teachers as much as designers of textbooks know that the young are attuned to a differently configured communicational world.

In that new communicational world, there are choices about how what is to be represented should be represented: in what mode, in what genre, in what ensembles of modes and genres, on what occasions. These were not decisions open to students (or teachers or textbook makers) some twenty years earlier. That change is tied more to economic, social, and political changes than to technological ones. Of course, with all this go questions not only of the potential of the resources, but also of the new possibilities of arrangements, the new grammars of multimodal texts. These new grammars, barely as yet emerging into conventionality, and certainly very little understood, have effects in two ways at least. On the one hand, they suggest the order of the arrangements of the elements in the ensembles; on the other hand, they suggest the functions that the different elements are to have in the ensembles. This leads to functional specialization of the modes, and that in turn has the profoundest effects on the inner organization and development of the modes.

Where before—up until twenty, thirty years ago—writing carried nearly all the communicational load of a message—and therefore needed to have grammatical and syntactic structures that were equal to the complexities of that which had to be represented in that single mode—now there is a specialization: each of the modes carries that part of the message for which it is best equipped. This brings with it the possibilities of great simplification of syntax for writing, for instance.

Clearly the question of genre is no longer a question of the written mode alone.

GENRE AND EDUCATIONAL STRATEGIES

The profound cultural diversity of all contemporary Western, post-industrial societies, as much as the new demands for education for participation in a fully globalized economy, has specific educational consequences. It means that the outcomes-based curriculum, or, to use a better formulation, a curriculum which focuses on skills, disposition, essential processes, and understanding of resources for representing and communicating, may be what all of us in the Anglophone and ever-more globalizing world will need to consider urgently. This will be a curriculum which focuses above all on giving students a full awareness of how to achieve their goals in the contexts of their social and personal lives, an ability for which I use the term "design." Much more goes with that change from content as stable knowledge to design.

A new theory of text is essential to meet the demands of culturally plural societies in a globalizing world. Theories of meaning need to be rethought and remade. While there is a reality to genre, the conceptions which come from former social arrangements with their (relative) stabilities have left us with both the wrong theory and the wrong vocabulary. The wrong theory led us to believe that stability of language or of text-form (as indeed of other social phenomena) was a feature of these phenomena in themselves, when it was—as is clear now—always a feature of these phenomena shaped in a period when relative social stability had been obtained. So, for instance, to speak of generic mixes is in fact still to conceive of genre in the older fashion, where stable genres could be thought to be and were mixed. A newer way of thinking might be that speakers and writers always newly fashion generic forms out of available resources, a much more generative notion of genre, one where you learn the generative rules of the constitution of generic form within the power-structures of a society. That will permit (and account for) constant change and makes the actions of the producer of the genre innovative and transformative. It encourages and normalizes design of text in response to the perceived needs of the maker of the text in a given environment. In such a theory all acts of representation are innovative, and creativity is the normal process of representation for all. The two texts that I have discussed are instances of just such a response.

NOTES

[1] A narrative, by contrast, makes a different claim: "this is how I have (re)constructed the world for you," and "actions and practices, and the order in which they are narrated here, in the narrative, may be different to those of the everyday world."

[2] For this and other terms used in the analysis, see Kress and van Leeuwen, *Reading*.

WORKS CITED

Burn, Andrew, and David Parker. *Analysing Media Texts*. London: Continuum, 2003.

Hodge, Robert, and Gunther R. Kress. *Social Semiotics.* Ithaca: Cornell UP, 1988.

Kress, Gunther R "Against Arbitrariness: The Social Production of the Sign as a Foundational Issue in Critical DiscourseAnalysis" *Discourse & Society* 4.2 (1993): 169-91.

—. *Before Writing: Rethinking Paths to Literacy.* London: Routledge, 1997.

—. *Literacy in the New Media Age.* London: Routledge, 2003.

Kress, Gunther R., and Theo van Leeuwen. *Multimodal Discourse: The Modes and Media of Contemporary Communication.* London: Edward Arnold, 2002.

—. *Reading Images: The Grammar of Visual Design.* London: Routledge, 1996.

Kress, Gunther R., Carey Jewitt, Jon Ogborn, and Charalamos Tsatsarelis. *Multimodal Teaching and Learning: The Rhetorics of the Science Classroom.* London: Continuum, 2001.

Part III: Resistance

7 What Do Pictures Want (of Women)? Women and the Visual in the Age of Biocybernetics

Catherine L. Hobbs

Biocybernetic reproduction is, in its narrowest sense, the combination of computer technology and biological science that makes cloning and genetic engineering possible. In a more extended sense it refers to the new technical media and structures of political economy that are transforming the conditions of all living organisms on this planet.

—W. J. T. Mitchell

The program of life—the system of DNA, genes, and genomes that governs every living thing—was written four billion years ago. It's time to rewrite the program.

—Tom Knight

And, above all, who is in a position to reflect on these questions, or rather, what disciplines have the tools to sort out these issues?

—W. J. T. Mitchell

The decoding of the human genome's roughly 30,000 genes in 2000 marked a new era of "biological literacy" in reading DNA. In early 2004, South Korean scientists reported they had cloned a human embryo. Further, scientists now say they are ready to "rewrite the program" of life, moving in a sense from biological literacy to productive rhetoric. None of this would have been possible without the power of the machine, the binary computer.

While metaphors of code and language dominate these new explorations in biological sciences such as genetics and the digital sciences that make them possible, vision is as key to orienting in this New World as the sight-based navigational technology of early modern ocean adventurers. Whether imaging the very small in DNA, atoms, or electrons, peering inside the body with magnetic resonance, or watching chemical processes in the brain with PET scans, new visual information emerges from computerized biological sciences. Translations from linguistic code to the visual image and back are the rule, making *ekphrasis* the central trope of this emerging cultural dominant. The work of visual artists steeped in this culture shapes a new imaginary responding to this rich semiotic world. In this chapter I focus on women's visual art, reading the bioinformatic traces that have changed and will continue to change human reproduction significantly. The aim is to follow women's participation in response to emerging and dominant scientific and cultural events.

The chapter began as a response to and extension of a talk by W. J. T. Mitchell, University of Chicago art historian and theorist. In his talk, Mitchell inquires into the cultural emergence of "biocybernetics," aiming at a visual "thick description of the present," asking, "What do pictures want?" Mitchell references Walter Benjamin, who in his key texts imagined a materialist aesthetic of modernity, summed up in part in his 1935 essay "The Work of Art in the Age of Mechanical Reproduction" (483). Twentieth century mechanical reproduction such as film and photographic methods transformed the near-religious cultic reverence previously held for the original: for example, the original oil paintings of the nineteenth century, which can be understood inhabiting a tradition in their own time and space. Benjamin attempted to understand art through a rich analysis of mass culture in the present moment, with its more secular, dislocated, commoditized art and advertising images. After Benjamin, Mitchell analyzes the present, pinpointing two technical determinants of our time: the double helix image and Turing machine (binary computer).

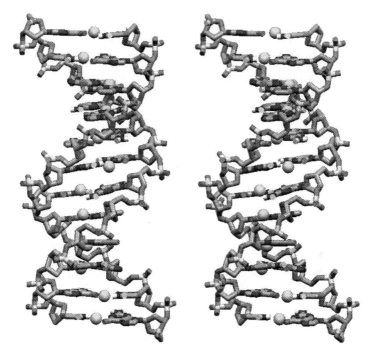

Fig. 1. DNA strand. Copernicus Project. 2004. <http://www.copernicus-project.ucr.edu> Used by permission.

Fig. 2. Dinosaur from *Jurassic Park*, © 1993 by Universal Studios.

These two images (Figures 1 and 2)—along with the media and structures supporting them—make up the founding concepts/images of
Mitchell's own "thick description of the present." The talk followed
closely on the heels of Mitchell's successful book *The Last Dinosaur
Book,* in which he takes as his icon the genetic code of the monster
in *Jurassic Park.* "Fused here in a single gestalt are the inseparable but
contrary twins of biotechnology, constant innovation and constant
obsolescence, the creation and extinction of life, reproductive cloning
and the annihilation of a species" ("Modern" 491), Mitchell says of the
image. The emergent scientific dominant of our time is biocybernetics, the center of his cultural analysis:

> I will state it as a bald proposition, then, that bio-
> cybernetic reproduction has replaced Walter Benja-
> min's mechanical reproduction as the fundamental
> technical determinant of our age. [footnote omitted]
> If mechanical reproducibility (photography, cinema,
> and associated industrial processes like the assembly
> line) dominated the era of modernism, biocybernetic
> reproduction (high-speed computing, video, digital
> imaging, virtual reality, the internet, and the indus-
> trialization of genetic engineering) dominates the age
> that we have called "postmodern." (Modern 486)

Unpacking the term bio-cybernetics in his talk, Mitchell noted that
cyber is Greek for the steersman of a boat, standing for control and
governance as well as communications. *Bios* is what is controlled,
or eludes control (484). Thus biocybernetics rewrites the dialectic
of nature/culture, image/word, idol/law, human/machine, mechani-
cal/biocybernetic reproduction and other founding binaries, he said.
Mitchell's theory interests me in part because the transformation of
these binaries—in particular, man/woman—previously was the concern of feminist and other theorists of the twentieth century. The deconstruction by elaboration or translation from one half to the other
half of the binary pairs was an effort to envision the world differently
and effect a shift in values.

I believe that Mitchell's thick descriptions of the age are needed and
relevant to visual rhetoric and gender issues today. His descriptions of
the age's emerging cultural dominants can be read in recent women's
art, which seems to abound thematically with reproductions of fleshly

and human bodies or bodies incorporated in new media represented in context and materiality as "other" than the bodies familiar to us today. Our culture's focus on reproduction and cloning certainly implicates and affects women. Yet it is not easy to ascertain a place or position for women in either our culture or Mitchell's analysis. If we accept and deploy his reading of cloning and its associated technologies as central to the present age, what can it tell us about women's visual responses to this culture today? What would it mean to factor gender as well as visual production and reproduction into the age of biocybernetics?

The field of rhetoric provides one vantage point for such an examination. From the standpoint of a materialist rhetorician, I take a perspective on art and images in general that is close to a conventionalist reading. These images and depictions of reproduction are created in a cultural context having a historical emergence and having interpretive and interactionist effects of the artists, viewers, materials, and other factors. Sex and gender along with other factors "matter" to me in images, texts, and hybrid forms. This is the basis of my exploration of the various examples below.

LOST LOVE

At the Modernism/Modernity conference, in examining his exemplary images from contemporary art, Mitchell presented the audience with several slides, including one of particular interest: a gynecologist's examining room in a ten-foot high glass exhibition cube filled with water, fish swimming around the steely frame. A computer monitor lurks in one corner. About this image, Mitchell says, "Hirst stages one of the critical scenes of contemporary biocybernetics, the control of women's bodies and reproductive processes as an archaic 'lost world' whose meaning is to be interpreted by the forensic imagination of the spectator" (496–97).[1]

What does this installation (Figure 3), titled ironically "Love Lost," want from the viewer? If rhetoric is the "art of positionality in address" (Bender and Welbery 6), what gender positions are available to viewers in this and other images seen through the lens of the emergence of biocybernetic culture? This is the kind of issue that interests me here. Is vision gendered, or are art history and visual interpretation sexed and gendered by the standpoint of the art producer and viewer in their cultural moment? How have and can women and various genderings

Fig. 3. Damien Hurst Exhibition. Gynecological table (Photo by John Schaefer). Used by permission.

from diverse rhetorical positions and situations be factored into vision theory or these visions of the future?

Discourses about visuals often still adopt a modernist universalistic point of view, with the assumed viewer a privileged male and the viewed, the *bios,* either controlled or resisting in an overt or trickster fashion (Haraway). Taking into account feminist theory of visual culture, I sense that much of the talk about biocybernetic imagery, if not the imagery itself, assumes a universalistic perspective, although perhaps the authors of such talk would agree and think that a good thing. (Perhaps theorists have posited a "good" universalism and a "bad," but the scope of that discussion is outside this paper.)

Perhaps the most interesting exemplar of this is Hirst's gynecological table, but I must also return to Mitchell's signature image of the test-tube cloned dinosaur in *Jurassic Park* standing in front of the slide projector, with a superimposed genetic code. This monster is gendered female, as is the fearsome replicator of *Jurassic Park II.* The universalistic perspective comes through because what interests Mitchell in this image is not gender but the symbolism of it: "This image provides a metapicture of the relation of digital and analogical codes, the script of DNA and the visible organism that it produces" (485). Yet, despite this brilliant bit of iconology, as miraculous as the biocybernetic technology reviving this lost species, was the nurturance of the young *in vitrines,* with no female matrix required. Reproduction is now a direct transcription of code to organism.

In Hirst's gynecological table installation, the female has similarly disappeared. We see a room, transparent because it is delineated by the sides of the glass box. The room is filled with water, as a womb in pregnancy. The water and glass may give some viewers the cold and unreal feeling often experienced in a gynecologist's office, and these viewers are likely to be female. Some women might feel otherwise: dismayed, as though we had gone back in time so that the care of modern medicine with its promise of relief from common suffering was no longer available to them. The water is like the sea, but unnaturally full of technological debris, so no longer entirely natural. Time enters the scene in the juxtaposition of the sea floor and the debris of the table. Perhaps the world has ended, and our everyday artifacts are covered by seawater.

Sharp-nosed fish swim through the space, staring out at viewers. Are they barracuda? The fish seem to menace. Perhaps, however, they live and reproduce here inside the box, becoming images of the continuity of life, fecundity? Where are the human actors, in particular the woman implied by the gynecological table? The woman is no doubt dead. The silence on this issue speaks to the aspect of cloning in which women seem to be absent in a process all about eggs, only obtained from reproducing females (but here be cautious—not all females).

Has the world ended altogether in a millennial bang? Are humans extinct, or is there only no longer the need for such a table because of advances in gynecological technology? If so, why not? Why is this artifact in a museum, where the viewers almost count as part of the installation? What does this want from these passers-by? Should they consider it an imaginary archeological site? Should they be nostalgic? Should they laugh? Somehow, laughter does not seem to be the right response to Hirst's piece.[2]

VOICING FEMINIST VISIONS

Feminist art theorist Jo Anna Isaak brings laughter, play, and the carnivalesque into her work on women's art, agreeing with Barthes that this is revolutionary because "a code cannot be destroyed, only played off"

(3). Thus play becomes revolutionary in her theoretical work, which seeks to reclaim images of women as well as analyzing pleasure as a "transfer point" of power relations in art. Isaak and other postmodern theorists reject any "global notion of feminist art practice," but investigate "gender positions across the field of signs" (4). Isaak also refuses any notion of margins or of center, saving the "Romantic outsider" position for male artists who believe in that myth. She and others using Lacanian psychoanalytic theory believe that "woman" does not exist essentially psychoanalytically but must be constructed "in relation to a series of representations" (4). Her work leads us to inquire how a "field" called women are constructed in biocybernetic representations or gaps silencing or erasing women's images. Mitchell's emphasis on speciation and post-humanism means he will not ask these questions, but others concerned with difference and power are still on the case.

Technology one day might help us answer the narrower questions: "How do women see?" and "Is it different from how men see?" At present, biological differences have not shown themselves in biologists' studies of the senses smell and sight, although cognitive psychologists have found differences, my specialist colleagues tell me. Nonetheless, even if we were to grapple with the actual science of biological difference, we would have to take into account that this admittedly more authoritative description of difference is not pure but is filtered through socially constructed biological knowledge. So thinking in cultural terms can help us explore the genderings of biocybernetics and contemporary visual imagery. Despite the great advances in biotechnology and informatics in our day, we still inhabit gendered human bodies (from birth biologically marked male, female, and also variously intersexed). Our culture still demands that each child (with some possibilities for later revision) insert him or herself into a structure of gender relations and partnerings. Where we place ourselves or are placed in the system has certain privileges and consequences, although these are sometimes modified by factors such as geography, ethnicity, and social class as well as our own self-identifications and positionings. A rhetorical view of images confronts an impossible breadth of symbols and structures in context. Nevertheless, sex and gender matter, perhaps in bodying forth the punctums, patterns, and foci of our experiences with vision.

In her collected essays, *The Pink Glass Swan,* feminist art critic Lucy Lippard writes of the aftermath of the explosion of "feminist imagery" from the seventies:

> Younger feminist artists continue to think, debate, image, and imagine what "woman" is, what she wants, what her experience is, and how that experience varies across class, culture, age; how it forms, is formed by, and can change society itself. Much of their "back-talk" is about affirmation, about talking back to the culture that tries to define women as the "other." (25)

Like Isaak, she rejects essentialist definitions, yet she argues that the "collage" aesthetic of postmodernism is "particularly feminist." "It is an aesthetic that willfully takes apart what is or is supposed to be and rearranges it in ways that suggest what it could be" (25).

Art historian Linda Nochlin refuses any notion of innate forms that are associated with women, such as curves or circular forms. She pays attention to how art, primarily in the eighteenth and nineteenth centuries, represents women. Her belief is that woman cannot be seen as a fixed, pre-existing entity or frozen "image," transformed by this or that historical circumstance, but as a complex, mercurial and problematic signifier, mixed in its messages, resisting fixed interpretation or positioning despite the numerous attempts made in visual representation literally to put "woman" in her place. Like the woman warrior, the term "woman" fights back, and resists attempts to subdue its meaning or reduce it to some simple essence, universal, natural, and above all, unproblematic (7).

I take as my starting point that women as a biological category do not produce a homogeneous art, but also that art and images are not economically, sexually, or politically neutral. Bioinformatics arises in a culture in which there is increasing political pressure to control women's bodies.[3] Also, within the history of art theory and criticism, unmarked viewers have been assumed to be male, and, in the Western tradition, white. In literature, feminist reader response theory has grappled with the implied male reader and the way women must imagine themselves as addressed as male in the canon of American literature (Fetterley). Laura Mulvey and film theorists have explored the power of the camera's naturalized male "gaze," and others have investigated how current films can change this phenomenon. In her

1975 essay "Visual Pleasure and Narrative Cinema," Mulvey argued that women were presented as objects to be consumed by men's visual "gaze" in movies produced by mainstream Hollywood studios. Women's visual appearance in these films "freezes the flow of action in moments of erotic contemplation" (62). Later feminist film critics have analyzed images of women in mainstream film, as well as films that presume women spectators. Many film critics and filmmakers now explore the possibilities of female spectatorship, analyzing how women can be agents in the face of these theories of the male "gaze." Along with the (once startling) representations of female genitalia, Judy Chicago's *The Dinner Party* in 1979 shocked as much over the assumption of a gendered viewer and the heretofore unexamined possibilities of female spectatorship.

In his version of the biocybernetic world, Mitchell responds in a sense to the feminist perspective in his statement of goals:

> Perhaps this, then, is one task of art in the age of biocybernetic reproduction, to reveal the codes and expose the illusion of the ultimate mastery of life. Another task would be the elaboration of what I have called a "paleontology of the present," a discipline that would begin by acknowledging that contemporaneity is perhaps even more mysterious to us than the recent or distant past, and that would proceed by insisting on the connectedness of all forms of life, a project that might put cybernetics to work for human values. Still another task is the re-articulation of what we mean by the human, by humanism, and the humanities, an inquiry in which all the things we have learned about "identity" and identity politics in the postmodern era would be applied to the ultimate question of *species* identity. Finally, there would be the question of the image, and the Imaginary, itself. ("Modern" 498)

This post-feminist, post-humanist stance focusing on universals, connectedness, and species to keep the world alive nonetheless rests on an understanding of differences. We may have deconstructed the category "women" or critiqued feminism as too Western or too white or too middle class, but feminist and gender theory continues because it explains something to a group/series/coalition of somethings that helps them live better, understand their sometimes common experience, and make changes for the better in their lives and society. As Kenneth Burke pointed out long before deconstruction, identifications produce the differences that make connectivity work (21). Positing sameness thus ultimately can work against connection. I turn now to the imaginary produced by cloning, the ultimate in reproduction of the same. Perhaps Mitchell is right when he says, "A certain tactical irresponsibility with images might be just the right sort of homeopathic medicine for what plagues us" ("Modern" 498).

DOLLY, A WORK OF ART IN THE AGE OF BIOCYBERNETIC REPRODUCTION

Famous Dolly (Figure 4), with her coffee cream wool and narrow head, rears up on hind legs, front legs resting on the rails of her pen, her silly putty tongue revealed as she bleats and bleats, while her lambs rest in the background straw. The next day, she is dead at six years of age (most sheep live twice as long). But Dolly was cloned with an egg from a six-year-old mother, which is all we know of her mother. Dolly herself was a "normal mother," having been bred and having birthed several lambs. But that was not the significant fact about Dolly; it was that she was man-made, unnatural as her name-sake,[4] made by and for man, a copy which superceded the original. At the same time, Dolly was an original, because she was a first.

Ethical and legal prohibitions aside, efforts to promote cloning, even of humans, go on apace. Now that we have deciphered the codes to "read" biological life, scientists want to go further to rewrite the programs (see Goho). Today, no longer satisfied to clone already given DNA, scientists are seeking to create organisms that have never before existed. Scientists have now created the polio virus from its molecules and are building new, never-before-seen molecules from the ground up with DNA. While there is much potential for doing good in this work, some projects seem to be done to push the envelope to see how far the science of life can be taken. Scientists are now working to selectively alter the human genome as if to improve consumer choice of babies. Marketplace forces shape notions of selection and ownership of new forms, changing the reverence formerly held for the "mysteries" of life. On the level of daily life, extensions of *in vitro* fertilization (IVF) make it possible for young women in college to surf the Internet checking out the highest prices for egg donation to defray tuition and

Fig. 4. Dolly (1997). AP Photo/Paul Clements, APA 1686633. Used by permission.

fees. Although well paid, the process is in no way comparable in ease or safety to that of male medical students who traditionally made deposits in sperm banks.

My imaginary scene of cloning and work on reproductive technology envisions male scientists and technicians, which, of course, is not true in every case. Yet, statistically, men populate the new field of biocybernetics or bioinformatics, setting the agendas and creating and naming their works, in women's names. Dolly, that icon of technological progress, of perfectability, is double-edged. As bioinformatics specialists work to perfect the human being, they are controlling women's fertility and reproduction, often empowering (usually upper-class) women in the process. Nonetheless, the double-edge could become a double-cross; Gilman's *Herland* may soon be technologically possible, and males could become luxury items in short supply, their reproduction curtailed to reduce world violence.

FLESH OF MY (PERFECTIBLE) FLESH

Shulamith Firestone's *Dialectic of Sex* argued a quarter century ago that men and women would not be equal until technology had relieved women's bodies of the burden of fleshly reproduction. Her work, wonderful in its ability still to shock undergraduates, represents the strong version of faith that reproductive technology will ultimately benefit women. Science fiction texts have long featured embryos grown in glass aquariums, as were the first dinosaurs in *Jurassic Park* in Mitchell's examples. We have also seen the extension of human abilities through hybrids, as in Donna J. Haraway's version of the cyborg, which celebrates the integration of technology and the human and what that might make possible. However, these earlier feminist versions of perfectibility are moderate in the tidal wave of assumptions of perfectibility on the part of the Human Genome Project and bioinformatics as a whole. The blending of cybernetics, nanoscience, and biology has great potential for good in curing illness and relieving suffering.[5] At the same time, this integration threatens to reproduce the ethical violations of the twentieth-century eugenics the Human Genome project grows directly out of. The impetus to perfect ourselves, with us since the millennialism of the seventeenth century, reproduces the religious, cult-like version of earlier art with our own bodies as the work of art. Mitchell's speech both celebrates and critiques this double-edge biocybernetic culture.

The cult of visual, televisual perfection, paradoxical in a country of obesity and visual imperfection, often culminates in the cult of the perfect child, especially in the upper-middle classes. The perfect child becomes the artistic product, with a Christ-like aura, and the "real" can be just as uncanny as Mitchell's description of Spielberg's David. This real-world perfect-child imaginary is, however, also only achieved with the aid of reproductive technologies, sometimes even from conception with IVF. Tested, preserved, and birthed technologically, the fleshly child is religiously cared for and placed in highly competed-for houses of worship and education. This perfect child, born from a per-

fectly scrutinized, perhaps even purloined egg, ought to have a perfect
mother (laser-haired and liposuctioned), and, although she may turn
out to be a Madonna, there is also a cultural slot available for Mommy
the monster (*Jurassic Park II*).[6] (The father is alternately Ozzie Os-
bourne or Tom Hanks.) The best examples of perfectability and cyborgian hope have for years been displayed on the covers of women's
magazines such as *Seventeen* or *Glamour,* where little or nothing is
"real."

Images of "Babies in Bottles" (Squier's title) and cyborgian hybrids
abound in late twentieth-century art. (Of course, it might also be productive and fun to reach back and read the paintings of Hieronymus
Bosch as fleshly cyborgian.) Women's art in particular has seemed ob-
sessed with the flesh in all its sensuous pleasures as well as with the
technologies of flesh. Early in the last century, Mary Cassatt's work
reveled in baby flesh, lovingly but less sentimentally represented than
in many male artists. Mothers, too, were fleshly creatures sensuously
moving through their daily tasks, with children or with their own artistic work of creating atmospheres for living.

In contrast, biocybernetic versions of flesh include the watery trans-
lucence of Joan Truckenbrod's work (Figure 5), with women's breasts
and bodies "shimmering through hours of dream time." This bio-col-
lage is different from previous paper and object collages, appearing to
hold biological essences static in their plasticity. In the watery images,
we once more see fish (including sharks?) associated with or menacing
the feminine. Truckenbrod is an especially good figure to consider, as
she creates her art via computer. However, she decries the visual and
intellectual emphasis of that medium: "Computing should be constructed with sensory experiences like touch," she writes, "rather than
the language of the machine. The connective tissue linking the natural
world with the virtual world through the body and mind is disjointed"
(qtd. in Candy and Edmonds 125).[7]

CYBERNETICS AND FLESH

In an installation by Eva Hesse, racks of flesh, like coats hanging at
the dry cleaners, also have a plasticized, watery appearance. The racks
could just as well be sides of beef hanging in a meat locker. Such a
vision reminds us starkly of the materiality and animality of our human flesh. This is not to say women's images of the body are necessarily different from the fleshly images produced by men. One macabre

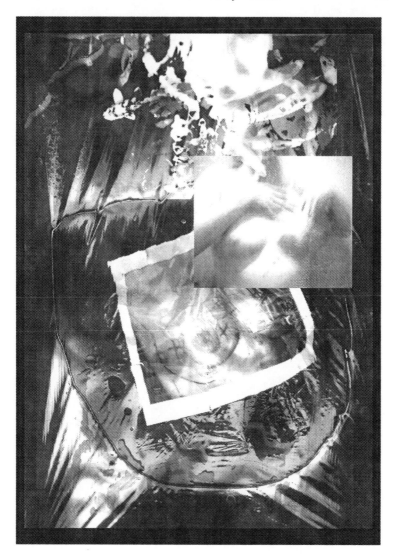

Fig. 5. Joan Truckenbrod, "Thresholding." Used by permission.

integration of science and art by a male physician displays plasticized corpses (volunteered before death), and, although there is plenty of flesh, it is again more plastic than moistly fleshly. Yet the flesh by Hesse hanging on the meat racks may be more human than the real flesh of Dr. Hagens, whose cadaver holds his own skin as if he has just taken off his pajamas (Figure 6).[8]

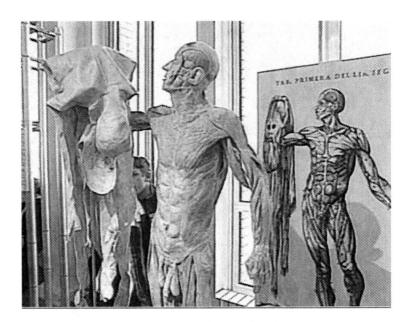

Fig. 6. Gunther von Hagens. Bodyworlds Exhibit <http://www.cnn.com/ HEALTH/9802/07/cadaver.art/photo.html>. Photo by CNN. Used by permission.

In contrast, a computer exhibit, "Clean Rooms," which claims to investigate the "audience reaction to genetic manipulation," was shown in Manchester, United Kingdom, in 2002 and again in 2003 in London. As the website describes it, "CleanRooms challenges our responses to biotechnology: a science often perceived as secretive and sinister. Exploring ideas of contamination and containment, ethics and accountability, CleanRooms asks the audience to decide how far they themselves would go with the emerging powers of genetic manipulation." Gina Czarnecki's installation *Silvers Alter,* part of the Clean Rooms exhibit, is described as follows on the website: "Life-size human forms 'live' within a large video projection in the gallery. They are the subjects for you to manipulate and mate. The 'beings' you create have never existed before. *Silvers Alter* raises a simple question; to what extent are we prepared to participate in all that we have made possible and that we aspire to make possible for ourselves?"[9]

In a more abstract vein, UCLA's Victoria Vesna's new media art explores how we shift our perceptions of our bodies when we incorporate ourselves in a networked environment.[10] More distanced, intellectual, and mathematical than the previous representational computerized project discussed by Czarnecki, Vesna's Bodies INCorporated, which she initiated as a collaborative project, was a solo exhibition at the San Francisco Art Institute in the late 1990s. She discussed her work in 2003 at Purdue's Computers and Composition Conference in a talk titled "Mind Shifting and Future Bodies: From Networks to Nanosystems," descriptive of the scope of her collaborative projects. Professor and chair of the Department of Design/Media Arts at UCLA, she explores issues of cybernetics, nanoscience, time, and social transformation spurred by technologies. She writes,

> Working on Bodies INCorporated completely shifted my creative process. I stopped thinking of producing work that was complete or finished. Indeed, to this day, people are creating bodies and adding their data to the project, thus changing it. It is dependent on the live network and could not possibly be collected in the usual sense of the word.

In Bodies INCorporated, guests can join the site and become "stockholders" in a playful, humorous game of "incorporation." As Vesna explains,

> At a deeper level, Bodies INCorporated addresses such issues as the legitimacy of cultural institutions as the only socially sanctioned site for display of art, and the ways in which structures of physical and ephemeral spaces effect our collectively embodied behaviour. From within computer networks we constantly project our selves, and play complicated identity survival games.

Once in the project, a member finds a Body Order Form reading, "Where you can be textually engaged or engaging." Members can create bodies from menus with limited selections of materials such as glass, water, bronze, rubber, and wood, and bodies can be male, female, or both, in varying sizes. It is possible to be heterosexual, homosexual, or asexual. Bodies in the project are living, dead, or in limbo. Once a body has been created, there is not a lot to do but view the body as well as others living there. A News feature announces the "birth" of new bodies, as well as deaths. Vesna said she intentionally designed the death process to be difficult, and it appears few have actually died, although many "bodies" that have been created seem to be languishing in limbo. Consumerism is centrally featured and played off of in the body creation process. After creating a cyber body, the participant is told: "CONGRATULATONS! You are now free to go anywhere and free to do and/or buy anything. TOTAL democracy reigns supreme, and happy consumers are handsomely rewarded."

In a subsequent project, Vesna added reproductive process to her repertoire with a collaborative project called 'n0time' (Building a Community of People with No Time). The complexly faceted project is reproductive, replicating memes, ideas that propagate themselves until the time is ripe, and they explode. Bodies are represented as tetrahedral, as avatars. As Vesna explains on the site: "The representation of the avatar as a human (or an animal, or even plant) is an outdated idea, just as cyberspace architectures based on our badly designed buildings are. We propose shedding the idea of the 'body' in cyberspace and starting over by building a tetrahedron."

Why does Vesna use a *tetrahedron*? Yes, why would Vesna represent the body as a geometrical shape, and if so, why this one? Her website, *n0time*, provides a host of good reasons, the first given being "Minimum system: the tetrahedron is the first case of insideness and outsideness."

As she explains on her home page:

> Exploring issues of time in relation to human networks and our bodies as elaborate networks has moved my attention to the molecular level. Working with tensegrity made me think more in terms of emerging patterns in nature. No matter how alienated we may become, we produce patterns that mirror the natural world. Consider the cell phones that are already being taken for granted. The technological infrastructure is designed to be most efficient by dividing cities into hexagons. Hexagons are found in many structures in nature, including beehives that fascinated mankind for centuries and the recently discovered buckyballs and buckytubes, the primary molecules driving nano-technology. My goal is to make these far reaching connections between the social structures we unconsciously build and the ones that are inherently the building blocks of nature.

> Making the invisible traces of our connectivity and
> mirroring of nature visible is my long term goal.

Vesna's work in many ways exemplifies Mitchell's description of visual culture's interaction with biocybernetic cultural values and goals. Her imaginary is more computational in feel, more intellectual, and perhaps closer to cybernetics than biology.

Imaging biocybernetics with vulnerable, naked human forms, even cybernetically produced, makes a difference in our conceptualizations and feelings about humans and the work. Vesna's more mathematical work is visually captivating and imaginatively bold. Nonetheless, the representations on computer feel visually thin compared to the rich complexity of just one small corner of the human world. Gender becomes just another consumer choice in cyberspace, with viewers, who may feel included and active, in reality being passive consumers offered narrowly preset selections. But perhaps this is the point. Such cyber exploration, viewing, and imaginative practice with human bodies for some may increase our confidence in our power to mold the future on a grand scale into a perfect or perfectly interesting world. Responses to and interpretations of these visual works come out of the situations of the beholder and are varied—so perhaps these visuals can also serve as homeopathic agents, as Mitchell suggested. A final example addresses the aspect that visual artists (and critics) need not use nontraditional materials and media to evoke in viewers the biocybernetic present and future. Rhetorical contemplations of other and older works in traditional media are also transformed by our current cultural dominants.

TOWARDS A GENDERED BIOCYBERNETIC FUTURE

Hollis Sigler's "To Kiss the Spirits: Now this is what it is really like," a traditional oil on canvas with painted frame, is part of her series on breast cancer.[11] (She died of breast cancer in 2001, after years of painting as a long-term survivor of the disease that claimed both her mother and her grandmother.) This faux naive work seems to accept and ironize patriarchal stereotypes of women as children. Sigler often paints themes from women's experience of love, domesticity, everyday life, and death (Heller 196). Nevertheless, the more traditional (and traditionally feminine) painting still bears the mark of the biocybernetic future. Here, in a work that references Van Gogh's "Starry Night," a woman ascends a gilt spiral staircase that appears wrapped in a glowing golden cloud. She leaves a warm and comfortable, "toylike" neighborhood where all is peaceful and orderly below and rises to an as-yet-unseen celestial promise, her color transfusing from a blood red to feminine pink and her wings growing as she wends her way up the escalier to the starry sky. In this age of biocybernetics, the staircase spiral evokes in many of us the spiral ladder of DNA, hearkening back to the cancerous replication of her disease as well as her hope for a cure, despite the inevitability of ultimate human death (but perhaps no longer inevitable in biocybernetic culture). Sigler's peaceful ascending angel contrasts with Paul Klee's watercolor *Angelus Novus* of 1920, a symbol of Benjamin's angel of history, in his famous passage from *On the Concept of History:*

> A Klee painting named "Angelus Novus" shows an
> angel looking as though he is about to move away
> from something he is fixedly contemplating. His eyes
> are staring, his mouth is open, his wings are spread.
> This is how one pictures the angel of history. His face
> is turned toward the past. Where we perceive a chain
> of events, he sees one single catastrophe which keeps
> piling wreckage and hurls it in front of his feet.

If biology's past visions of progress can be as horrifying and cataclysmic looking backward today, women's literary visions of a biocybernetic future can look just as bleak. Canadian Margaret Atwood presents her end-of-time vision in her recent book *Oryx and Crake,* giving us a sublime and heart-rending imaginary world. Atwood and others who are reasonable argue that we should be more aware and wary about our embrace of biocybernetic technologies. Yet just like the characters in her book, we may not find it easy to resist as we share the hopes of ending human suffering held out by the meld of computation, biology, nanotech, and related technologies. When our present ethical and agreed-upon technological progress endows us with God-like powers, as it seems to be doing today, it is probable that sooner or later, an individual like Atwood's Crake will come along, and, with the best of intentions, play God. In the effort to improve the world, such an individual or a group may unbalance and destroy the world. In Atwood's book, the role of woman, Oryx, like Eve, once again was to bring evil into the world unwittingly while intending only to support her man, the God-like genius that evoked near-worship. *Bios,* that which is controlled or eludes control in Mitchell's earlier definition, was both controlled and eluded control to bring down humans in Atwood's novel. Mitchell's argument that biocybernetics is a new cultural dominant was on target and timely: outside fiction, in 2004, the South Koreans, acting against the ethical wishes of the world, cloned a human being. Others in biocybernetics are working to improve the species and its world, in projects much like those Atwood describes that produce the dangerous pigoons and wolvogs. What do pictures want (of women)? Perhaps to help us all as we create and save the world. As we have seen, the wide arc of women's visual production captures both the hopes

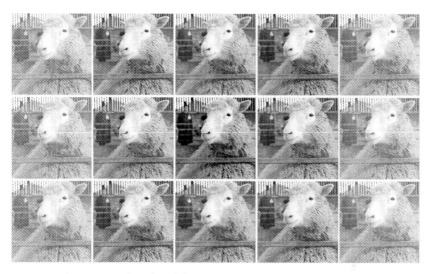

Fig. 7. The Dream of Perfectability. © 2007 by James Miles. Used by permission.

and the cautions of this cultural moment, troping on the codes and icons that make up its historical debris. The dream of perfectability is embraced as well as exploded through laughter in the field of human women's vision.

NOTES

[1] View image at http://www.mediadivide.org/WEB Downsizing Galleries/New York City WEB/pages/Damien Hurst Exhibition.htm

[2] I say this in spite of the fact that I have only seen it photographed on the web, mechanically reproduced. Perhaps it has an "aura" in physical space that has been lost on the screen. (I was not present at its original production

or showing. However, the fact that I could see the slide in a talk in Madison, Wisconsin, and later retrieve it from an exhibition website shows just how dislocated the representation of the installation is from the show and how it can take on a life of its own apart from the context of showing.)

[3] Benjamin has written about how war affects art. The new video-guided war images a twentieth-century masculine war, while neutralizing the need for the strong male soldier it depicts. Yet the culture developing around the Gulf conflict re-introduces WWII gender relations, with all their ambiguities, from the pin-up girl to Rosie the Riveter. The movement to limit abortion rights grows out of this culture of nostalgia.

[4] We should consider the complexity of the rhetorical positioning of women bioinformaticists associated with the laboratory that named Dolly the cloned sheep after the complex figure that is Dolly Parton.

[5] Traditional defense production has converged at times with cybernetic war machines and biological warfare. Nanotechnology converges with biocybernetics, as in this website description of Rensselaer's new program involving "nanobiotechnology": "The study of materials at the atomic and molecular scale is enabling the synthesis of new materials with radically different properties and functions.

- The self-assembly of thin films with special optical properties has already been adopted in several industries.
- The assembly of complex molecular structures, such as nanotubes, has applications as varied as nanocomposite materials with extraordinary strength, nanoconducting wires for electronic interconnects, and nanomatrices for supporting active biological molecules in medical applications.
- Visualization and manipulation of individual molecules has special importance in the biological realm, and the rise of nanobiotechnology as a recognized scientific pursuit has been rapid and stimulating. Rensselaer core strengths in this arena form the basis for future research opportunities" (Rensselaer).

[6] Art history is replete with images of perfect mothers. See Isaak for contemporary women's visions of mothers and motherhood.

[7] View image at http://old.siggraph.org/artdesign/profile/Truckenbrod/1999_4.html.

[8] Mannheim's Museum of Technology and Labor exhibited corpses without skin, produced by injections of plastic by Dr. Gunther von Hagens, the exhibit curator.

[9] View this image at http://www.artscatalyst.org/htm/cleanrooms.htm. Also in the exhibit: "Neal White's *Uncontrolled Hermetic* recreates one of the controlled areas or clean rooms used in industrial biotechnology and pharmaceuticals. You, the visitor, fulfill the final part of this system, as the

contaminating or contaminated body, the weakest link in the ultraclean technology chain: a human being."

[10] See http://vv.arts.ucla.edu/projects/current_events_frameset.htm.

[11] This piece should be able to be viewed at http://www.nmwa.org/collection/ after it is transferred to the National Museum of Women, where it has been promised as a gift.

WORKS CITED

Bender, John, and David E. Wellbery. "Rhetoricality: On the Modernist Return of Rhetoric." *The Ends of Rhetoric: History, Theory, Practice.* Ed. Bender and Wellbery. Stanford: Stanford UP, 1990. 3–39.

Benjamin, Walter. *Illuminations: Essays and Reflections.* Ed. and intro. by Hannah Arendt. Trans. Harry Zohn. New York: Schocken, 1968.

--. *On the Concept of History, or Theses on the Philosophy of History.* Lloyd Spencer's Web Site. 14 Sept. 2004._<http://www.tasc.ac.uk/depart/media/staff/ls/WBenjamin/CONCEPT2.html>.

Burke, Kenneth. *A Rhetoric of Motives.* Berkeley: U of California P, 1969. 19-27.

Candy, Linda, and Ernest Edmonds. *Explorations in Art and Technology.* London: Springer, 2002.

Fetterley, Judith. *The Resisting Reader: A Feminist Approach to American Fiction.* Bloomington: Indiana UP, 1978.

Firestone, Shulamith. *The Dialectic of Sex: The Case for Feminist Revolution.* New York: Morrow, 1970.

Gilman, Charlotte Perkins. Herland. 1915. Electronic Text Center, University of Virginia Library. 14 Sept. 2004. <http://wyllie.lib.virginia.edu:8086/perl/toccer-new?id=GilHerl.sgm&images=images/modeng&data=/texts/english/modeng/parsed&tag=public&part=teiHeader>.

Goho, Alexandra M. "Life Made to Order." *Technology Review* 106.3 (2003): 50–57.

Haraway, Donna J. *Simians, Cyborgs, and Women: The Reinvention of Nature.* New York: Routledge, 1991.

Heller, Nancy G., ed. *Women Artists: Works from the National Museum of Women in the Arts.* New York: National Museum and Rizzoli, 2000

Hirst, Damien. "Love Lost." *John Schaefer. MediaDivide.* 14 Sept. 2004 . <http://www.mediadivide.org/WEB Downsizing Galleries/New York City WEB/pages/Damien Hurst Exhibition.htm>.

Isaak, Jo Anna. *Feminism and Contemporary Art: The Revolutionary Power of Women's Laughter.* London: Routledge, 1996.

Jurassic Park. Dir. Steven Spielberg. Universal, 1993.

Lippard, Lucy R. *The Pink Glass Swan: Selected Feminist Essays on Art.* New York: New Press, 1995.

Mitchell, W.J.T. "Are We Modern Yet? The Work of Art in the Age of Biocybernetic Reproduction." *Modernism/Modernity* 10.3 (2003): 481–500.

—. *Iconology: Image, Text, Ideology.* Chicago: U of Chicago P, 1986.

—. *The Last Dinosaur Book: The Life and Times of a Cultural Icon.* Chicago: U of Chicago P, 1998.

Mulvey, Laura. "Visual Pleasure and Narrative Cinema." In *Feminism and Film Theory.* Ed. Constance Penley. New York: Routledge, 1988. 57–68.

Nochlin, Linda. *Representing Women.* London: Thames and Hudson, 1999.

Rensselaer Polytechnic Institute. "Nanobiotechnology." 13 December 2004. <http://enzymes.che.rpi.edu/nano.html>.

Squier, Susan Merrill. *Babies in Bottles: Twentieth-Century Visions of Reproductive Technology.* New Brunswick, NJ: Rutgers UP, 1994.

Truckenbrod, Joan. "Thresholding." *Joan Truckenbrod Portfolio 1999.* 2004. (14 Sept 2004) <http://old.siggraph.org/artdesign/profile/Truckenbrod/1999_4.html>.

Vesna, Victoria. *Victoria Vesna Home Page.* 14 Sept. 2004. 1 Aug. 2007 <http://vv.arts.ucla.edu/projects/current_events_frameset.htm>.

—. *n0time.* 1 Aug. 2007 <http://notime.arts.ucla.edu/notime3/>.

8 Far Encounters: Looking Desire

Mieke Bal

The verb "looking," without preposition, points to an act performed on a direct object: desire is "looked" into being. This phrase, which I coin for the purposes of this paper, is necessary in order to analyze something that is *stricto sensu* unspeakable. The desire at stake is both unconscious, or, in a less psychoanalytical sense, unreflective, and "closeted." I am referring to a subtle and complex, yet quite frequently experienced, feeling that entails a high risk for the subject. I will argue that the look that generates such feelings is the systemic opposite of voyeurism, although it is also an erotic look. To grasp this "sexogenic" look, I turn to Marcel Proust.

One sentence from Proust is worth a thousand insights (on images, gender, and sexuality), to inverse an anti-literary cliché on art that proclaims an image to be worth a thousand words. The object of this paper is a single sentence. In studying Proust's novel I have often found that many of the concerns that preoccupy us today in the practice of teaching in any of the cultural disciplines were already the object of imaginative thought in *A la recherche du temps perdu*. Among them are the nature and impact of images, how we look upon gender, and how we perform sexual transactions through images. Given the current interest in visuality in cultural studies, and the tendency to construe literature as a less relevant field than, say, film or the new media for the understanding of sex-related issues in society, I am particularly interested in the relevance of this modernist masterpiece for today as an infinitely rich source of thought on today's culture, so replete with visual stimulation.

I will argue that the most unlikely theoretical theme to be gleaned from a literary text—vision—is central to Proust's work. More precisely, I look to Proust for thinking about what "hip" art historians call

visual culture. For, as unlikely as it may sound, this 4,000-page trea-
sury of words foregrounds the visual nature of the kind of encounters
that generate sexuality. Those sexual interactions that are banned, for
reasons of cultural taboos, from verbal expression, especially, find their
way into what I will here call a closeted visual imaging of desire. In a
novel dedicated primarily to the exploration of desire and its unavoidable consequence, jealousy, imaged desires stand out as a kind of heroics or magic of semiosis, the literary art that visualizes what words cannot say, without either saying or denying it. Hence, images that both
reveal and conceal unspeakable desires, thus negotiating the tension
between the individual subject and the social environment that we call
"culture," are emblematic of the complexities of visual culture.[1]

As opposed to many who flag this term and design curricular activities on the basis of it, Proust offers profound and utterly relevant
thoughts on what it is to be surrounded by images and to have visual
stimulation as the predominant, everyday experience of contemporary
cultural life. Paradoxically, (re)reading this old classic is the thing to
do if one wishes to ground visual culture studies in a theory of looking. In a volume devoted to images, I contend that such an analysis
is indispensable for a full understanding of the intricate relationships
between images and sexuality within culture.

The fragment I have chosen can be called an image-sentence: a
sentence that produces an image—that "images"—and that allows its
readers to witness the production process itself. This image-sentence
helps us to understand the intricate bond between image and imagination, but also between the latter and thought. In that sense, it is also a
thought-image. The sentence produces an encounter:

> Une après-midi de grande chaleur, j'étais dans la
> salle à manger de l'hôtel qu'on avait laissée à demi
> dans l'obscurité pour la protéger du soleil en tirant
> les rideaux qu'il jaunissait et qui par leurs interstices
> laissaient clignoter le bleu de la mer, quand, dans la
> travée centrale qui allait de la plage à la route, je vis,
> grand, mince, le cou dégagé, la tête haute et fière-
> ment portée, passer un jeune homme aux yeux péné-
> trants et dont la peau était aussi blonde et les cheveux
> aussi dorés que s'ils avaient absorbé tous les rayons du
> soleil. (I 728)

> One afternoon of scorching heat I was in the din-
> ing-room of the hotel, plunged in semi-darkness to
> shield it from the sun, which gilded the drawn cur-
> tains through the gaps between which twinkled the
> blue of the sea, when along the central gangway lead-
> ing from the beach to the road I saw approaching,
> tall, slim, bare-necked, his head held proudly erect,
> a young man with searching eyes whose skin was as
> fair and his hair as golden as if they had absorbed all
> the rays of the sun. (I 783)

I propose to look at this sentence: at what that which it produces looks
like—what it "images"—and what the mechanisms, processes, and
politics of vision are that the sentence itself represents—what it imagines about vision, and more specifically, about a visual "take."[2]

Let me first say that I recognize the ontological divide that sepa-
rates text from image, a divide substantiated by the very attempts to
produce "intermedial" texts. The essentially mixed discourse of cinema does not in the least contradict that distinction. And although
the visual aspect of reading cannot be denied, nor does the visual act
of reading allow comprehending the text at a single glance.[3] The question of literature's visuality does not reside in the use of the eye, but
in the deployment of visuality as a complex cultural form of behavior.
Discussions of intermediality often begin and end with the question
of delimitation and definition. But, as I will argue through Proust's
sentence, the productive question is not if literary texts are capable of
generating visuality, but how vision "writes itself." I will argue that
Proust's visual writing offers a more subtle view of what it means to
look at an image than any of the ontological debates has managed to
suggest so far.

What is the "theory" of vision that *La recherche* constructs, and
what can we learn from it? The theory contains several propositions.
First, the look, unique among the senses, is an approach of an other,
be it a fragment of the exterior world or the people inhabiting it. But,
second, it is an approach that permits no proximity. This has never
been put forward more emphatically than in the famous scene where
the young Marcel approaches Albertine's cheek for a kiss for the first
time: "Mes yeux cessèrent de voir" (II 365 / II 661) (suddenly my eyes
ceased to see) (II 379). Looking becomes impossible when proximity precludes the work of the senses. Third, as a result, the look is

the sense-based act *par excellence* through which sexual encounters are initiated, while, at the same time, it embodies the fundamental difficulty of those encounters. In this triple sense, the question "what is an image?" is best transformed into the question, "how is an image produced?" This question foregrounds both the cultural and the dynamic nature of looking, and what I call, therefore, *acts* of looking. What we can learn from this theory is no less than a mode of "good," socially productive, and abuse-free behavior.[4]

The Predicament of Vision

Marcel complains bitterly about this fundamental deficit of the human body.[5] He couches his complaint in terms of a bodily epistemology, a form of knowledge that integrates sensuality and sense-perception but remains out of reach. I will argue that it is the pursuit of this knowledge that frames the book's imaginative theorizing of vision. The failed kiss leads to the following reflection, which is crucial for the interpretation of the importance of our sentence for a theory of looking:

> Je me disais cela parce que je croyais qu'il est une connaissance par les lèvres; je me disais que j'allais connaître le goût de cette rose charnelle, parce que je n'avais pas songé que l'homme, créature évidemment moins rudimentaire que l'oursin ou même la baleine, manque cependant encore d'un certain nombre d'organes essentiels, et notamment n'en possède aucun qui serve au baiser. A cet organe absent il supplée par les lèvres, et par là arrive-t-il peut-être à un résultat un peu plus satisfaisant que s'il était réduit à caresser la bien-aimée avec une défence de corne. Mais les lèvres, faites pour amener au palais la saveur de ce qui les tente, doivent se contenter, sans comprendre leur erreur et sans avouer leur déception, de vaguer à la surface et de se heurter à la clôture de la joue impénétrable et désirée. [. . .] car dans cette zone désolée où elles ne peuvent trouver leur nourriture, elles sont seules, le regard, puis l'odorat les ont abandonnées depuis longtemps. (II 364 / II 659–60)

I told myself this because I believed that there was
such a thing as knowledge acquired by the lips; I
told myself that I was going to know the taste of this
fleshy rose, because I had not stopped to think that
man, a creature obviously less rudimentary than the
sea-urchin or even the whale, nevertheless lacks a
certain number of essential organs, and notably pos-
sesses none that will serve for kissing. For this absent organ he substitutes his lips, and thereby arrives
perhaps at a slightly more satisfying result than if he
were reduced to caressing the beloved with a horny
tusk. But a pair of lips, designed to convey to the pal-
ate the taste of whatever whets their appetite, must
be content, without understanding their mistake or
admitting their disappointment, with roaming over
the surface and with coming to a halt at the barrier
of the impenetrable but irresistible cheek. Moreover
at that moment of actual contact with the flesh, the
lips, even on the assumption that they might become
more expert and better endowed, would doubtless be
unable to enjoy any more fully the savour which nature prevents their ever actually grasping, for in that
desolate zone in which they are unable to find their
proper nourishment they are alone, the sense of sight,
then that of smell, having long since deserted them.
(II 377–78)

This complaint about the inadequacy of the senses has nothing metaphysical about it. The irony—"a horny tusk"—is counter-balanced by
the discourse of emotion—"zone of desolation"—anchored in a physicality firmly beyond the mind-body split—"food for the lips."

The fundamental inadequacy of the senses put forward here cannot but solicit the ideas of Proust's younger contemporary, Lacan, who,
like Proust, was also a theorist of desire. Both writers belabor the notion that lack feeds desire. The desire to see, particularly to see close
up, that is frustrated in the narrator's kiss, is the desire to overcome the
incapacity to approach the other through the instrument that lends
itself least to proximity: the essentially distancing sense of vision. The
insistent attention to vision, and the near-obsessive attempt to bring
about the integration of imaging and imagining to which much of

La recherche is devoted, is, I will argue below, a form of modesty. In our crowded contemporary world, which has over-invested the image with pleasure, the disabused recognition of the limitation of the senses makes a new exploration of vision's anchoring in distance a highly appealing proposition.[6]

Although the reflections on kissing might suggest that for Proust, desire and love go hand in hand, it is not through Albertine, the narrator's "official" love object, that Proust's lesson in visuality is best approached. Albertine represents love and desire both on the level of the fabula, and negatively, embodying as she does the radical impossibility of ever achieving a level of proximity that will satisfy the desire to know. The character who feeds the narrator's desire on the level of writing, and positively (and this as early as when the first image of him presents itself) is Robert de Saint-Loup. Desire's instrument is the sense of vision; the result is neither proximity nor possession, but the image. To look at how Marcel looks at Robert, to borrow the narrator's look, so to speak, is to learn something about visuality that helps us see better what Rembrandt, Vermeer, and Chardin—Proust's declared favorites—have to offer, but also what photography, the new medium of Proust's time and still the ancestor of today's new media, can do for our encounters with the other, which haunt social life in contemporary Western culture.

It is worthwhile, then, to look at how the protagonist, that expert in focalization, enters into a visual engagement with Robert; how he comes to *see* him, beyond the mirage of the glance, a mirage he describes in terms of linear perspective's tricks:

> Que de fois en voiture ne découvrons-nous pas une longue rue claire qui commence à quelques mètres de nous, alors que nous n'avons devant nous qu'un pan de mur violemment éclairé qui nous a donné le mirage de la profondeur ! (II 419 / II 712)

> How often, when driving, do we not come upon a bright street beginning a few feet away from us, when what we have actually before our eyes is merely a patch of wall glaringly lit which has given us the mirage of depth. (II 435)

The eye deceives, as the term *trompe-l'œil* has it, and visual art is nourished by this capacity to produce fictions. Linear perspective uses lines to produce its deceptions. Elsewhere, Proust denounces the dangers of visual art's opposite tendency, which is to superpose layers and layers, until a thickness comes about of the kind that kills the writer Bergotte ("Ses étourdissements augmentaient; il attachait son regard, comme un enfant à un papillon jaune qu'il veut saisir, au précieux petit pan de mur," III 187 / III 692) ("His dizziness increased; he fixed his gaze, like a child upon a yellow butterfly that it wants to catch, on the precious little patch of wall," III 185). The two basic media of the painter, lines and layers of color, are thus met with suspicion. They appear to be deadly.

How to look in a manner that is fatal neither to the subject, as in the hyperbolic parable of Bergotte's lethal move outside of himself to stick to the image (of the patch of yellow wall, or the yellow patch of wall, in Vermeer's painting of Delft), nor to the object, as in the case of Albertine, who is retrospectively killed by her status as object?[7] In order to answer this question, it is crucial to examine the different phases of the act of looking, beginning with the beginning.

SAFELY SEEING THE SUN

The moment in the afternoon sun is the beginning. This beginning inaugurates an interaction between two subjects as a definition of vision. Far from killing, this act arouses, feeds, and defines desire. It is a material act, even if vision cannot achieve proximity. It constitutes a domain, a space that gives space to both the subject and object who share it and leaves it open for a variety of possible identifications. According to the sentence to which this paper is devoted, Proust discovered this space-giving seeing when he first encountered the image of Robert.

The first part of our sentence presents vision; not the object of seeing but the visual situation. With this term, I mean the visual equivalent of the narrative situation, which specifies where the words and images in the narrative come from. The visual situation is delimited in time and space, as a chronotope in miniature, in a descriptive passage that no narrative verb has yet interrupted:

> Une après-midi de grande chaleur, j'étais dans la salle
> à manger de l'hôtel qu'on avait laissée à demi dans

l'obscurité pour la protéger du soleil en tirant les ri-
deaux qu'il jaunissait et qui par leurs interstices laissaient clignoter le bleu de la mer, . . .

One afternoon of scorching heat I was in the din-
ing-room of the hotel, plunged in semi-darkness to
shield it from the sun, which gilded the drawn curtains through the gaps between which twinkled the
blue of the sea, . . .

This beginning carries an aesthetic, leaning as it does on Impressionism. Even before we get to see anything, everything here lets us surmise that the object of vision will be gloriously beautiful. The situation in which the protagonist finds himself, and within which his act of looking will be performed, prepares him for the positive aesthetic that he will project on the object. The man who is about to enter his field of vision and who will be his best friend for long stretches of the fabula is bound to be a source of visual pleasure. Marcel will never stop underlining Robert's physical beauty. This beauty is essentially a quality of color. Like the Impressionists, therefore, Proust paints Robert with color. Blonde, Robert is the man of after-lunch sunshine; he is sunlight.

Narratively, the entrance on stage of this sun-man has been pre-pared through a fantasy on friendship that precedes this passage. Hence, the apparition of the sun-man has nothing surprising about it. Nevertheless, I would like to submit that the image-sentence is an example, both extreme and representative, of the power of images in a massively literary text. This power can be so great as to produce an alternative reading of *La recherche,* parallel to and often detached from the narrative one, sometimes even overruling it. This power resides in the *mise-en-scène* of the visual situation. How, then, is this visual "take" staged?

First, Marcel is situated in a way that materially determines what of the outside world he can see, that limited fragment of the world that is visually at his disposal. It is a hot day, the family has just eaten, and one imagines the silence of the *siesta,* replete with odors of the food just consumed, sounds of insects and waves of the sea. Yet none of these sensations are mentioned. Only vision, the sense of distance, and the sense of touch (heat), that sense situated at the other pole of the gradation between distance and proximity of body, join forces to create the image.

Second, the opposition between the situation in which the subject of the look is immersed and the spectacle given to him to see is articulated in terms of a motivated opposition. It is dark in the room because it is bright outside.[8] This opposition and its causality keep us aware of the insight, after all quite ordinary, that one sees better if one is not blinded by an excess of light. Yet, at the same time, this opposition that structures the field of vision is the visual equivalent of the narrative motivation that "explains" why description interrupts the flow of the narrative in which it intervenes.[9]

This paradox of chiaroscuro is familiar to us from the painters who deployed it long before Proust came along. Although the uncontested master of the chiaroscuro, Caravaggio, does not feature in Proust's work, others do. We know, and Proust exploited that insight, that Rembrandt's paintings play with light and darkness to reinforce our concentration of what we are offered to look at. The hat whose flap obscures the eye is there to force us to put more effort into our act of looking. As a reward for our effort, we can encounter the eye of the figure in a true encounter, not in a quick glance that ignores the figure's subjectivity of which the eye is the seat. Rembrandt thus deploys chiaroscuro so as to promote a look that instores equality. Similarly, the drawn curtains take on color through their contact with the outside light, so that they, in turn, can color the space yellow. Hence the subject of the look is bathing in soft yellow, like a figure of Vermeer. Yet it is not these references to painting and its traditions and masters that make our sentence a visual artifact.[10]

The particular visual quality at stake here is the one that defines the status of the subject. What is being written in this case is the subject, enclosed in space, in a three-dimensional frame. He is cut off from the world that, by virtue of this spatial opposition, constitutes the image: a cut-out fragment radically divorced from the eye which is condemned to distance. But if the visible world is infinitely open, whereas the space of the subject is limited, we can also say that the latter constitutes the spectacle, the cut-out image. Again, Lacan has made many of us familiar with this situation, but Proust wrote this before Lacan theorized it. What we see represented, then, through this bath of yellow warmth, is the state of the subject captured in the look of the other.[11] But in distinction from Lacan's rather bleak conception of this captured state, the "take" on the subject—his being captured by the frame—is happy, libidinally charged, and affective; it is set in a golden tone. This positive tone sets Proust off from the Lacanian theory of desire.

The soft light in which the subject is bathing not only determines how—in what light, precisely—he will pose the object of his act of looking, an object no longer the other who is outside but the image that this other being constitutes for the eye inside. This soft light also offers, actively so to speak, what remains outside it. The curtains, in their function of mediating screen, the curtains that "par leurs inter-stices laissaient clignoter le bleu de la mer," also function literally, ma-terially, as frame. They allow the subject to see a bit of the world, a *travée,* where the light, precisely, is not softened, not made to appear yellow, but where light is instead, if I may put it this way, "absolute." The framing power of the curtain even produces a "moving" image ("clignoter").

That ribbon of light—cut out from the exterior world, which the curtains leave visible in its absolute and live brightness—is an effect. Yet we construct it before our reader's eye, as duplicated by the di-egetically concrete ribbon, the "travée centrale qui allait de la plage à la route" ("the central gangway leading from the beach to the road").[12] This ribbon intervenes, textually, between the temporal conjunction "quand" and the punctual verb form "vis," which together inaugurate the narrative dimension of the act of seeing.[13] For nothing forces us to make an ontological distinction between the vertical ribbon of light, with its explosive blue, and that other ribbon, horizontal, on which the object of vision is walking. Paradoxically splitting the two elements of Derrida's supplementary nature of the frame, the former ribbon con-stitutes the frame, whereas the latter ribbon is framed by it; unless, of course, we elect to think of the former ribbon simply as the vertical sides of the frame, and the latter as the horizontal limit, the bottom of the frame.[14] If the man coming into the image needs the *travée* in order to be able to walk, then the subject of the look needs it in order to position the figure on the screen that is his image, in other words, to give the figure, in the technical sense of visual art as well as in the social sense, (a) support.

Already we realize that there is nothing simple about looking. The belabored framing staged here, that visual set-up whose narrative function it is to motivate the description that follows, does more than just persuade the reader trapped by realism that the thing seen can ef-fectively be seen by the focalizer, in a literary version of linear perspective, even if it is "really" impossible to see body hair at such a distance. On the opposite side, the side of the object, the framing fulfills the function of inflecting the image, of specifying its nuances that no detailing of the object would be able to render. Moreover, by specifying what is in the image by distinguishing it from what is not, this set-up also specifies the visual quality of the image in its materiality. This materiality is not of physical matter, since the distance inherent in vision "dematerializes" it in that sense. Instead, it is a visual materiality beyond diegetic, narrative matter in which one can say what one sees. The image's materiality is also of primary matter, such as "paint"—or ink, or letters and words. It is into this materiality that the looking subject must enter—as one must enter into the symbolic order—in order to be able to see materially, outside of Platonic idealism as well as outside perspectival colonialism. Both these alternative modes of looking are damaging. The former deceives and, hence, blinds the subject of the look, the latter appropriates and thus captures and potentially disempowers the object. Instead, Proust's theory of looking, according to this beginning, draws the subject out into the field of vision, where he can truly meet the object of seeing.

ILLUMINATION

Of what does the material domain of vision consist? First of all, there is the opposition between soft mediated light and raw "absolute" light. The light-space that envelops the subject already draws him out of himself so that he can endorse his placement inside the framed fragment of the world he is about to see. That quality of summer-afternoon near the beach results in the beginning of a description that will soon be continued. All of this is a precious substance that mediates not only between subject and object, between the look and what is seen, but also between the media, of which one is in charge of furnishing the words, and the other, the visual set-up. That domain is most adequately indicated with a qualifier that does not establish hierarchies between the two sides of the mediation: semiotic. Semiotics is the theory of signs, sign production, and sign use. A semiotic event can be produced in any single medium, but also in several at once. It is in this semiotic domain, which refuses ontological boundaries, that literary visuality takes place.

"Taking place": the phrase is eminently suitable because it refers to an event, as in narrative, and to the spatial coordinates of that event, its location and environment, both, by definition, visible. The extraordinary innovation that Proust's sentence wrought is that it makes this materiality of visuality, fugitive as it may be, substantive, almost palpable. The sentence gives this materiality place so that it can "take place." In its wake, this materiality redefines the meaning of fiction. No longer confined to the mind that imagines it, the fictional event links that mind to the body, through which the concrete, visible, albeit imagined, place receives sensual presence.

Proust's tactile, warm light achieves this. His light defines the quality of the seeing subject, of the subject as seer, not only through the retina but also through his entire body bathing in warm yellow light. Hence the indispensable presence of tactility within visuality. Moreover, this light is a trace. The noun "trace" is to be taken in a sense that negotiates between Peircean programmatic semiotics and Derridean unwitting semiotics.[15] It is the sun outside, with its Platonic resonances, that projects the trace like writing in colored pencil. Through its efficacy, the sun captures the subject, puts him within a spectacle, and affects his body and emotions. Marcel, who produces the frame in which the image is locked, with his look subjected to the restriction of the visual field we have seen, does not himself manage to stay outside his product. This is the first lesson in visuality the sentence proposes.

But what is the "proper" image here, the image within the frame thus produced out of that illumination made up of chiaroscuro?

> je vis, grand, mince, le cou dégagé, la tête haute et
> fièrement portée, passer un jeune homme aux yeux
> pénétrants et dont la peau était aussi blonde et les
> cheveux aussi dorés que s'ils avaient absorbé tous les
> rayons du soleil.

> I saw approaching, tall, slim, bare-necked, his head
> held proudly erect, a young man with searching eyes
> whose skin was as fair and his hair as golden as if they
> had absorbed all the rays of the sun.

"Je vis": a verb form finally comes to rule the sentence's grammar. The verb and its narrative tense signal the end of the set-up and the beginning of the second level of focalization that is to follow, embedded within the retrospective memory. An event of vision is happening, and what is described is the act of looking performed by the sentence's "first person," the subject of writing. "Je vis" is a shifter with a long history, of which certain episodes have dubious overtones.

One such dubious case is Caesar's *veni, vidi, vinci* of the colonizing look of conquest. Another that may give pause for thought is Freud's look as promoter of sexual excitement, a view that potentially attributes actual agency to the pornographic look. In view of that dual history, it seems important to realize that the Proustian look, in contrast, teaches us a mode of looking, a visual activity, which, in spite of the multiple scenes of voyeurism in *La recherche,* has nothing colonizing about it.

Instead, the almost tactile quality of this warm yellow light precludes any possible attempt at voyeurism. Even if we define voyeurism quite generally, as is often done, as a look whose subject stays out of reach and whose object is not aware of his status as object, hence, as a look that objectifies and keeps firmly in place the opposition between subject and object that so often turns out to be damaging, one cannot impute such a look to Proust's imagining of vision.

Even if we apply that definition to the *prise de vue* at hand, we cannot turn the resulting image into a voyeuristic one.[16] This is impossible because the light, like a syrupy substance, attaches itself to the subject, who is irremediably implicated as a result. The thing seen, itself distant but seen through this light, situated beyond the boundary of the dining room, looks like this: "grand, mince, le cou dégagé, la tête haute et fièrement portée, [passer] un jeune homme [. . .]." Nothing would enable the subject of the look to appropriate this object, seen in profile and walking.

The distance inherent in vision contributes to allowing two seemingly contradictory things to happen: the light replete with desire emanates from the two subjects, mutually—even if so far, the desire is Marcel's only, since he initiates the visual act—and at the same time, the object-subject that is seen remains autonomous. The act of looking is undeniably "cruising," but without appropriation. Here lies, precisely, the importance of Robert for the libidinal economy of *La recherche.* Contrary to Albertine, Robert is not *pris sous garde,* put under surveillance. For, it is through this male character, this future intimate friend, this ideal of physical beauty and role model for the subject under the felicitous banner of "je est un autre," that this economy will develop. This economy is first and foremost visual in this novel, which so massively invested in love and/as knowledge.

FRAMING

Love, indeed, guides the protagonist, but also the narrator, whose vast ambition it is to comprehend. This verb is to be taken in both the intellectual and literal sense of embracing, of taking together, both epistemology (how to know the other) and poetics (how to write the other) under the aegis of love (how to approach the other). And this ambitious endeavor is played out in the interstices—a word whose visual impact as frame we have already seen—between the adult focalizer, whose visual memories are being narrated, and the young one, his former self, who participated in the scene that is the substance of the memory. This substance is altogether visual, but it complicates the nature of the visual domain. Hence, it is on the level of the visual that we must interpret the reach of vision, the domain where, through the impossibility of ever achieving the desired proximity, desire materializes.

Like the curtains, love is a frame, and, as such, it frames the image just as it frames the ribbon of light left by the opening between the curtains and crossed by the path, in the literary space, on which the character is seen to be standing out. Like our sentence as a whole, this imaginative, yet sense-based framing can be read as a theoretical object, a phenomenal artifact with theoretical relevance. Frames and framing, in this sense, polemically assert the importance of the concept of framing as a better alternative to "context."

In a Derrida-inspired plea for abandoning the notion of context in favor of that of the frame, Jonathan Culler lists the problems of the former and the advantages of the latter where he writes:

> But the notion of context frequently oversimplifies rather than enriches discussion, since the opposition between an act and its context seems to presume that the context is given and determines the meaning of the act. We know, of course, that things are not so simple: context is not fundamentally different from what it contextualizes; context is not given but produced; what belongs to a context is determined by interpretive strategies; contexts are just as much in need of elucidation as events; and the meaning of a context is determined by events. Yet when we use the

term *context* we slip back into the simple model it proposes. (xiv)

No context is given; in other words, there are only other texts, neighboring ones, which are as much in need of interpretation as the one we are looking at. This is the reason why Culler, who follows Derrida but applies the notion of framing to the concrete situation in which literary studies are practiced in North America, prefers "frame" over "context."

It is also the reason why the indispensable intellectual frame is semiotics, "Since the phenomena criticism deals with are signs, forms with socially-constituted meanings, one might try to think not of context but of the framing of signs: how are signs constituted (framed) by various discursive practices, institutional arrangements, systems of value, semiotic mechanisms?" (Culler xiv). Culler's phrasing "forms with socially-constituted meanings" seems a perfectly adequate definition of the sign, compatible with Peirce's definition but placing the emphasis elsewhere. This formulation solicits thought about the oppressive aspect of the visual order even under an allegedly liberal regime. For the field of vision, the frame that delimits the object seen has always already defined the look. Hence, the image is a sign.

Love, that emotion whose contagious nature we know, which keeps the person in love from staying "himself," is involved in the same formulation. Far from staying aloof from the social, economic, intellectual, and institutional constraints that Culler mentions, love is intertwined with them, even if it colors them pink, or, as the case may be, yellow. Love is here proposed as sensuous, material, even in its incipient stage confined to vision—but it is a vision thick with warmth as a body-enveloping "world."

Does this mean that the young Marcel is already in love with Robert? Of course not; in fact, he never will be, at least not openly, not on the level of the fabula, where the events are situated. It is true that even before knowing Robert, Marcel had decided he wanted to make him his best friend. But the question of love as frame is not posed on the level of the fabula, only on the level we are examining—of focalization. It is the luminous nature of Robert, a feature that will be attributed to him all along and that sticks to him like a skin, that is established here. The soft yellow light is not a mere warm ambiance in which the subject bathes and which colors the object. It is also the projection, the writing, in the precise Derridean sense, that the object emanates and projects onto the subject. Hence, the near-redundancy at the end of the description: "un jeune homme aux yeux pénétrants et dont la peau était aussi blonde et les cheveux aussi dorés que s'ils avaient absorbé tous les rayons du soleil." As early as the beginning, when he installs himself under the sign of the sun, the young protagonist-focalizer liquidifies in a sentiment that resolves distinct identities, a sentiment we can only imagine as "falling in love."

If the description of the man seen is framed by light, this light, mentioned again at the end of this long sentence, continues to project its framing effect on the next sentence. This sentence contains the first mention of the second feature that stays with Robert indelibly as a character, a feature that embodies light's fugitivity in a more drastically diegetic manner: speed.

> Vêtu d'une étoffe souple et blanchâtre comme je n'aurait jamais cru qu'un homme eût osé en porter, et dont la minceur n'évoquait pas moins le frais de la salle à manger, la chaleur et le beau temps dehors, il marchait vite. (I 729)

> Dressed in a suit of soft, whitish material such as I could never have believed that any man would have the audacity to wear, the thinness of which suggested no less vividly than the coolness of the dining-room the heat and brightness of the glorious day outside, he was walking fast. (I 783)

Robert walks so fast that it seems as if he is chasing his monocle. This characteristic speed is the lightness of vision translated into temporality. What binds the two features, according to the young focalizer, is sexual ambiguity: "blanchâtre comme je n'aurait jamais cru qu'un homme eût osé en porter," he muses, before continuing with tactile fantasies described in visual terms of light and predicated "glorious."

These two traits of the "closetedly" central character join forces in what I have elsewhere dubbed the "photo-effect," which is so fundamental to the Proustian text. Robert is the protagonist of this effect. The art of photography is the art of light, so light it barely seems to bring to its products the materiality of paint, or of lead, carbon, ink, or marble. This art, because it is only the effect—of light—defines substance as the mediator between the subject and object of Proustian sensation.[17]

If photography, at least in Proust's time, is the domain of black and white, the brightness and lightness of Robert establish a revealing contrast with the obscurity that, as we will see shortly, will envelop him in the last "take," right before his death. This makes the two descriptions together a properly photographic portrait. And, as if to attract attention to this semiotic function of the character, Robert is also the appointed photographer of the diegetic world. It is Robert who takes the photo of Marcel's grandmother that will haunt the protagonist for the rest of his life. Moreover, it is in his function as family photographer that Robert makes love to the liftboy at Balbec, when he is developing the photograph in the darkroom. Thus, in the darkroom, he is engaged in an act of revelation, not only literally in the act of developing the photograph, but also figuratively, when he reveals—but still "closetedly"!—his homosexuality.

In order to measure the importance of the second feature, the temporal version of Robert's lightness, let me quote the fragment that is symmetrically contrasted to the sentence I have analyzed. Marcel now sees Robert for the last time, just before his death as a military hero. Again, the description is introduced by a "je vis" that follows a "quand," and, again, against all realistic expectation, the object seen is unknown:

> quand je vis sortir rapidement [. . .] trop loin pour que dans l'obscurité profonde je pusse le distinguer, un officier.
>
> Quelque chose pourtant me frappa qui n'était pas sa figure que je ne voyais pas [. . .] mais la disproportion extraordinaire entre le nombre de points différents par où passa son corps et le petit nombre de secondes pendant lesquelles cette sortie, qui avait l'air de la sortie tentée par un assiégé, s'exécuta [. . .] . Le militaire capable d'occuper en si peu de temps tant de positions différentes dans l'espace avait disparu [. . .].
> (III 810 / IV 389)

> that is to say too far off for me to be able to make him out clearly in the profound darkness, I saw an officer come out and walk rapidly away.

>Something, however, struck me: not his face,
>which I did not see, nor his uniform, which was
>disguised by a heavy greatcoat, but the extraordi-
>nary disproportion between the number of different
>points which his body successively occupied and the
>very small number of seconds within which he made
>good this departure which had almost the air of a
>sortie from a besieged town. So that my mind turned,
>if I did not explicitly recognise him—I will not say
>even to the build, nor to the slimness or the carriage
>or the swift movements of Saint-Loup—but to the
>sort of ubiquity which was so special to him. This
>military man with the ability to occupy so many dif-
>ferent positions in space in such a short time disap-
>peared [. . .]. (III 838)

Yet, despite the absence of the proper name, that linguistic signifier
par excellence of identity, the identity of the officer is beyond doubt. It
is Robert, here framed in the negative, the darkness. Without the sun,
without light, only his speed remains as a tool to signify himself visually: to put himself in the image.

The image described here, in a language not without geometrical
connotations, brings to mind Peirce's definition of the icon: "An *icon* is
a sign which would possess the character which renders it significant,
even though its object had no existence; such as a lead-pencil streak
as representing a geometric line" (10). The line that the pencil draws;
here, the line is drawn not on paper but in space, a space, however, of
which we see nothing but the plane on which the positions occupied
are drawn in such rapid succession. Is this, then, an iconic image, not
because it is visual but because the movement fixated on the sensitive
plane of the photograph derives its existence from that act? That remains to be seen.

The unknown officer is known; his movement becomes the "sign
which would possess the character which renders it significant, even
though its object had no existence." Pure product of the look, Robert
is constructed as a sign not by the focalizer, who does not acknowledge
that he knows him, but as a sign for the reader who has been nourished
by the images outside of which Robert has no existence. The first one
of these, as we have seen, is the bath of light in which Marcel and
Robert exist together. The frame, here the infinitely large darkroom

of the curfewed city, envelops them together yet again. The dimension that makes the frame a three-dimensional space liable to implicate the subject and the object together, in equality, within a contagious look, is the dimension of the index rather than of the icon.

Photo-Memory

Sexuality and the desire that inaugurates it are favorite topics in cultural studies, especially within the framework of gender, feminist, and queer studies. Since the so-called "visual turn," named by one of its key contributors, W. J. T. Mitchell, much has been written on the power inequalities that permeate the visual domain in which desire is so often acted out. In a somewhat unfortunate medium-essentialism, cultural studies or, as I prefer to call it, cultural analysis, has seen the separate development of "visual culture studies." I have deployed a single sentence from Proust's encyclopedia of literary wisdom to compose a lesson in visual culture.

If, in the end, this lesson is convincing, it seems to me that adepts of "visual culture" as a new and better approach to the study of culture than either art history or literary study will find themselves in a logical predicament. If a literary text has more fundamental things to say about vision than their own textbooks, and if, to boot, that text dates back to the time in which both rejected disciplines were in the process of being established, the divide between literature and visual studies that this new movement is predicated upon makes no sense at all. But it is not to gain points in an academic polemic that I continue to see the relevance of *La recherche.* Beyond the "intermedial" analysis of literature, what Proust makes the image do is of wider importance.

In the seminal study I evoked above, Kaja Silverman mapped out the ethical implications of Lacan's theory of vision. In the last chapter of her book, she studies the Lacanian concept of the screen. This can be imagined as an opaque obstacle that hampers direct access to the object of vision. It stipulates beforehand the conditions of perceptibility according to the direction of the dominant, anonymous, enveloping gaze, outside of which no subject can withdraw, and which is best understood as the visual symbolic order. Elsewhere in the study, Silverman opposes photography to memory in terms with strong Proustian resonances: "Whereas photography performs a memorial function by lifting an object out of time and immortalizing it forever in a particular form, memory is all about temporality and change" (157). Both photography and memory function in relation to the past, that lost time that *La recherche* declares is its project to search. But if the latter has an unstable, fast temporality that inscribes loss (*perdu*) within the search, the former stabilizes, even if at the cost of the life that alone renders the past desirable.

A bit later, after analyzing the implications of Walter Benjamin's and Roland Barthes's ideas on the subject, Silverman proposes the relevance for the subject of a look impregnated with memories charged with desire—"libidinally saturated associative clusters which act like those mnemic elements which, as a result of a psychic working over, have been made the vehicles for the expression of unconscious wishes" (185). Can we imagine an image that might be able to reconcile photography and memory? I submit that this is what Proust does in sentences like the one I have analyzed here.

Let me state explicitly the importance of the social productivity of an act of looking that is anchored in such a libidinal, "photographic" memory. This importance lies not so much in the desire that propels it as in that art's ability to connect on the level of the screen, in a public domain where that art is at the disposal of innumerable subjects, marginal elements along with the most significant ones. This connection brings those images most charged with sentimental and sensational impact for the reader or looker, to bear on the marginal, so that the latter can begin to radiate desirability, to shine. The term Silverman uses for this decisive act of looking is "heteropathic memory": the "memory" of other people's memories. Hopefully it is clear by now that, in the case of Robert, this character is introduced in the novel through a "remembered" image, a "photograph" of his younger self, when he radiated desirability. The desire in question is homosexual, which positions it in the margin of the cultural screen.[18]

This is precisely why Proust has not been able, or did not wish, to boast this feature. As a result it transpires only in sexually ambiguous imagery. The words "comme je n'aurait jamais cru qu'un homme eût osé en porter" (as I could never have believed that any man would have the audacity to wear) hint at this possibility. The image of Robert that envelops Marcel in its rays is the one that will much later enable the latter to give himself over to heteropathic identification, not with Robert but with the desire for Robert that a stranger in the street feels (II 182 / II 480). There, too, geometry offsets sensation:[19]

je vis qu'un monsieur assez mal habillé avait l'air de lui parler d'assez près. J'en conclus que c'était un ami personnel de Robert; cependant ils semblaient se rapprocher encore l'un de l'autre; tout à coup, comme apparaît au ciel un phénomène astral, je vis des corps ovoïdes prendre avec une rapidité vertigineuse toutes les positions qui leur permettaient de composer, devant Saint-Loup, une instable constellation. Lancés come par une fronde ils me semblèrent être au moins au nombre de sept. Ce n'étaient pourtant que les deux poings de Saint-Loup, multipliés par leur vitesse à changer de place dans cet ensemble en apparence idéal et décoratif. (II 182 / II 480)

when I saw that a somewhat shabbily attired gentleman appeared to be talking to him confidentially. I concluded that this was a personal friend of Robert; meanwhile they seemed to be drawing even closer to one another; suddenly, as an astral phenomenon flashes through the sky, I saw a number of ovoid bodies assume with a dizzy swiftness all the positions necessary for them to compose a flickering constellation in front of Saint-Loup. Flung out like stones from a catapult, they seemed to me to be at the very least seven in number. They were merely, however, Saint-Loup's two fists, multiplied by the speed with which they were changing place in this—to all appearance ideal and decorative—arrangement. (II 186)

To feel like the other—that is the literal meaning of the notion of heteropathic identification. If the Lacanian symbolic order joins forces with the Peircean symbolic in order to limit what is thinkable to what the screen lets us see and language say, the visual composite—which allows the icon to contribute its "geometry" and the index its light so that the abstract form becomes legible as if through a secret code—makes it possible for the marginal to shine. Once this identification succeeds with the help of a visuality that incorporates what it both shows and hides, it makes all the sense in the world to identify Robert as the real hero of *La recherche*. Thus, if he dies a hero on the battlefield, the irony, never far away when Proust invokes cultural grandeur, tends to fade.

Notes

[1] Of the many publications that discuss the imaging potential of literature, Ernst Van Alphen's is the most directly relevant here. In poignant contrast to the desiring look I discuss here, though, his analysis concerns experiences of looking in concentration camps.

[2] The appropriate French term would be "prise de vue." This term derives its specific relevance here from its systematic contrast to "prendre sous garde," which is one possible etymological understanding of the verb for "to look," "regarder." See Norman Bryson for a discussion of the implications of this meaning of the verb.

[3] Nor can a single glance comprehend an image, but one can easily *think*—illusionarily—that one sees an image at a glance.

[4] For a brilliant, in-depth account of Freud's theory of the production of images, see Silverman (75–100).

[5] In accordance with habit but strictly speaking, incorrectly, I refer to the narrator-protagonist as "Marcel" only when this figure's particular function as either narrator or protagonist, or younger or older focalizer is not at stake.

[6] Malcolm Bowie has explored the Proustian resonances in Lacan's work in great depth. His notion of "theory as fiction" forms a relevant counterpart to my argument here, which considers fiction as theory. See Catherine Lord for an elaboration of the related notion of "theoretical fiction." Lord's study is devoted to what she calls, in a critical intimacy with Harold Bloom, "the intimacy of influence," a concept that fits nicely with Lacan's unacknowledged relation to Proust's writing.

[7] After serving as a series of photographs, Albertine is eliminated from the story when she becomes redundant. See my study on visuality in Proust (*Mottled Screen*).

[8] In this respect, the description parallels the earlier one, made famous by Paul de Man, in which Marcel enjoys the summer outdoors more profoundly because he is in his half-obscure room.

[9] See Hamon's classical study on description, and my own contribution on the subject in Franco Moretti's (ed.), *Il Romanzo* (V 2).

[10] It is no more obvious, in fact, that Proust made these references consciously, reflectively, or voluntarily. Neither can we impute to Rembrandt's will the egalitarian look solicited through his chiaroscuro. I am reading these texts, not their author's mind. For an extensive critique of intention as an analytical concept, see Bal (*Narratology*).

[11] See Lacan. For a clear explanation of Lacan's theory of vision and its ethical implications, see Silverman (*Threshold*).

[12] Diegetic is what pertains to the fabula, the string of events that appear to underlie the narrative text but in fact is produced by that text. For all narratological terminology, see Bal (*Narratology*).

[13] The term "punctual" refers to the event of the moment, as distinct from durative events, which take time.

[14] See Derrida (*Truth*) on the frame. Underlying my remark here is also his discussion of supplementarity in *Of Grammatology*.

[15] In "Writing and Difference," Derrida abstains from positioning his ideas on trace, difference, and differing in relation to a semiotic framework, although his engagement with Saussure makes this abstention almost odd; Peirce defined the domain of the semiotic in a way that could have persuaded Derrida (most clearly in Innis).

[16] See chapter 4 of my book on Rembrandt (*Reading "Rembrandt"*) for an in-depth discussion of voyeurism and non-voyeuristic images.

[17] In her brilliant book on Proust, Julia Kristeva fails to notice the special centrality of vision in the domain of sensation.

[18] Not coincidentally, Silverman, whose theorization of visuality is among the most subtle, complex, and brilliant, also offers an extremely fine theorization of the kind of marginalized experiences of male desire (*Male Subjectivity*).

[19] For an extensive analysis of this passage, see Bal (*Mottled* 214–37).

Works Cited

Bal, Mieke. *The Mottled Screen: Reading Proust Visually.* Trans. Anna-Louise Milne. Stanford: Stanford UP, 1997.

—. *Narratology: Introduction to the Theory of Narrative.* 2nd (revised) ed. Trans. Christine van Boheemen. Toronto: U of Toronto P, 1997.

—. *Reading "Rembrandt": Beyond the Word-Image Opposition.* New York: Cambridge UP, 1991.

Bowie, Malcolm. *Freud, Proust and Lacan: Theory as Fiction.* Cambridge: Cambridge UP, 1987.

Bryson, Norman. *Vision and Painting: The Logic of the Gaze.* London: MacMillan, 1983.

Culler, Jonathan. *Framing the Sign: Criticism and Its Institutions.* Norman and London: U of Oklahoma P, 1988.

Derrida, Jacques. *Of Grammatology.* Trans. Gayatri Chakravorty Spivak. Baltimore: Johns Hopkins UP, 1976.

—. *The Truth in Painting.* Trans. Geoff Bennington and Ian McLeod. Chicago: U of Chicago P, 1987.

—. *Writing and Difference.* Trans. Alan Bass. Chicago: U of Chicago P, 1978.

Hamon, Philippe. *Introduction à l'analyse du descriptif.* Paris: Hachette, 1981.

Innis, Robert E., ed. *Semiotics: An Introductory Anthology.* Bloomington: Indiana UP, 1985.

Kristeva, Julia. *Le temps sensible: Proust et l'expérience littéraire.* Paris: Gallimard, 1994.

Lacan, Jacques. *The Four Fundamental Concepts of Psycho-Analysis.* Ed. J.-A. Miller. Trans. A. Sheridan. Harmondsworth: Penguin, 1979.

Lord, Catherine. *The Intimacy of Influence: Narrative and Theoretical Fictions in the Works of George Eliot, Virginia Woolf and Jeanette Winterson.* Amsterdam: ASCA, 1999.

Man, Paul de. "Seminology and Reading (Proust)." *Allegories of Reading: Figural Language in Rousseau, Nietzsche, Rilke, and Proust.* New Haven, CT: Yale UP, 1979. 57–78.

Mitchell, W. J. T. "The Pictorial Turn." *Picture Theory.* Chicago: U of Chicago P, 1994. 11–34.

Moretti, Franco, ed. *Il Romanzo.* Vol. 1–5. Torino: Einaudi, 2001–2003.

Peirce, Charles Sanders. "Logic as Semiotic: The Theory of Signs." Innis 4–23.

Proust, Marcel. *A la recherche du temps perdu.* 3 vols. Paris: Gallimard, 1954.

—. *Remembrance of Things Past.* 3 vols. Trans. C.K.Scott Moncrieff and Terence Kilmartin. London: Penguin, 1989.

Silverman, Kaja. "Apparatus for the Production of an Image," *Parallax* 6.3 (2000): 12–28.

—. *Male Subjectivity at the Margins.* New York: Routledge, 1992.

—. *The Threshold of the Visible World.* New York: Routledge, 1996.

Van Alphen, Ernst. "Caught by Images." *Art in Mind: How Contemporary Images Shape Thought.* Chicago: U of Chicago P, 2005. 163–79.

9 Blood, Visuality, and the New Multiculturalism

David Palumbo-Liu

One of the main points I always try to emphasize in all my classes is that ethnicity is relational: it is produced as one marker of difference between and amongst all of us, albeit unevenly and variously; it is produced laterally across all races and ethnicities, and it is deeply embedded within the social, historical, cultural, and political fabric of our lives. It is not easily separable out into individual components, at least not without some cost to analytic richness and political efficacy. That is all to say, I am against ethnic enclaving. And yet, if we scrupulously bring in whiteness, or any other ostensibly normative category, the chances are that we will then be forced to grapple with that relationship in often complex, troubling, and uncomfortable ways. For instance, what happens when we are instructed to read past race by an at least temporarily "reconstructed" white male? What should we do as we listen to him argue for a reading of humanity that moves past the visible surface of the skin and into the depths of blood ties? Should we greet that anti-racist call with a sense of solidarity, or suspicion, or something else? And what sort of judgment would our reaction bring upon us, as well? In this essay I will be addressing precisely this question, assessing a rather interesting anti-racist film coming from a perhaps unlikely quarter. I am speaking of that eminent American social critic, Clint Eastwood, and his 2002 film *Blood Work*. The film, based on the 2002 novel of the same name by Michael Connelly, seems to ask us precisely to read past the surface of life (and that would include racial markings) in order to apprehend some common blood coursing through the collective social body. This isn't easy, the film seems to say; you have to work at it.

I start by tackling the issue of surface and depth, and race. The interiority of the racial subject has long been attributed a specific set of sexual, economic, political, and moral traits and behaviors that is both signaled and manifested by its exterior. In this case, the equation between appearance and essence, which has always been a highly thematized problematic in western philosophical thinking, is deemed unproblematic for the racial subject—what you see *is* what you get. There is no mystery here, rather, a broad transparency. Such a reading of surface as essence and essence as manifest in behavior is dramatically evident in the writings of Augustus Henry Keane, whose work is characterized by such assertions as those found in his 1908 study, *The World's People: A Popular Account of Their Bodily and Mental Characters, Beliefs, Traditions, Political and Social Institutions.* According to Keane, for example, members of what he called the "Negro/Black Division" were "sensual, unintellectual, lacking a sense of personal dignity or self-respect, hence readily bending to the yoke of slavery; fitful, passing suddenly from comedy to tragedy; mind arrested at puberty owing to the early closing of the cranial sutures, hence in the adult the animal is more developed than the mental" (qtd. in Haney-Lopez 97, n. 51). The members of the "Mongolic or Yellow Division" were "generally somewhat reserved, sullen, and apathetic (Mongols proper); very thrifty, frugal, and industrious (Chinese and Japanese); indolent (Malays, Siamese, Koreans); nearly all reckless gamblers; science slightly, arts and letters moderately developed" (qtd. in Haney-Lopez 97, n. 52). These pronouncements sound typical enough coming from the discourse of scientific racism; what is notable is that this text was cited as authoritative evidence by the US Supreme Court in its landmark cases of the early twentieth century.[1] It becomes patently clear that the surface and the interior are commensurate in these cases precisely because both are social constructs. Not only are they both social constructs, they are in fact mutually constitutive, to the point of solipsism.

Nevertheless, this assumption of transparency, and its ideological function, has been put into crisis by historical contingencies that evince shifts in the political and material historical environment. In this unsettling of what might be called *interior/exterior commensurability,* the ideological functions freighted upon "race" become visible in ways unavailable before, as naturalized categories are opened up for re-examination. For example, in recent years the Human Genome Project has brought in its wake countless attempts to plumb the new sameness which nanoscience has given us all to share; we move beneath the epidermis and beyond phenotypical determinism to explore a common and essential human genome. And science offers us, through the usual middleman of capitalism, a personal interface with this new knowledge base—we can use science to tell us, authoritatively, who we really are. Consider the case of Wayne Joseph, who, according to a 2003 story in the *LA Weekly,*

> was a 51-year-old high school principal in Chino, California whose family emigrated from the segregated parishes of Louisiana to central Los Angeles in the 1950s. He is of Creole stock and is therefore on the lighter end of the black color spectrum, a common enough circumstance in the South that predates the multicultural movement by centuries. And like most other black folk, Joseph grew up with an unequivocal sense of his heritage and of himself; he tends toward black advocacy and has published thoughtful opinion pieces on racial issues in magazines like *Newsweek.* When Joseph decided on a whim to take a new ethnic DNA test he saw described on a *60 Minutes* segment last year, it was only to indulge a casual curiosity about the exact percentage of black blood; virtually all black Americans are mixed with something, he knew, but he figured it would be interesting to make himself a guinea pig for this new testing process, which is offered by a Florida-based company called DNA Print Genomics Inc. Joseph [found out he] was 57 percent Indo-European, 39 percent Native American, 4 percent East Asian—and zero percent African. After a lifetime of assuming blackness, he was now being told that he lacked even a single drop of black blood to qualify.
>
> "My son was flabbergasted by the results," says Joseph. "He said, 'Dad, you mean for 50 years you've been passing for black?'" [2]

Here, I want to explore how *Blood Work* attempts to break down the notion of exterior/interior transparency as it is specifically tied to issues of race, gender, and social visuality. This ambition is intimately attached to a larger question: how does the problematic of the visible and the invisible, the phenotypical and the essential, function to secure a sense of what it means to be human? And to be human together with others?

Blood Work was only a moderate success in terms of its reception by the general audience.[3] While reviewers largely agreed that cinematically it was well produced, directed, and acted, many felt the plot was both too contrived and at other times obvious. Most thought that this latest attempt at portraying an elegiac, allegorical battle between good and evil paled before one of Eastwood's finest films, the relatively proximate *Unforgiven* (1992). And in many respects these critics were right. But they missed (or perhaps ignored) a truly unusual element in *Blood Work,* and that is its focus on race.

In its basic narrative structure and ideology *Blood Work* is perhaps most similar to Eastwood's *In the Line of Fire* (1993), a story about a Secret Service agent who feels responsible for not having prevented the assassination of John F. Kennedy. The protagonist is drawn into a dangerous cat-and-mouse game by a killer who dares him to prevent an assassination that he is planning. In *Blood Work,* Eastwood again plays an aging, retired law enforcement officer who is lured back into the field by a peculiar set of circumstances and a particular kind of antagonist. And again, the antagonistic relationship that drives the film is one between personified notions of good and evil, and life and death. This Manichean division becomes complicated by the idea that the two figures that play out this drama are actually not so dissimilar: both are equally alienated from society at large. These elements are found in many of Eastwood's films, of course. Again, what is significant about *Blood Work* is the way in which the protagonist is drawn back into the social, a process that takes him through a labyrinth of race, biology, and ethics, in which the scopic gaze is at different points critical, deceptive, and irrelevant. And this ultimately speaks to the status of the visible in public life.

Blood Work presents its case against racism precisely within a critique of social visibility. The film argues that our current mode of being-together largely takes place via the consumption of mediated images, most conspicuously the constant proliferation of "news." This imaging of human connectedness, and of "human interest" that is the affective glue, reifies actual being-together. Knowledge of others is channeled along a production-line of sentiment, desire, and, most of all, fear. The visible here is hyper-visibility: distortive, sensationalistic, and alienated. *Blood Work,* to the contrary, attempts to articulate a normative, human visibility in which subjects can actually share in the determination of the significance of the visible. But to do this we have to recognize and then unlearn how the visible is read, and this in turn includes relearning the visual indexes of race and gender. *Blood Work's* reconfiguration of the Eastwoodian (anti)hero centers upon two motifs. First, the film not only charts the alienation of the anti-hero, but, critically, it also creates a positive alternate social space that is emphatically intersubjective, domestic, and normative. Its constitution is diametrically opposed to a pathologized and alienated public arena of hyper-visibility and male violence.

Eastwood's films are known for their depictions of alienated, sociopathic types who perform the dirty little duties that liberal society requires and sponsors but at the same time disavows. But these films customarily leave the protagonist dangling outside the social, clothed but also trapped in idiosyncratic nobility. *Blood Work* re-integrates its protagonist, but back neither into the fold of society in general nor into some singular private sanctuary. Instead, we find the protagonist installed in a particular microcommunity constituted within a non-racist, non-rationalized, multicultural and multiracial ethos of shared mutual obligations. The outside world is rejected for its obsession with the hyper-visible, panoptic, voyeuristic gaze, whose requisite luminosity bathes everything in a blinding white light that leeches out human goodness and particularity for the sake of configuring either lurid and violent sensationalism or pre-fabricated "goodness." This reconstitution of the heroic figure is important not only in so far as it is itself an allegory for the transformation of the cinematic persona for which Eastwood is famous, but also the means by which this transformation feeds back to critique the public *habitus* of contemporary American visual media.

This is set up in the opening sequence, which begins with an aerial view of a crime scene; the spectator seems an occupant of the police helicopter that both circles and illuminates the scene. The visual in this case is attached to top-down power relations, of seeing and arresting objects, pinned down in its light. The end point of this opening tracking shot is the heroic figure, framed visually but also isolated verbally by an assessment voiced by a Mexican American detective, who proleptically names the figure to emerge from the car, and then declaims, "no matter what happens, it will be his face we'll see."

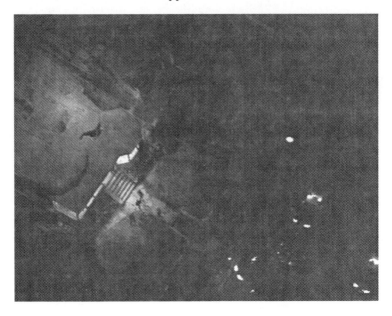

Fig. 1. Aerial view of crime scene. © 2002 by Warner Bros. Pictures.

Eastwood plays Terry McCaleb, a famous FBI profiler who has been involved in trying to solve a number of highly publicized serial killings. His current nemesis is given the name of the "Code Killer," on account of the fact that he leaves the same nine-digit number (903472568) at the scene of each of his killings. Upon chasing down a suspect, the aging McCaleb suffers a massive heart attack, but not before shooting the suspect—but it is unclear whether the wound is fatal or not. Nearly two years later, now retired, McCaleb undergoes a heart transplant. Two months after his operation, he is approached by a young Latina woman who asks him to come out of retirement long enough to solve the murder of her sister, Gloria, who was killed during the hold-up of a Korean convenience store. Though McCaleb at first refuses, the woman persuades him to take the case: it was her sister's heart that was transplanted into his body. It is not only for her sake, but also for the sake of the victim's young son, Raymond, that the woman asks McCaleb to do this. Reluctantly, he agrees to look into the case.

Fig. 2. Hero figure. © 2002 by Warner Bros. Pictures.

After obtaining access to the police files on the case, McCaleb begins to believe that this was no ordinary robbery; it seems strikingly similar to the killing of a man, Cordell, at an ATM machine that took place a few weeks before. As McCaleb delves deeper into their respective cases, he comes to believe that the police have been going at this all wrong; they have been concentrating on the locations of the two killings. McCaleb argues that the place is irrelevant, what is important is the relation between the two victims. After a number of attempts, he finally hits upon a similarity: both victims had recently donated blood. He discovers that Gloria's blood type is the same as his own, highly rare blood type. Thus he knows that the odds of the first victim's blood type being the same as Gloria's and his are infinitesimally small, and yet that proves to be the case: against all probability, all three of them share the same rare blood type.

The second break in the case comes when McCaleb reviews both the security camera's recording of Gloria's murder and the audiotape of the 911 call that was made to report the crime and ask for an ambulance. It so happens that right after Gloria and the Korean merchant are shot, a shadowy figure the police have dubbed "The Good Samaritan" enters the scene, tries to bandage Gloria's wounds, and calls

911. He then disappears. The police say that he "sounds Hispanic, [is] probably illegal, and that's why he doesn't want to come forward." But upon comparing the precise time of the shooting with the placement of the call to 911, McCaleb discovers that the call was placed shortly before the murder. This means that the Good Samaritan is anything but that—he in fact is the murderer—the image of good is revealed to be a mask for an inhuman evil. The question then becomes, why would the murderer call an ambulance before the fact, why would he try to keep Gloria alive? McCaleb now knows that the killer has chosen his victims carefully: he wants to be sure they live long enough for their hearts to be transplanted. By the rare similarity between all their "blood work," McCaleb understands which body the heart is to be donated to: his own.

The final break in the case comes when Gloria's son Raymond inadvertently breaks the code. Looking at an old newspaper clipping he has found in McCaleb's boat, he notices that there is "no one" amongst the nine digits, while all the other digits occur exactly once. At the time, McCaleb doesn't think much about this, but later he notices a check he has written his neighbor. He has made the check out to "Buddy Noone." A number of small incidents and intuitions come together: when did Buddy move in, why is he so interested in the case, etc. McCaleb draws a line in the middle of the last name and it becomes clear: No/one.

It should be clear that the point of emphasis in the film is the notion of connection. What connects people together, for better or

Fig. 3. McCaleb's check. © 2002 by Warner Bros. Pictures.

worse? How do good and evil create and draw on such connections? Who is the Buddy of No-One?

The film follows these questions on a number of different levels: the manifest action of the characters, their hidden motivations, fears, doubts, and desires. And, critically, the film attaches such meditations to the consideration of the racialized body. That is, as well as the inner spaces of psychic and social disequilibrium, the film focuses on the material, the corporeal, the phenotypical, the visibility of the surface. This is what "profiling" is all about, a movement betwixt and between the visible and the invisible, geared to police the line between the socially acceptable and the criminal. Again and again the film intercuts shots of McCaleb where he seems tanned and relatively fit with shots of him deathly pale, as if to monitor the narrative's ebb and flow. This trajectory is directly linked to his body's accommodation of the transplanted heart. Throughout, McCaleb clutches "his" heart, breathes laboriously, and others continually tell him that he looks tired. But at the same time, the film repeats the notion that he should "follow Gloria's heart." The actual and metaphorical revivification of McCaleb is attributed to both the transplant, but also his renewed connection to the social world, and that connection is read in terms of sentiment and sympathy, sexuality, the transcendence of racial difference and the commitment to social ethics.

In *Blood Work,* there are countless allusions to McCaleb having the heart of a "Mexican" woman; the Mexican detective Arrango deplores, for example, the "waste of a good Mexican's heart." But the film reads race in a more capacious, even cosmic sense, and deploys it as a marker of difference that is to be, if not transcended, at least rendered less consequential. Paul Gilroy's discussions of "epidermal" and "nano-scientific" notions of race and species being, and the visual, are useful in this regard. In *Against Race,* he writes:

> The critical notion of "epidermalization" bequeathed to our time by Frantz Fanon is valuable here. It was born from a philosopher-psychologist's phenomenological ambitions and their distinctive way of seeing as well as of understanding the importance of sight. It refers to a historically specific system for making bodies meaningful by endowing them with qualities of "color." It suggests a perceptual regime in which the racialized body is bounded and protected by its

enclosing skin. The observer's gaze does not pene-
trate that membrane but rests upon it and, in doing
so, receives the truths of racial difference from the
other body. (46–47)

He then asserts, "Today skin is no longer privileged as the threshold of
either identity or particularity. There are good reasons to suppose that
the line between inside and out now falls elsewhere. The boundaries
of 'race' have moved across the threshold of the skin. They are cellular
and molecular, not dermal."[4] Following the historical shift Gilroy asserts, it would seem that the film is also arguing that the phenotypical
has to be set aside, the visual prevented from determining the content
of character. What matters instead are our common species genetics,
those deep similarities below the surface that do not follow the delin-
eations and differentiation of the epidermis.

   However, there is a critical difference between DNA and blood-
type, and interestingly, *Blood Work* insists we work through that distinction before we reside comfortably in Gilroy's recommended commonality. This is the crucial point that takes us out of the realm of
genetics and into the realm of human variability. It does so by raising
the question of accommodation, of tolerance. The issue becomes not
genetic commonality of species but rather the capacity of one person
to "tolerate" an organ transplanted from another's body. Besides the
fact that the two bodies of the recipient and the donor have to have
the same blood type, there is the need to guard against the rejection
of the foreign body. As Sherwin Nuland notes, the story of transplants
becomes "the story of our evolving comprehension that the cells of
each of us harbored within them something that is theirs alone." The
question then becomes, "How can a potential recipient be made less
xenophobic, less destructive of protoplasm from a donor?" (465). Just
as this phrase borrows a sociopolitical term as its metaphor, so does
Blood Work use the question of protoplasmic "xenophobia" to stand as
a metaphor for McCaleb's "tolerance" of Gloria's heart, and this points
as well to the larger issue of connection and shared moral obligation.

   We discover that what ultimately binds people together is not race,
nor even blood, but a mode of "being together." Gloria donates blood,
and this leads ultimately to her murder, as the killer has discovered
that she and McCaleb share the same blood type by looking into the
records of the clinic. McCaleb receives her heart, and is thus responsible for giving her justice. While the film has McCaleb and his doctor

constantly taking his temperature and recording the ebb and flow of his body's tolerance of the heart to make sure his body is not rejecting the heart, the film suggests that any physiological danger is offset by the fact that McCaleb is indeed moving closer and closer to being like Gloria in essential ways. Conversely, McCaleb's relation to "Buddy" appears first to be an amiable sort of tolerance, but as Buddy is identified as the killer, it becomes clear that their relation is the inverse of McCaleb's and Graciela's (and by extension, Gloria and her son). Whereas the first set of relations, between McCaleb and Graciela, is predicated on sympathy, generosity, and love—expressed as it is in the "blood" they all share in one way or another—McCaleb and Buddy Noone's relation is based on an inner connection to violence and alienation from society at large—as represented by the dual acts of killing and extracting, that is, the killer's ex-appropriating the blood from the victim's body in order to scrawl his visual clues, the "code" of the killer, for McCaleb to decipher.

Consider two sets of scenes. Each clip articulates a scene of recognition. But the first of each pair is a scene of partial or mis-recognition. It is followed by its completion or correction: we get the "right" connection between people. Both sets of clips represent the two, different, private worlds that lie beneath the surface. The first one will be the ethically responsible, inter-ethnic human community championed by the film; the second is the sociopathic, violent world.

First, we have the initial encounter between Graciela and McCaleb (Figure 4). At their first encounter Graciela presents McCaleb with a photograph of her sister and Raymond. McCaleb's initial response is purely professional:

> "Your sister?"
> "Yes, and her son."
> "Which one?"
> "What?"
> "Which one is dead?"

Graciela then explains the circumstances of her sister's death, and the results for both herself and for Raymond. This scene is elaborated in detail in the novel through the following dialogue, which is absent from the screen play. McCaleb senses that Graciela is trying to elicit a specific reaction from him:

Fig. 4. First Meeting. © 2002 by Warner Bros. Pictures.

"Look, this isn't going to work," he finally said. "I know what you're doing. It doesn't work on me."

"You mean you have no sympathy?"

He hesitated as the anger boiled up in his throat.

"I have sympathy. You read the newspaper story; you know what happened to me. Sympathy was my problem all along."

He swallowed it back and tried to clear away any ill feeling. He knew she was consumed by horrible frustrations. McCaleb had known thousands of people like her. Loved ones taken without reason. No arrests, no convictions, no closure. Some of them were left zombies, their lives irrevocably changed. Lost souls. Graciela Rivers was one of them now. She had to be or she wouldn't have tracked him down. He knew that no matter what she said to him or how angry he got, she didn't deserve to be hit with his own frustrations as well [. . .]. (9)

Graciela finally tries one last time: "Look at it again. Please. Just one more time and then I'll leave you alone. Tell me if you feel anything else?" He shook his head and made a feeble hand gesture as if to say it made no difference to him. "I was an FBI agent, not a psychic."

There are a number of things to note in this passage from the novel—elements that are only indirectly articulated and highly nuanced in the film. First is McCaleb's gradual coming back into sympathy. As he reveals here, the reason he left the force is not only because of his heart, but also because he has withdrawn out of self-protection. He is in fact too sympathetic, too close to the lives of the wounded and bereft, and their lack of "closure." But this withdrawal has denied him closure: it is exactly "closure" that McCaleb needs in order for him to move on to a new life, and in the course of the film we discover that the narrative to be closed involves bringing Gloria's killer to justice, finding the Code Killer, and, finally, ending McCaleb's alienation. The second aspect of this passage to be noted is the way the novel and film both show the slow building of affinities and sympathy between McCaleb and Graciela, as found not only in their bond of sympathy, which is evident here already, but also in their shared "work": both are detectives. Graciela has read the newspaper accounts of McCaleb's retirement and heart transplant, but that is not all; she also matches the date and hour of his transplant with that of her sister's murder. She has "tracked him down" not only to do a particular kind of blood work, but also because she has good reason to believe that he has a special stake in the case. However, at this early point in the narrative McCaleb is unable to make that "psychic" connection, and Graciela finally has to tell him "she's the woman who saved your life [. . .] . Your heart [. . .] it was my sister's" (10–11). This knowledge allows McCaleb to begin to piece together the mystery of Gloria's murder in from a different perspective, and finally to acquire a particular chain of perceptions upon watching the security camera's graphic and complete registering of Gloria's murder.

Critically, this thematic of bonding, so explicitly detailed in the novel's dialogue, is presented symbolically and visually in the film. One night, McCaleb dreams that it is he who is being shot. But crucially, what he envisions is not an exact replication of the video camera's recording, in which his body is merely substituted for Gloria's, and that is what makes it interesting. For McCaleb's dream alters the situation and the sequence of events. Whereas Gloria is held close by the killer, who points the gun to her head and presses the trigger twice, McCaleb's nightmare has him at a short distance from the killer, who shoots him repeatedly in the chest. McCaleb falls down in slow motion, and as the killer continues to fire, McCaleb reaches into his shoulder harness and pulls out his gun, and attempts to fire back.

This last element replicates exactly the segment from the beginning of the film, when McCaleb, felled not by a killer's weapon but by a heart attack, is lying on the ground, drawing out his gun and firing at the fleeing figure of the Code Killer. What Eastwood has done as director is to fuse the two "realities"—that of Gloria's death, and that of McCaleb's near-death—within McCaleb's nightmare vision. Again, as we will see throughout the film, the visual, the evidentiary, is transmogrified and metaphorized into a synthetic image that discloses the interior, the psychic connecting tissue between characters. Eastwood has exploited the genre of the detective story (and film noir) which emplots detection of the surface against a narrative of coming-into-consciousness.

The film thus revolves around the issue not only of "connection"— what brought these people together to act this way—but also of the different modalities in which people are connected. For instance, read in this light, the blood, and blood type, shared between Gloria, Cordell, McCaleb, and Raymond, links them biologically. But this biological relation is complemented by, and perhaps even eclipsed by, their shared goodness: Gloria and Cordell both give blood (and Eastwood has Cordell's widow repeat the line, "He was a good man"). He begins to "get" his connection to Graciela, Gloria and her son, and indeed, the rest of humanity. Again, this knowledge allows McCaleb a particular chain of perceptions upon watching the security camera's graphic and complete registering of Gloria's murder; in fact, it allows him to solve the case.

We can contrast this pair of scenes with a second set, which again narrates a coming into recognition, but instead of positive human bondedness and sympathy—McCaleb being shot as Gloria was—it is a sequence of pathology and violent bonding, one which McCaleb has to renounce. Re-engaging in his work draws him back into the human world in a way that endows him with one sort of connectedness that the film depicts as both exciting and borderline sociopathic. Again, Eastwood employs a standard narrative strategy of detective fiction—that of the red herring. While we are supposed to be looking for a Mexican as a murder suspect, we are misdirected away from Eastwood's white male buddy. Nevertheless, the film is directed well in this regard, and Jeff Daniels does a good job of leaving just a hint of weirdness to his character, who is cast as a kind of ne'er-do-well bum, drinking beer, fishing, and living off an allowance from his "old man." When it finally comes out that Buddy is the killer, the common ground shared by Buddy and McCaleb shifts radically. No longer living "together" as male buddies on neighboring boats because of a shared distance from the "real world" of land and labor and families, the two men are linked together by a shared pathological alienation that feeds off violence.

The film suggests that there is a specific reason the Killer has selected McCaleb as his antagonist: it is because the two are both diametrically opposed and yet so similar (the news reporters keep asking McCaleb, "Why is he singling you out?"). When asked by Buddy what it was like to be a celebrity "profiler," McCaleb says, "At the top of my game I was connected, a part of everything, victim, killer, crime scene, all part of me. It's starting to feel that way again." Obviously,

Fig. 5. McCaleb shooting. © 2002 by Warner Bros. Pictures.

Fig. 6. Buddy Noone. © 2002 by Warner Bros. Pictures.

society needs profilers, detectives, police to guard it against evil. But, as in many of Eastwood's films, the line between good and evil is blurred precisely at the point where the mentality needed to view, decipher, and rectify justice comes to imitate exactly that of criminality: a profiler tries to "see" the crime through the eyes of its perpetrator, the killer becomes "part of him." This results in the alienation of the profiler, his absorption into a strange symbiotic relationship with his opposite number, who turns out to be more like him than not.

As it turns out, just as McCaleb needs this particular pretext to feel "connected," so too does the Code Killer. And when McCaleb diagnoses Buddy, he is in part commenting upon his own social pathology: "[The Code Killer] missed the action, he wanted to get it back, so gives me a new heart, but not a new life." The film stages the relation between the Killer and McCaleb in not only homosocial ways, but erotic and sentimental ways as well. Taunting McCaleb to identify him, the Killer mouths the words "Happy Valentine" into the security camera's eye, and leaves "Happy Valentine's Day" messages in the victim's blood by the murder scenes. And in the scene when McCaleb finally recognizes Buddy as the Code Killer, Buddy refers to the speech McCaleb gives about "being connected," saying that that is exactly how he himself feels. He tells McCaleb that when he said that, "Man, I almost came." Again mocking the rhetoric of romance, he tells McCaleb: "You're mine forever." Hence, McCaleb's "buddy" will be "no one."

The particular sociopathic space in which these two characters cohabitate is deeply interior ("Every beat of that stolen heart is the echo of my voice in your head," says Buddy), and dependent upon the deciphering of visible acts of evil. The "friendship" between the two men is staged as an allegorical struggle. McCaleb asks Buddy, "What do you want?" To which he replies, in a tone of incredulity, "I want you to live, I want it to start again, the battle between good and evil." At the end of the revelatory scene, Buddy asserts to McCaleb: "We're Cain and Abel, Kennedy and Oswald, we are the shit on the bottom of somebody's shoe." It is at this point that we are given to understand McCaleb's transformation. He opts out of the game: "I'm not interested [. . .] I don't need you at all." It is exactly that equation that is broken apart by the introduction of Gloria's heart and the ethical connection that reanimates McCaleb, as evinced in the first set of scenes. Here the companion piece to this last clip of social pathology is McCaleb's denunciation of that particular bond he had with Buddy, and his execution of Buddy via an explicit intertextual allusion to *Dirty Harry*.

Most germane for the film's address to the visual, the visual gone terribly wrong as mediated by the media, which attends only to the surface, Graciela reaches over to, in the same gesture, close Buddy's eyes and press his face under the water, sealing his death. Buddy's death is coterminous with the termination of the sociopathic vision. This would be a poetic ending to the film, but Eastwood does not let it end there. Importantly, he returns to the issue of race, as if remembering that he needs closure there, too. So he reverses the dark and brooding direction of the film, having killed the killer and given Gloria her justice, to end on a comic note that seemingly resolves the messy business of race and essence.

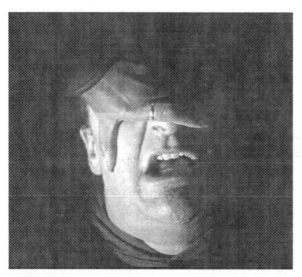

Fig. 7. Buddy's death. © 2002 by Warner Bros. Pictures.

Ultimately, we have a comic ending to this disquisition on race—race is seen as superficial, arbitrary, indeterminate, and racial thinking outmoded and destructive. Boundaries are meant to be crossed, and they will be because this is morally sanctioned, indeed, it is morally necessary to do so. The Mexican detective is a relic, stuck in denying McCaleb the status of being one of "us"; McCaleb doesn't need that legitimation, the film seems to say, his moral victory is all the proof that he needs that he and Gloria are one in body and spirit; call it Mexican, or whatever. McCaleb and his partner share a laugh as the Mexican detective is led off stage, sputtering obscenities in Spanish, upon which McCaleb comments in false surprise, "I didn't even know he spoke Spanish." McCaleb's body receives Gloria's heart, but the film leads us to believe that the important part is not the medical transfer, but that the heart of the other and the body of the Self have *remained* fused and viable, not because of their shared blood, but because of McCaleb's coming into being with Gloria's moral goodness, which allows him to tolerate, to accommodate, the formerly racial and gendered other.

The final scene is a distance shot of Graciela, Raymond, and Mc-Caleb riding on his boat as it transects the horizon and moves into invisibility. They are all fishing. It in this closing scene that race is left behind for a grander message about not only not being alone, but being together in a particular manner. The reconstituted multicultural, multiracial, and multigenerational "family" (Raymond's father had deserted their family years ago) is our final image, but the film is not finally about culture, race, or age, but rather a capacious notion of human sympathy and social life that transcends all those categories. It seems to move us from the logic of surface and depth, from top to bottom, to a lateral democratic egalitarianism. And as such, it seems to have at once made a powerful, but also horribly clichéd statement. The question becomes whether the film's technique offers anything that would raise it above the merely competent and ordinary?

Fig. 8. View of Boat. © 2002 by Warner Bros. Pictures.

I conclude this essay with two points for consideration. First, Eastwood is rather clever in the way he manipulates the idea of the visual. As we have seen, he shuttles between surface visibility and meditations on the hidden, the unmanifested, the immanent. But this is so generic for the detective story. Let's get more specific. The motive for so doing,

I suggest, is to highlight again the development of McCaleb's new perspective. McCaleb leaves behind the sensationalistic, sociopathic relation he has with the Code Killer, leaves behind the spotlight of hyper-visible media notoriety, and enters the private, invisible sphere of personal community. He accepts willingly the idea of being "nobody," not in the half-complete manner of his initial retirement, but now with not only closure, but also with a set of human relationships that more than compensates for his loss of public fame. It would take more space, and detract from the main purpose of this essay, to follow all the film's references to Homer and that particular heroic tradition, but let me just point to the use of the conundrum of "Nobody" ("No one"), and Odysseus's clever use of anonymity and names in the Cyclops episode ("Tell them 'Nobody' blinded you"). But besides this easily identifiable allusion there is the equally important allusion to Achilles's sour remark in the afterworld that he would rather die in old age, anonymously, than have made the choice to die young with glory. While the novel sets out the first allusion in its narrative, Eastwood is clearly playing with the second as he tracks McCaleb sailing into the sunset with Graciela and Raymond. But, finally, the intent behind articulating "no one" as "There is no *One* anymore" instructs us to read it as arguing against the atomizing of social identity, and for recognizing instead the argument made by Jean-Luc Nancy that the emergence of being is at once singular and plural. Indeed, this philosophical position so consistently set forth in Nancy's work becomes dramatized in his remarkable essay, "The Intruder," in which Nancy speaks of his own heart transplant: "The intruder exposes me excessively. It extrudes me, exports me, expropriates me. I am the malady and the medicine; I am the cancerous cell and the transplanted organ; I am the immune depressant agents and their palliatives" (I, 42, my translation). Clint Eastwood as conveyer of Jean-Luc Nancy, maybe not, but not altogether distant, either.

Nevertheless, we cannot get away from the precise nature of the sacrificial element in the film. When Buddy says to McCaleb that Gloria was his "valentine" to McCaleb, this sick "love" is, I suppose, intended to evoke its negation. That is, like Jesus, Gloria must give up her life to bring about the redemption of McCaleb. But she is not a sacrifice, despite all the heavy Christian imagery that Eastwood puts before us—of grace, of glory, of blood. She is an unwitting and unwilling victim. The film thus retreats back into the realm of the white male survivor, hero, rescuer, redeemer, justice-maker. The fact that he is a reconstructed one, whose reconstruction depends on three women of color, leaves us dangling at the edge of multiculturalism's critical edge at the turn of the century.

Here is what that edge or toggle point looks like dialectically, which is really, to my mind, the best way to evaluate *Blood Work*. First, let us say it is a positive articulation of anti-racist, multicultural thinking, a critique of white male violence, of the society of the spectacle, a social critique of the commodification of the visual. We could say that it replaces this social pathology with a utopian vision of common moral bondedness, of "blood" that works if we can tolerate difference. Buddy is killed, McCaleb lives, as a Mexican, but what does that word mean, anymore?

On the other hand, it is only the reconstructed white male who can bring this about, albeit aided and abetted by a child and a slew of women (his doctor, played by Angelica Huston, the black female sheriff who bends the law to help McCaleb, and of course Graciela, and absolutely, Gloria). To accomplish justice and moral rectification, McCaleb must give up his title, his rank, his fame, but Gloria has to give up her life. And even more problematic perhaps is the fact that the allegory works precisely because it dematerializes and dehistoricizes the production of racism, focusing instead on some general, ahistorical psychic pathology of primal violence and media obsessiveness.

But let's take one more dialectical turn, though I would not insist at all that it be the last twist. But here it is. It may well be that Eastwood cannot, precisely because of his gendered and racialized historical subject position, adequately address the issues of gender and race, and because of his class position the issue of the material production of violence and specularity. But the step forward that he has taken is, in perhaps the most comprehensive way possible, to dismantle a critical part of his own screen persona in such a way that allows for a different reading of race, of being together, of morality and social ethics. And that may not be all that bad, for we should see this in the rigorous way that Kenneth Burke taught us to read ideology and rhetoric—with scrupulous attention to the ratios of performance, audience, scene, history. Who would see a Clint Eastwood film, anyway?

NOTES

[1] Keane is quoted in Ian Haney-Lopez. See for instance Haney-Lopez's discussion of how Keane's work was deployed in the Ozawa and Thind cases.

[2] See Erin Aubry Kaplan, paraphrased from her first person narrative. I thank Michael Omi for this reference.

[3] The film is based on the novel of the same name by Michael Connelly. Trade publications noted that the film opened with an "anemic" $7.3 million gross, and ranks as one of Eastwood's lesser films.

[4] See Paul Gilroy. Against this optimistic proposition, see Sally Lehrman: "Race doesn't exist, the mantra went. The DNA inside people with different complexions and hair textures is 99.9 percent alike, so the notion of raced had no meaning in science. At a National Human Genome Research Institute meeting five years ago, geneticists were all nodding in agreement. Then sociologist Troy Duster pulled a forensics paper out of his briefcase. It claimed that criminologists could find out whether a suspect was Caucasian, Afro-Caribbean, or Asian Indian merely by analyzing three sections of DNA."

WORKS CITED

Burke, Kenneth. *A Grammar of Motives.* Berkeley: U of California P, 1969.

Connelly, Michael. *Blood Work.* New York: Warner Books, 2002.

Gilroy, Paul. *Against Race.* Cambridge: Harvard UP, 2000.

Haney-Lopez, Ian. *White by Law: The Legal Construction of Race.* New York: New York UP, 1996.

Kaplan, Erin Aubry. "Black Like I Thought I Was." *LA Weekly.* Oct. 3, 2003. 1 Aug. 2005.

Lehrman, Sally. "The Reality of Race," *Scientific American* online, Jan. 13, 2003. 1 Aug. 2005.

Nancy, Jean-Luc. *L'Intrus.* Paris: Galilee, 2000.

Nuland, Sherwin. *Doctors: The Biography of Medicine.* New York: Knopf, 1988.

Conclusion: Interinanimation

10 The Cyborg's Hand: Care or Control? Interview with Trinh T. Minh-ha

Valentina Vitali

Born in Vietnam, Trinh T. Minh-ha is a key figure in American independent cinema.* Her multidisciplinary work (films, essays, poetry, musical compositions, and installations) has been the subject of several retrospectives around the world. *Reassemblage* (1982) is a documentary on women's lives in Senegal as well as a critique of the anthropological eye. The status of women, the politics of identity, and the exploration of Asian cultures are recurring themes in her work, as in *Shoot for the Contents* (1991) or *Surname Viet Given Name Nam* (1989). Screened in Berlin in 1995, *A Tale of Love* is a fictional feature film about a Vietnamese writer living in the USA who works as a photographer's model in order to help her family back home.

The title of her latest video, *The Fourth Dimension* (2001, 87 min), screened at the Locarno Film Festival, alludes to time and the processes it involves: the traveller's subjective experience, the sacred time of ritual, mechanical time, film time. In this film-essay, Trinh T. Minh-ha immerses herself in contemporary Japan to examine the crystallized tensions between modernity and tradition, the present and the past, and the fusion of Eastern and Western cultures. Combining shots of cityscapes, ceremonies (funeral processions, theatre, religious festivals, and rituals), and everyday life, she delivers a reflection on the temporalities we live by. Avoiding any hint of didacticism, the documentary also explores the relation between sound and image, functioning as a recurrent melody that appeals to all senses (from the Locarno Film Festival catalogue, 2001).

VV: I used to teach film theory to aspiring filmmakers. One day the students were told to find an idea for a documentary. One of the students—incidentally, a woman from Korea—said that she wanted to make a documentary about a dream she had dreamt, and proceeded to tell her dream. The teacher told her that she could not make a documentary about a dream because documentaries were about facts and reality. So the following week the same student went to the teacher and, explaining that that she had now found a good subject for her documentary, simply retold her story without, however, saying that it was her dream. This anecdote was told to me by my colleague, the teacher of the documentary module. His intention was to show me that some students really are confused. Contrary to my colleague, I thought that the student had grasped the central problematic of documentary filmmaking and, more generally, the problematic of realism. I wanted to start this interview with this anecdote because your work, and particularly *The Fourth Dimension,* questions the conventional boundary between fiction and documentary, by explicitly confronting the issue of narration, and therefore of history and temporality.

TMH: We keep encountering these classifications—fiction, documentary, and experimental—everywhere in the film world. I don't feel as if I belong to any of them. Even the terms "art" and "avant-garde" raise questions among artists. In making these distinctions, the tendency has often been to reiterate a preconceived hierarchy, and hence to harden a fundamentally explorative activity into a category of work. There is no real experiment when "experimental" becomes a genre of its own; "avant-" and "arrière-garde" are but the two sides of the same classification. In "documentary," one has to go through fiction to show reality, just as in fictional narratives, one has to go far into the realm of documentary to document one's own fiction. That's why, rather than endorsing these categories by which the film world largely abides, I produce films that I consider to be first and foremost "boundary events." One can view them as different ways of working with freedom in experiencing the self and the world.

The documentary aspect of *The Fourth Dimension* has less to do with the non-staged nature of the material shot than with the process of documenting its own unfolding: it documents its own time, its creation in megahertz, the different paths and layers of time-light that are involved in the production of images and meanings. Our life situations are regulated by time—by instituted work-time or television-time for example; our bodies and daily activities tell us with precision how time takes on specific forms and leaves its marks in our landscape. And yet, when I introduce the work as a video or a D-film[1] on time, it is like saying it is about nothing. This is a bit similar to the case of the student you just mentioned: a documentary has to be about something factual and verifiable. But, a sum of facts does not necessarily lead to truth.

Time defines and dominates new technology. It conditions every aspect of our lives and is often invoked as a criterion to determine the "quality" of media works. Films that are quickly dismissed as "too long" by film reviewers are often those that let us feel time in its operation and materialization. So, when people tell me the subject of *The Fourth Dimension* is abstract, okay, but, depending on how we live it, what is more concrete than time? Is "too long" an abstract reality? Film is time, and, if time is a fiction, so are we—a fictional field that can be acted on, but one that is also hosting us and changing us as we inhabit it.

In the realm of cinema, "the fourth dimension" refers to the dimension of time. In spiritual practice, it can refer to the dimension of light—light not as the opposite of darkness, but light within darkness. Whenever one encounters a wall, or a space called darkness, one is not merely dealing with a finite boundary. The function of a wall or a boundary is not simply to stop you. It can also be to signal a departure and the possibility of a different presencing. So every time you hit a wall or an impasse, that impasse can tell you a lot about yourself: having nowhere to go, you're "in"—at the beginning of something new that is happening.

For me, rituals (in Japanese culture and in digital technology, for example), which concern one aspect of the film, delineate a very strong boundary defining the worlds of past and present, light and darkness, outsiders and insiders, or form and content. But when one really enters this boundary, really deals with it, it becomes a revolving door, something that opens both ways and allows you simultaneously entrance and exit. We can understand "the fourth dimension" in this sense. And there is also a third meaning to "the fourth dimension": when some Japanese novelists use this term, it is usually to refer to that dimension of reality not immediately perceptible through "normal" sight. In other words, one has to lose one's "normal eye" in order to enter the fourth dimension.

VV: When you discussed the film after the screening, you were asked about representing tradition and Japanese rituals. You explained that you were not representing tradition as old and modernity as new. The film documents the dialectical relation between interrelated ideas of tradition and ideas of modernity. One dimension that is very present, even tangible, in your film is the mobility of the camera, by which you trace, in your own terms, this relation between two realms that are habitually conceived as separate. For example, at one point the camera focuses on women dressed in traditional garb and more particularly on the paraphernalia worn on the face, which look like a gag, possibly because they were conceived as a way of constraining the woman and her voice. And yet, as the camera scrutinizes or, rather, caresses the face of a woman, something comes through, in the woman's expression and in her eyes, in spite of the mask or, perhaps, because of the mask, something which is unique to that woman.

In this scene, as in many others, the camera performs a telescoping between ostensibly traditional custom and modern life, so that the woman's mask appears in an entirely new way. As you put it, it appears as a boundary which, as boundary, makes something new happen: here it produces the image of an individual woman in modern-day Japan. Could you say something about this "telescoping," and, more particularly, about the fact that such mobility does not so much stop but change at a specific moment in the film, so that half-way through, the initial inventiveness—a very mobile camera, masked and split frames, sound de-spatialization, and an interesting use of the voice-over, which leaps, as it were, from voice-over to diegetic but off-screen voice and vice-versa—turns into what seemed to me a more conventional, or perhaps just a more "well-behaved," mode of filmmaking. From that moment onward, the voice-over stabilizes, even if it is still not the voice-over of conventional documentary film.

TMH: What new technology has always promised us is speed, portability, and mobility. Everything is going wireless, faster, smaller,

and lighter. This is where tradition and modernity meet. Smallness, which remains an important quality of tradition, was what
modernization despised as it equated prosperity and development
with expansion in size and in scale (bigger, taller, the more the
better). What its grand-scale, universalising enterprise—and colonialism is here a grand example—sought to achieve was to make
a clean sweep of all traditions and to raise everything anew from
the ground. Today, in postmodern times, it is the return of smallness and portability that we're witnessing, albeit a return that promotes not convivial tools but self-destruction at ever-faster speed.
Guerrilla network and warfare in old and newly re-appropriated
forms is the only way smaller nations have to fight the big powers.
So mobility is, in effect, double-edged: the artificial return to the
past via new technology may lead to further institutionalization
of individualism, or it may contribute to new forms of decentral-
ization.

It seems most adequate to attack this problem in relation to
Japan, a society whose genius often reveals itself in the way its cre-
ations—of old and new—manifest these values: maximum function, maximum productivity within minimal space, and volume.
Smallness and mobility characterize all aspects of cultural and
economical life. This is why I turned to digital technology in vi-
sualizing Japan. For me, the two are very linked. The mobility of
the camera in *The Fourth Dimension* can be said to be effortless—
literally, because I was using a small, very lightweight camera; and
culturally, because of what I saw as prominent in Japanese aesthetics: the frame within the frame whose mobile, reflexive repetition,
like the revolving door I mentioned earlier, encases and confines
reality while it also allows infinity to come into view. It is through
the finite, through the rituals of imaging (or of framing, scanning, panning, travelling, and editing, for example) that infinity
is made tangible. Devices suggestive of the mobility and multiplicity of framing are used throughout this digital film (more easily
noticeable in the first part and last part), but as you've implied
in your response, there's an important instance in its unfolding,
which may bring about a shift in one's reception of the visual and
aural material immediately following it.

There, where the film takes on a "well-behaved" tone, to use
your term, is when chronological time intervenes. In other words,

the turning point in the film comes about with the evocation of Kamba Michiko's death.[2] In the midst of this fluid, multi-layered time of travelling and image surfing, there's suddenly something like an arrest in the flow of events: without warning, the viewer confronts the linearity of a date ("May 19" then, "June 16, 1960"), the specificity of a proper name (Kamba Michiko), and the stillness of a face recaptured from a framed photograph. It is as if things have temporarily stopped in time or, as a statement in the film says, as if "time [were] frozen in its movement." This direct information on a political figure, this straight narrative of a historical event, or this representative arrest in the course of a film that otherwise makes no use of the conventional explicative mode of informing is linked to what is being invoked on screen at that moment: a death, albeit a death that tells of the passing of a historical epoch and its people. There is more than one way to make history. What seems important to me is to retain history's thickness and cultural dissemination in its unconcealed architecture. Here, however, in the midst of that spatial thickness, you suddenly have a linear temporality evolving with the single name and face of a woman.

I chose Kamba Michiko as the one political figure to evoke precisely because of what I see as most representative in her death. With the struggle she led, her death may be said to have marked the turning point for the image the world had of Japan. Here, the emphasis is on image, since the film is not about (unmediated) Japan but about the image that one construes of Japan. Rather than trying to bypass its own reality as image, as time and light, the film deals with its production of "Japan's likeness." It is in this context that Kamba's death takes on its full significance as it tells us of a crucial passage in Japan's appearance: with the repression of a civic society, what was launched was a new image of Japan as a corporate society, for which the Western way became the way to progress. Given in a very straightforward manner, this historical information is then followed by a number of related statements, such as those on Japan's isolation from other Asian nations and on the lot of its immigrants—all selected for their contribution to Japan's image as a modern traditionalist society and a global economic power. By now, the viewer's ear is tuned to a different kind of narration and the rest of the film can continue with a denser, accelerated rhythm between music, text, and image. The verbal fragments in voice-over are heard at much tighter intervals, while the visual returns, towards the end of the film, to some of the images presented at the beginning. Time is here being compressed, but the mobility of the camera remains.

VV: There is a wonderful image in the first half of the film: a long, panoramic shot of a Japanese *torii* gate in a lake and, behind it, skyscrapers. Slowly the camera moves out and down into the lake, with the shimmering waters reflecting the gate as well as the skyscrapers. The camera then closes in on the reflection, to show us its substance, as it were, that is, the many glistening streams of water and light that produce the reflection. It seemed to me a wonderful representation of history in all the density of the voices that constitute it. With the naming of Kamba Michiko, it is as if you arrested the camera to take a snapshot of that fluttering reflection. This does not mean that the water freezes: the glistening and the flowing continue, even if the snapshot is still. That is why, as you point out, the camera keeps on being mobile after the naming of Kamba Michiko, but in a different way. You are a multidisciplinary artist, but the interesting aspect of your activity, for me, is that, by being an artist and a cultural historian, you operate at the intersection of practice and theory. I wonder if the structure of *The Fourth Dimension,* the personal or subjective half and the historical or objective half, is related to this aspect of your work. And, more generally, how do you handle the relation between practice and theory?

TMH: I write poetry and theory, I teach and make film, and was trained as a musical composer. To many viewers, these are the strong dimensions in my films.

VV: Sound is indeed a very important aspect of *The Fourth Dimension,* not to mention music. I particularly appreciated the fact that, in the film, music has a visual as well as a sound dimension. I am thinking of the long and wonderful scenes showing drumming performances. First, during the ceremony, you show the men beating on very large, standing drums, the rhythm to which the women dance, dressed in traditional costume and wearing what looked like very painful wooden shoes. You then show the same ceremony with women at the drums. Next are a group of women drummers training: their bodies are immobile, only the arms move in impeccable synchronicity, while their faces, turned to the camera, are expressionless, in spite of their considerable effort involved in the exercise and the individual differences. The extent of their energy is conveyed by the potency of their music. You then cut to a street parade of bare-chested men drummers. In contrast to the women, their bodies are all over the place, they walk and jump in a disorderly manner, but their music is less potent; it does not hold the spectator in the same way because it is on a different narrative level. And then, to finish it off, you cut to a military parade, or, rather, a line-up of soldiers training in the street. They have their pants down, and, as the commander blows the whistle, they start dressing as fast they can. That was a wonderful sequence in which the music plays an important part, as music, sound, and visual performance. Or, again, in your use of the voice-over, which does not provide a comment [on] the image and which, moreover, leaps inside and outside the visual.

TMH: I am glad you mention the military sequence. You see, people talk about ritual as traditional, but the soldiers lining up to simulate an aspect of military training is a ritual that has nothing "traditional" about it, neither in the look nor in the action. It's rather hilarious when you think that, of all possible representations of military bravery, it is that sequence which they choose to re-enact in the Sendai festival: sleeping with their underpants in a line on the street and competing in speed to regain a soldierly appearance at the sound of their commander's whistle—all of this carried out with the grandiose music of *Star Wars* in the background. People apparently have no qualms inserting similar scenes in a festival which, like many other local festivals, is meant to reinforce social cohesion through tradition. The more one looks closely at these festival performances, the more one sees them as cultural hybrids and as meeting ground for the interaction of past, present, and future times.

The film abounds with examples of ritualized events that may have the look of tradition, but the action and performance of post-modernity, and vice-versa. I'm tempted here to say, who would do that but Japanese people? It's such a unique blend of utter conformity and odd liberty in both the revival and the modernization of tradition. But the reality is that, whether we're Japanese or not, we all incorporate rituals and live by them in our everyday existence. Just look at rave culture (there's a sequence of it at the beginning of the film) or other youth cultures of our time: tribalism and its rituals are definitely part of this "new form of kindness," to use a statement in the film. Small and singular are what characterizes the faces of resistance in the age of globalization. Rather than seeing rituals only in terms of tradition and religion, it is interesting to widen the scope of our view and to expand the term to the daily activities of secular life.

To return to your question about theory and practice, there's a predominant tendency to see tradition as past and "timeless" and to equate modernism with the present and linear time—clock time or chronological time, for example. This is the way compartmentalized knowledge deals with reality: it can only speak in dualities and in pre-established hierarchies. Numbering our days, dating events, dividing, and counting as an end in itself seem to be the normative way of grappling with time. And yet suffice it to say that time does not come in one unifying form; it not only exists in a multiplicity of forms and rhythms (biological, physiological, geological, and so on) at any single moment, it is also not limited to what humans can perceive. Time leaves traces in a multitude of layers and scales in the realm of life. Everything is time—stone, tree, mountain, ocean, thoughts, doubts, clouds. We *are* time. So it's absurd to talk about timelessness in this realm. You're "in time" when present and eternity meet. The "real" time—the one we tend not to see because we are caught up in it—is the "eternal present" that contains both past and future. This is how I would contextualize the relation between theory and practice in my work.

My activities as filmmaker, theorist, poet, and composer are tightly interwoven while they also constitute distinct, independent tracks. Making films or videos, composing with sound, writing and dicing with verbal language, each has its own unique reality to deal with. As I've been told, it is not uncommon that viewers of my films sometimes prefer, for example, to turn their attention primarily to the experience of hearing. They use a good sound system and just turn up the volume full blast, and they really enjoy listening to the musicality of the sound track, which can stand on its own, as do the visual and the verbal commentary, while being interwoven. You see, that's the notion of independence. Independence is not separation. It means to stand on one's own, independently, and yet relate.

I don't work with mere opposition. But, to some people's minds, it's still difficult to accept a relation of multiplicity without immediately turning it back into one of subordination and domination. For example, just look at what happens between the verbal and the visual or between sight and sound in both mainstream and alternative media. No wonder, from time to time, I encounter aggressions from viewers who, puzzled by my ability to work through the question of politics in artistic realization and to offer a social view of the properties of an artistic medium, can only react negatively to the dynamics of theory and practice. Sometimes their questions may denote mere curiosity, which I welcome; other times they already imply a preconceived idea of what the practice of filmmaking should be, which is very stifling.

What bothers them is the hearing eye, the image that hears what it says, looks at itself, and tells of the instance of consumption while being consumed—the "pensive image," as Roland Barthes calls it, or the "boundary image" as I would prefer to put it. For the mainstream, theory and practice can only stand in mutual exclusion or submission: either your practice illustrates your theory, or your theory illustrates your practice. No independence.

If such logic is to prevail, then I would like to keep this question alive: which illustrates which? Is it theory or practice that comes first? It's like asking that consciousness be divided so that it can be fitted into the preconceived compartments of linear time, with a clear "before" and "after." Only people who don't really engage with theory would come up with the idea that a film can illustrate a theory and vice versa. It's funny, and I would challenge any filmmaker, "the best on the market" as they say, to do such a thing. Try as much as you wish, you can't make a film out of a theory. (One recognizes immediately in montage, for example, that when an edit doesn't work, it's mainly because it is based on an idea.) Similarly, there is no theory that can entirely capture a practice. They are two different realities, each with its own light, its own precise workings. Always in excess, they escape one another. It is that challenge between the two that one keeps alive in the process of filmmaking.

If my inter- and multi-disciplinary background is reflected in any way in my work, it is in the desire to maintain that independence among activities of production and among film elements. I don't remember having begun a film even with an idea; it has always been with a strong, mute feeling triggered by an encounter or by resonance between events. It's from there that everything happens. In "documentary" I don't work with a preconceived treatment or a well-outlined subject; and in "fiction" I write a very precise script with all the production details minutely indicated and drawn—but if the scenes are all there, they have no set order. They're like the pieces of a puzzle that will find their own order as the film takes shape. In both approaches, things come together through the process of shooting and editing, by putting yourself on the spot, as bound to a particular situation.

VV: What is interesting for me is that in doing so you document the process of "putting together things." I have seen many films that give this impression of fragmentation and immediacy, especially work that uses digital technology. And yet, the majority conceal the process of "putting together things," the narrative, by erasing its marks. This is what is missing in a lot of digital work. There is a lot of fragmentation and pasting, but then the hand that fragments and pastes, the collating agent, is absent, or rather, is totally reified and presented as "technology," which leaves no margin for questioning the modalities of collation, the order of discourse. It is a kind of narrative that claims absolute power because, by compressing time and space, it allows no objection.

TMH: I think you really put the finger on what largely goes unquestioned in new media works. When some programmers heard that I'd completed a digital video, they were extremely interested. But when they saw it, nothing of what I did quite fit into what they were expecting to see in digital "experimentation." The work, which fares in the grey zone of in-betweenness, often seems recognizable at first sight, although it remains with further sight "a non-recognizable entity" (a label that has been applied to both my artistic and scholarly works, and to myself). The kind of silent rejection with which it sometimes meets has mainly to do with what people perceive as "innovation": disturbances of the image that primarily, if not exclusively, involve the retina. Most of what has been prized in the field of digital visual production is limited to effects on the retina. All the other questions are taken for granted, such as the hand and brain that manipulate these effects, the social scope of art and technology, the politics of "forms" and of aesthetic decisions, in brief the question of the work's location and positioning.

The power at work and the cyborg's hand remain ultimately invisible. Digital effects that decompose and disintegrate the image abound in new media works and become an end in themselves. But how this process of returning to the void—to no-image—leads us further in understanding ourselves, the world of virtual reality and of datascapes, and the system that promotes this technology, does not seem to enter certain criteria for "innovation." In the reflexive play of my films, the space created to expose the making processes involved is not there for the mere sake of reflexivity—a notion whose significance is often taken in a very shallow way—but as a means to deconstruct the context in which we operate. And this is what affects us down to the smallest details of our lives. For example, the way we frame people tells not only about how and what we see, but also about the off-screen, the space excluded or not visible in the frame. *The Fourth Dimension* is said to open with a "panoramic" image: that image "on the move" (as differentiated from the "moving image") is at the same time a reference to the possibilities of filmmaking and to its limits. The focus is on both the literal and the figural limit of the image. I show this by offering a mobile re-framing, tracking the rectangle left and right, up and down, letting it trace its own boundary while hitting against the boundary of the screen frame.

VV: That is why I think your work is very interesting, and important. My students use the Internet, at times only the Internet, to do their research. When I tell them that the 'net has to be used carefully, because some of the sources know less about cinema than the students themselves, they look surprised. Not because they are told that they know more than someone else, but because of my reminder of that "someone." It does not seem to enter into their heads that the material available on the 'net is chosen (or not) and compiled by human beings.

TMH: This attitude, which my film addresses, dwells on the persisting opposition between machine and humans. Of common acceptance is the belief that machines are objective and untainted by the subjectivity of human beings. This is all a question of boundaries. I am not aiming at achieving either one—objectivity or subjectivity. As discussed earlier, boundary breaching and crossing fosters new beginnings. In film and video, it is in the encounter of the organic and the technological that images of self and other are literally created. Like language, technology speaks of she (or he) who speaks it. We are captured in whatever we try to capture. What we face in this double co-existence is the two-times-two-ad-infinitum reality that regulates our everyday existence. We keep on thinking of objectivity and subjectivity as separate, but when the objectivity of a subjectivity comes into play or when a subjectivity within a subjectivity is set in motion, new horizons open up and we can deal with the relation differently.

This is also what I've brought out in *The Fourth Dimension,* with the exploration of machine-time and human-time in Japan's context of mobile forms and minute care and control. The modalities of such a mode of co-existence permeate every aspect of life, even the most mundane. For instance, in Europe, if you buy a train ticket and then decide to travel further than your ticket allows, you are immediately suspected of cheating and punished for your "misbehavior" if you're caught. In Japan this is no problem: you pay a fare (the lowest if you wish) at the ticket machine so you can get on the train; then, if you decide otherwise, you just wait for the conductor and pay the additional portion without anyone suspecting you in any way. Or you can get on first class with a second-class ticket and pay the difference later; there's no wrongdoing when there's no distrust. It is a different relation to machine. Here, changing your mind, changing your itinerary at any moment in your journey, does not make you look suspicious, because the system is not based, in this case, on the mutual exclusion of man and machine, but on their mutual co-operation. Instead of promoting competition, domination, and subordination, it emphasizes the interactive and the collective in achievement. At another level, the same can be said of the relationship between tradition and modernity. Tradition is very present in Japan.

VV: But the same is true in European and, generally, in Western countries, even if there tradition can be, and often is, presented as very modern.

TMH: Yes, it is hidden or denied even as it is carried on, whereas in Japan, whether peaceful or antagonistic, the co-existence of the two is put forward as an asset of the culture. This is what I gather from the struggle that many artists, architects, and writers from Japan are carrying on in their works and in their desire to "synthesize the global and the particular" (their terms). And I'm saying this, despite the wide tendency in Japanese politics to equate Western with modern, to confuse "Japanism" (the nostalgic flight to tradition) with "Japaneseness," and hence, to reject, for the sake of modernization, everything deemed to belong to "the past."

A die-hard image that results from the perpetuation of this old divide between tradition and modernity is precisely the image of Japanese culture as an imported commodity, of Japanese creation as derivative—excelling only in imitation—and of Japanese spirit as fiercely xenophobic. Arguments from both the "ultra right" and the "ultra left" are based on such a partition. But what I find far more baffling or disquieting is the intimate pairing of care and control, the blurring of their differences in every aspect of the culture, which I strongly experience while living in Japan. What *The Fourth Dimension* offers, then, is an interval that allows one to work at shifting Japan's image, by focusing on the encounter while playing with these contested representations (which are narrow-minded but not false). With the current events of our times and with the on-going questions raised around the so-called "clash of civilizations," it is important to return anew to "tradition" and "modern," to question our normative sense of time, and to open to a more expansive and inclusive feel of "being-time."

NOTES

* This interview is a revised version of the one first published in *Metro Magazine,* www.metromagazine.com.au. Used by permission.

¹ The term "film" is deliberately used here, not because of a lack of differentiation between the two media (video and film), but because of the "bridge" digital technology has extended between them.

² Kamba Michiko was a student of Tokyo University and a well-known leader of the 20,000 Zengakuren students who demonstrated against the Government of Prime Minister Kishi and the signing of the renewed Japan-US Security Treaty.

Works Cited

Mihn-ha, Trinh T., dir. *The Fourth Dimension.* Prod. Jean-Paul Bourdier and Trinh T. Minh-ha. Digital video. 2001.

—. *Reassemblage.* Prod. Jean-Paul Bourdier and Trinh T. Minh-ha. 1982.

—. *Shoot for the Contents.* Prod. Jean-Paul Bourdier and Trinh T. Minh-ha. 1991.

—. *Surname Viet Given Name Nam.* Assoc. prod. Jean-Paul Bourdier. 1989.

—. *A Tale of Love.* 1989.

Star Wars. Dir. George Lucas. Composer John Williams. Twentieth Century Fox. 1977.

Index

Contributors

Mieke Bal, a well-known cultural critic and theorist, holds the position of Royal Dutch Academy of Sciences Professor (KNAW). She is also Professor of the Theory of Literature in the Faculty of Humanities at the University of Amsterdam. Her many books include *Travelling Concepts in the Humanities: A Rough Guide* (University of Toronto Press, 2002) and *Narratology: Introduction to the Theory of Narrative* (University of Toronto Press, 1997). *A Mieke Bal Reader* just came out from the University of Chicago Press (May 2006). Mieke Bal is also a video artist.

Linda T. Calendrillo is Dean of the College of Arts and Sciences at Valdosta State University. In addition to publishing and presenting in rhetoric and composition studies, she enjoys co-editing *JAEPL: The Journal of the Assembly for Expanded Perspectives on Learning* with Kristie Fleckenstein; they also worked together on *Language and Image in the Reading-Writing Classroom* (Erlbaum, 2002).

Kristie S. Fleckenstein is associate professor of English at Florida State University. She is the author of *Embodied Literacies: Imageword and a Poetics of Teaching* (Southern Illinois University Press, 2003; recipient of the 2005 Conference on College Composition and Communication Book of the Year Award) as well as the co-editor of *Language and Image in the Reading-Writing Classroom: Teaching Visions* (Erlbaum, 2002). She co-edits with Linda T. Calendrillo *JAEPL: The Journal of the Assembly for Expanded Perspectives on Learning*. Her work on material rhetoric, imagery, and digital technology has appeared in such journals as *College English, Rhetoric Review, JAC: Journal of Advanced Composition, Computers and Composition,* and *College Composition and Communication.*

Alan Gross is professor of rhetoric at the University of Minnesota. He has a long-term interest in scientific communication and is the author of *The Rhetoric of Science* (Harvard, 1990; 1996) and of *Starring the Text: The Place of Rhetoric in Science Studies* (Southern Illinois University Press, 2006). He is also the co-author of *Communicating Science: The Scientific Article from the 17th Century to the Present* (Oxford, 2002) and co-editor of *The Scientific Literature: A Guided Tour* (Chicago, 2007). His interest in rhetorical theory and criticism has led to the co-authored *Chaim Perelman* (SUNY, 2002) and two co-edited collections, *Rereading Aristotle's Rhetoric* (SIU Press, 2000) and *Rhetorical Hermeneutics* (SUNY, 1996).

Catherine L. Hobbs is professor in the composition/rhetoric/literacy program in the English Department at University of Oklahoma. She is the editor of *Nineteenth-Century Women Learn to Write* (University of Virginia, 1995), and the author of *Rhetoric on the Margins of Modernity: Vico, Condillac, Monboddo* (Southern Illinois, 2002) and *The Elements of Autobiography and Life Narratives* (Pearson/Longman, 2005). Her essays on the history of rhetoric, language, and literacy have appeared in *Rhetoric Society Quarterly* as well as journals including *Rhetorica, Rhetoric Review, JAC: Journal of Advanced Composition, Historical Reflections/Reflexions Historiques,* and *JAEPL: The Journal of the Assembly for Expanded Perspectives on Learning.*

Sue Hum is an assistant professor of English who teaches undergraduate and graduate courses in writing at the University of Texas at San Antonio. Her research interests include composition theory and pedagogy, modern rhetorical theory, critical race theory, gender and language, and contrastive rhetoric. Her publications include *Relations, Locations, Positions: Composition Theory for Writing Teachers* (co-edited with Peter Vandenberg and Jennifer Clary-Lemon, NCTE, 2006) as well as essays in *JAC: Journal of Advanced Composition, Readerly/Writerly Texts,* and *Journal of Curriculum Theorizing.*

Don Ihde is Distinguished Professor of Philosophy at Stony Brook University. He directs the Technoscience Research Group and its affiliated Technoscience Research Seminar, a graduate and postdoctoral program. He is the author of thirteen books and the editor of many others. His interests have been in phenomenology and hermeneutics and in their relationship to science and technology. His most recent books are *Bodies in Technology* (University of Minnesota, 2002) and co-edited with Evan Selinger, *Chasing Technoscience* (Indiana University, 2003). His current research is in imaging technologies and the multicultural roots of technoscience.

Gunther Kress is professor of Semiotics and English at the Institute of Education, University of London. He has a specific interest in the interrelations in contemporary texts of different modes of communication—writing, image, speech, music—and their effects on shapes of knowledge and forms of learning. He is also interested in the changes—and their effects and consequences—brought by the shift in the media of communication from the page to the screen. In relation to that, he is presently engaged in a research project called "Gains and Losses: Changes in Representation, Knowledge, and Pedagogy in Learning Resources." Recent books include *Reading Images: The Grammar of Graphic Design* (Routledge, 1996), *Multimodal Discourse: The Modes and Media of Contemporary Communication* (Edward Arnold, 2001) (both with Theo van Leeuwen), *Before Writing: Rethinking the Paths to Literacy* (Routledge, 1997), *Early Spelling: Between Convention and Creativity* (Routledge, 2000), *Literacy in the New Media Age* (Routledge, 2003), *Multimodal Teaching and Learning: The Rhetorics of the Science Classroom* (Continuum, 2002), and *Multimodal Literacy* (Peter Lang, 2003), edited with Carey Jewitt.

David Palumbo-Liu is professor of comparative literature at Stanford. He is the author of *Asian/American: Historical Crossings of a Racial Frontier* (Stanford, 1999), among other books. His latest publications—in journals such as *boundary 2* and *The New Centennial Review*—include articles on multiculturalism and "civilizational thinking," theoretical and academic writing, art and the "post-border" city, and Jean-Luc Nancy.

Trinh T. Minh-ha is a writer, filmmaker and composer. Her work includes two large multi-media installations (*The Desert Is Watching*,

2003, with Jean-Paul Bourdier and *Nothing But Ways,* 1999 with Lynn M. Kirby); six feature-length films that have been honored in thirty retrospectives around the world (including the international art exhibition Documenta 11 in Kassel, Germany 2002); and seven books, of which the more recent are *Cinema Interval,* (Routledge, 1999) and in collaboration with Jean-Paul Bourdier, *Drawn from African Dwellings,* (Indiana, 1996). She is professor in the departments of women's studies and of rhetoric (film) at the University of California, Berkeley. She has just completed a new feature, *Night Passage* (2004).

Valentina Vitali teaches film theory and history at the University of East London. She is the author of *Hindi Action Cinema* (Oxford University Press, forthcoming) and the co-editor, with Paul Willemen, of *Theorising National Cinema* (British Film Institute, 2006). Her work has appeared in *boundary2, Inter-Asia Cultural Studies, Kinema, Framework, Southern Review, Women: a Cultural Review, Journal of Asian Studies, Filmwaves* and in a number of collections, including *Hong Kong Connections* (Duke University Press, 2005) and *Shirin Neshat: 'Women without Men'* (Stiedl Verlag, 2005).

Anne Frances Wysocki is an Associate Professor of English at the University of Wisconsin-Milwaukee where she teaches courses in visual and digital rhetorics and new media theory and production. She is lead author of Writing *New Media: Theory and Applications for Expanding the Teaching of Composition,* which won the Computers and Writing Distinguished Book Award. Her compositions have appeared in *Computers and Composition, Kairos,* and the *Journal of the Council of Writing Program Administrators,* as well as in many books. With Dennis Lynch she has published *Compose/Design/Advocate: A Rhetoric for Integrating Written, Visual, and Oral Communication.* She has designed and produced software to help undergraduates learn 3D visualization and to introduce them to geology. Her interactive new media pieces "A Bookling Monument" and "Leaved Life" have won, respectively, the Kairos Best Webtext award and the Institute for the Future of the Book's Born Digital Competition.

Printed in the United States
204720BV00001B/100-108/A

9 781602 350328